Actual Factual Magic

The Simplified Guide to Walt Disney World

The Walt Disney World — 50th Anniversary Edition

By Joseph Pillsbury and Kat Garbis

Actual Factual Magic: The Simplified Guide to Walt Disney World

Actual Factual Magic: The Simplified Guide to Walt Disney World may be ordered through any bookseller.

Join our social media communities!

www.actualfactualmagic.com

Facebook Group: ActualFactualMagic Group

Instagram: ActFactMagic

YouTube: ActualFactualMagic

TikTok: Actualfactualmagic

ISBN/SKU: 9780578307091

ISBN Complete: 978-0-578-30709-1

Table of Contents

Introduction

People who have not yet experienced Walt Disney World® often have some common misconceptions. Walt Disney World® is super expensive, right? It is just a big amusement park. It is just for little kids. All we will be eating are burgers, hotdogs, and chicken strips. We can just take the monorail everywhere, right?

The truth is Walt Disney World® can be affordable or opulent. It can offer endless distractions, thrills and entertainment for all ages. And it is so much more than one big amusement park! Knowing your options can mean the difference between enjoying the vacation of a lifetime or being a frustrated person lost in the crowd.

This can all be overwhelming for someone visiting for the first time or if you have not been to the parks recently.

This guide is not intended to cover every last detail of the Disney experience – I think half the fun of visiting Walt Disney World® is discovering things for yourself! But if you know what is available to you, what you want to see and how to get there, you will have a much better time than the folks who are uninformed, overwhelmed, and lost.

I will point you toward the very best that Walt Disney World® has to offer but it's up to you to decide exactly what you want to experience.

Along the way, I'll throw in some suggestions, tips and tricks to help you stay a few steps ahead of the crowds.

When I started planning this fourth edition of *Actual Factual Magic-The Simplified Guide to Walt Disney World*, I was hoping to focus solely on the 50th Anniversary of this amazing vacation destination. That officially begins in October of 2021 and will presumably run through the entire year. I had not expected to have to write a guide that contends with all the challenges of a global pandemic. But here we are.

I plan to write this with a sense of optimism. Hopefully most of the Cast Members that were released in 2020, can be called back to resume their roles making magic soon after this book is published.

The cruel reality is it might take longer for safety restrictions to be lifted. So this book will include sections that deals with the realities of the pandemic too, of course. 2021 is bound to be a year of transitions as Disney carefully restores operations to something closer to normal.

In full transparency, it's very difficult to write a "perfect" guide book during these ever-evolving months. Things may change fast before and during your time at Walt Disney World®. All the more reason to have a good guide book to help you. Change is the enemy of any guide book, and the year ahead is going to be jam packed with changes as Disney transitions out of its pandemic protocols and as they introduce all the new attractions they hope to roll out in time for their 50th Anniversary celebration. Whether you are a newcomer or a Disney vacation veteran, there is a lot you are going to need to know.

You can try to tell people The Walt Disney World® Resort spans more than 43 square miles – the same footprint as the city of San Francisco. It contains four major amusement parks, an incredible sports complex, two of the country's largest water parks, an entertainment district and dozens of marvelous themed Disney Resort hotels. But even knowing all that, it is hard for people to comprehend what they are in for.

WALT DISNEY WORLD® IS GIGANTIC!...

THE MAGIC KINGDOM

THE CONTEMPORARY

THE GRAND FLORIDIAN

THE POLYNESIAN

TRANSPORTATION AND TICKET CENTER

SHADES OF GREEN

YACHT CLUB

BEACH CLUB

THE DOLPHIN

THE SWAN

DISNEY'S ANIMAL KINGDOM

CORONADO SPRINGS

DISNEY'S BOARDWALK

ANIMAL KINGDOM LODGE

THE ALL STAR RESORTS

BLIZZARD BEACH

DISNEY'S HOLLYWOOD STUDIOS

GALACTIC STAR CRUISER

ILLUSTRATIONS BY JOSEPH PILLSBURY

Walt Disney World® and the Global Pandemic

Disney has been operating in the middle of a global pandemic since the summer of 2020. They pioneered safe procedures during a health crisis by famously helping the NBA finish their season with no outbreaks of the virus. This success led into the careful, phased re-opening of the parks and resorts to the public, again with great results keeping guests and cast members healthy.

The majority of this book is going to be written as if Disney is under its regular operating procedures. There is reason to hope that with the coming vaccines and treatments, the pandemic may end soon. We hope Disney can continue a careful re-opening process that steps its way back to its normal, less restricted, form of magic. But this guide book would not be doing its job if it did not address the world as it is today. Though we have taken dramatic steps forward, resurgence of the virus has happened in other countries. There is a possibility that steps backwards might be necessary too. So this section is going to be a brief but necessary bit of guidance that will help you have a successful vacation during complicated times.

Connect with a Disney Certified Travel Agent

During the pandemic, not all Disney hotels were open. Not all the popular restaurants were serving guests. Fireworks and parades were halted. Most big auditorium shows were closed down and character greetings were stopped. These are some of the best parts of the Disney experience. You're going to want to know as these things are offered again. I'm telling you all this because things are changing very fast throughout the Disney Resorts.

A Certified Disney Vacation Planner is an independent travel agent or agency who's been through special Disney training. Once they complete their training they are granted access to Disney's unique internal reservation systems. The same systems Disney itself uses to book your stay if you call Disney directly or if you book your vacation online through the Disney app or website. The very important difference is that once you have booked your trip, Disney probably is not going to monitor changes for you that happen in the time between booking and the start of your actual
vacation. Typically these independent agents *will* monitor Disney's changing offerings and if a better deal is offered after you booked your trip, they can try to rebook parts of your vacation to get you that better price.

Disney Certified Travel Agents typically are travel agents in your own home town or nearby who work on a commission from Disney. You do not pay them anything more than you might if you booked directly through Disney.

The bottom line is you may be missing out on a lot of great stuff if you do not partner with a Disney Certified vacation planner this time around. Use this book as a reference to all the things that are possible at Disney, but let them do the hard work for making those wishes come true.

Get Your Park Pass Reservations

Unlike any other time before in Disney history, Disney is monitoring and controlling the overall attendance of all their theme parks by requiring visitors make a park reservation called a "Park Pass". This is NOT your admission ticket to the park. You will need that too. A Park Pass

Reservation is a way you can reserve the day you wish to visit a park in advance. You will not be allowed entrance to a park without a Park Pass Reservation even if you do have admission for that day. Even if you have a dinner reservation for a restaurant inside a park you will not be allowed entrance without a Park Pass Reservation. I know this is complicated, which is why I am laying this out as clearly as I can. It is also one of the main reasons I am recommending the use of a Disney Certified Travel Agent this time around. Disney is trying to make this simpler by linking the Park Pass system right on the same page where you can buy your Park Admission tickets. Park Passes are free. Again this is a measure born out of the need during the pandemic to control the size of the crowds in the parks, and with the pandemic still looming over us all, it looks like this system is going to remain in place as a precaution. If you plan far enough ahead getting a Park Pass is easy. If you discover all the passes are gone for a day you want, keep checking. Disney has been adding passes into the system as pandemic measures lighten and since people's plans change constantly a small amount of passes might pop up for any given day at any given time. It is also not a bad idea to check for Park Passes 24 hours ahead or even the morning of a day you might want to attend. This system is in constant flux.

Get Vaccinated

I am not recommending this to start some political debate. Vaccines have been a proven effective way to combat viral infections since the 1700s. For example, vaccines are why we no longer face mass outbreaks of Measles, Chicken Pox, Small Pox, Polio and particularly nasty cases of the flu. Preparing your immune system to be elbow to elbow with tourists from all corners of the world when you are enjoying Walt Disney World® is one of the best ways to ensure you can continue enjoying your vacation of a lifetime in the parks and pools rather than stuck sick in bed.

Masks!

During the worst part of the health crisis, Walt Disney World® did not mess around with the safety of its guests or its Cast Members. The rules around face coverings are disappearing, but then, rules may step backwards where masks are required everywhere again if there is an unfortunate surge in the virus. Disney may require every guest wear a fitted surgical style cloth or disposable mask (scarfs, neck gators, and valved masks are not allowed) within every public area of the Walt Disney World® parks and resorts. Or they may ask you to wear face coverings just for indoor attractions or on crowded transportation options. During this time of transition come to Disney prepared for sudden changes in these mask policies. Keep a set of masks with you. Rules or not, masking up in a crowded area might just be the prudent thing to do for the foreseeable future.

Of course Disney will sell you masks, but it is my recommendation that you find a comfortable set of masks for everyone in your family before your trip. Perhaps one mask for each day of your vacation. It's Florida. It's hot. It's humid. Masks will get sweaty and maybe smelly over the course of hours of use. Switching out reusable or disposable masks occasionally might be the key to enduring this most obvious change to the Disney experience. **Tip!** Bring a mesh bag that you can use to rinse and wash reusable masks in your hotel sink at the end of your day. A travel sized bottle of Woolite or some other brand of gentle detergent can really freshen up those masks. Let them dry either with the help of a hair dryer or the air conditioner vents in your room. Disney hotels offer laundry facilities too. Reusable masks can be sanitized for reuse with a quick run through the gentle cycle of a washing machine. Hopefully you will have fresh clean masks for your next day of adventuring in the parks.

Social Distancing

While things are starting to return to normal, any unforeseeable surge in the virus might bring back the need for distancing precautions. Plan to be flexible and understanding. Remember these rules are there to protect your health. While the plexi barriers might be removed now and the six-foot distancing markings might be gone from the ground, be smart about crowded places. Continue to use hand sanitizers and mask up if you find yourself packed tightly into a show or the fireworks viewing areas. Disney is re-opening many more of their resort hotels and, in phases, bringing the theme parks back to their normal capacities. Disney Parks during peak periods can be downright claustrophobic. It's going to be up to your own discretion how you protect yourself and your family. Remember, world wide, this crisis is not over. Disney can decrease access to their parks if they feel the need to bring back these precautions to keep you and their Cast safe.

There are places where you can still remove yourself from the major crowds at Disney. Position yourself in Frontierland closer to Splash Mountain where the parades kick off. Crowds are usually a little smaller along the route through Frontierland and Liberty Square. Watch the fireworks from the Fantasyland side of the castle where crowds are considerably smaller. You'll see that the fireworks are launched from two different points but you will not be packed into a crowd like a can of sardines. Watch the Magic Kingdom's fireworks from the shoreline of the Grand Floridian, or the beach at the Polynesian. This can really put some distance between you and the massive crowds. Eventually Epcot's redesign will create a lot more space for viewing their night time spectacular offerings. Hollywood Studios is a little more compressed than other parks. Fantasmic nighttime show happens in an enormous outdoor amphitheater and cannot really be enjoyed out of that area. The *Star Wars* spectacular and the Tower of Terror projection shows have narrow sight lines right down the streets. However if you are ok missing out on some of the lower special effects, some people 'in the know' like to avoid Epcot® and Hollywood Studio congestion by watching the high fireworks from Disney's Boardwalk® area. Animal Kingdom no longer offers Rivers of Light but soon Kite Tails will grace the large waterside amphitheater. The projection show on the Tree of Life can be seen from different angles throughout the area. But since this show cycles people will come and go from the viewing area. Crowd sizes can vary throughout the night.

Dining during the pandemic.

During the health crisis, Disney severely limited access to its dining spots. The number of restaurant tables were reduced to allow spacing. Guests were asked to take a quick temperature check before entering a restaurant. Disney brainstormed how they could continue to efficiently serve guests great dining experiences during these challenging times. One positive by-product of these pandemic adjustments was how Disney reinvented how they might serve you. Some really clever solutions were introduced. Menus can be magically brought up on a smart phone by scanning a QR code. In some cases you can have your meal pre-ordered before you arrive. Buffets have been modified with all-you-can-enjoy family-style experiences where platters of different items are brought to your table rather than you leaving your seats to shuffle through a buffet line. I hope they keep some of these innovations now as we return to normal operations.

Mobile Ordering through the Disney smartphone app made things easier at counter-service venues before the pandemic. During the pandemic, the app has become the preferred way to arrange dining throughout all of Disney. The Disney app is making it easier than ever to book last minute plans too. Reservations are more important than ever as restaurants may be required to meter how many guests they can serve.

Disney Transportation During the Pandemic

One of the ways Disney was most impacted was in their free transportation offerings. To allow safe distancing between customers, capacities had to be lowered which led to longer wait times to get from point A to point B anywhere within the massive Disney property.

During these challenges Disney announced they were discontinuing the Magical Express shuttle bus system between the Orlando International Airport and the Disney Resort Hotels. Baggage handling services were stopped early in the pandemic. Magical Express services will officially stop on January 31st, 2021.

The company that has always run Magical Express behind the scenes is Mears Transportation, They will continue to offer resort shuttle services under new branding as "Mears Connect". This service will no longer be free to get to and from your resort hotel. Estimated pricing for Mears Connect to the Disney Resort hotels is $32 round trip per person, $27 round trip for children. Mears will offer a private van service too for $200 round trip.

Disney has announced a partnership with the City of Orlando and the Brightline Rail company to create a train service between the Orlando International Airport to a train station soon to be located at Disney Springs®. I assume this will become the most popular way to shuttle between the airport and Disney in the near future. Predictions for the completion of this high speed rail line is 2024. Brightline pricing today for existing lines is surprisingly affordable so we think this will become the best option to get to Disney from the airport once the Disney Springs® station is open for business.

Of course there are numerous car services in the area including taxis, Uber®, Lyft®, Disney's Minnie-Van service (which is offered through the Lyft® app via their premium car offerings) and of course, most major car rental companies are available too. Keep in mind while shuttling to and from the airport, you may need to demand a larger vehicle to accommodate your luggage. These car services can scoot you around the Disney property faster than the free Disney transportation offerings. So if you are running behind for a reservation, it might be smart to keep these options handy on your smart phone. For the interim, while we all wait for the high speed rail service to be completed, these ride share services might be the most cost-efficient way to shuttle to and from the airport.

Once on Disney property there is an expansive free transportation system making use of buses, boats, monorails, and cable gondolas to whisk you between resorts and attractions. Disney is resuming normal capacity now but again, should there be an outbreak of the virus, they may return quickly to limiting capacity within all these vehicles. Be prepared for the possibility of longer wait times and allow extra time to get to reservations.

Bring your patience.

Disney is not the place to make your political views known in protest. This is 43 square miles of very secure private property and Disney has made it very clear that they intend to aggressively enforce their mask and social distancing rules. Failure to follow their rules might well mean you are ejected from the park and perhaps the entire resort.

Remember, while conditions might be improving; mask and distancing rules might be lessening and even disappearing, this has been an unpredictable virus and it is possible that mask rules and spacing restrictions could suddenly come back if there is an unexpected surge in Covid cases in the area. Be prepared to follow Disney's instructions and be as accommodating and patient as possible.

Disney has a monumentally difficult task: They are trying to protect their tens of thousands of guests and Cast Members from a virus that flourishes in crowded, enclosed spaces, and on commonly touched surfaces. It is a virus that travels within droplets emitted by breathing, coughing and sneezing. These droplets can be inhaled out of the air several moments after someone expels it. Imagine Disney's challenge trying to keep everyone safe when almost everything they do is the perfect opportunity for the virus to spread. They have been doing a herculean job and succeeding only because Cast members and guests all cooperate. Please help Disney keep the magic open. Be part of the solution. Cooperate.

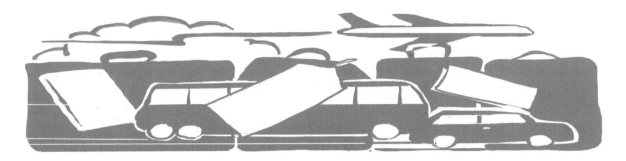

Planning Your Trip

The way I see it, the perfect Walt Disney World® vacation is a combination of smart planning and spontaneity. Sure, you need to make some hard plans ahead of time: Travel dates, airline tickets, hotel reservations, park tickets, park passes, and familiarize yourself with the new Disney Genie automated planner in the app. But in between all that you should still try to carve out time to relax and explore.

Disney's systems allow you to make dining reservations up to 180 days (60 days during the pandemic) in advance of your arrival. The sooner you make reservations for the special experiences you want to have, the better your chances will be of securing them. Book those early!

Giving a little thought to some of the basics can assure things will go smoothly throughout your vacation. Making travel plans well in advance and being a little flexible can save you some serious money with airlines and car rental agencies. Booking your hotel months in advance ensures you can stay where you want to stay and get the rate you hope to pay, as opposed to scrambling at the last moment for whatever may still be available.

Know Disney's Official Vacation Planning Tools

You can call Disney directly to plan most of your entire vacation either through their main number 1-407-W-DISNEY, the MyDisneyExperience app or through the WaltDisneyWorld.com website. Disney is unveiling their new vacation planning app called Disney Genie. All these tools can help you stay on top of the numerous changes happening before you leave for your vacation and adjust as necessary. You can plan an entire Disney vacation using any one of these methods, but right now, I suggest using a certified Disney Travel Agent.

Use A Disney Certified Travel Agent

I know this is a little confusing. Forgive me for repeating myself on this. Usually I advise you to take the reins on most of your pre-trip planning. But Walt Disney World® is changing its offerings rapidly as it reopens in carefully planned phases, a ride or event that might be closed today, might open tomorrow. That famous character dining experience you dreamed about might suddenly be offered again. By working with a certified Disney travel agent, they can track all these changes for you. They can pounce on those reservation dates as they become available and they can alert you to changes in policies as soon as they happen so you can make adjustments as needed. Best of all, using these services costs you nothing more than booking with Disney itself.

They could actually save you a lot of money by finding discounts and packages that might be hard for others to find.

Coordinate your park tickets with the Park Pass Reservation system.

This is new, thanks to the pandemic. But it is VERY important. Coordinate your park admission tickets with Disney's Park Pass Reservation system. In an effort to control the over-all attendance in all their parks, Disney now requires an advanced reservation to hold you and your party's spot within the limited space of each park. They say it is to hold down over-crowding and to give every guest a premium experience. Which is nice. But it is a headache if you do not make these free reservations for your time in the parks. To make things as simple as possible the Park Pass Reservation system is linked right from the site where you can purchase park tickets. Do NOT miss this very important extra step.

Bring Comfortable Shoes

This might seem like a no-brainer to some, but the amount of people I see trying to make a fashion statement while in the Disney Parks with new or unproven shoes still makes me cringe a little. Unless you run marathons, you will likely never put in more steps in a single day than you will during a Disney vacation. This is not an exaggeration. A normal Disney day can put 5 to 8 miles of wear on your shoes. Sometimes much more. There is something in the magic of every park that can make you walk more than you ever dreamed you could. And the size of these parks are so much bigger than most first time visitors can fathom even with me telling you the tidbits like the entire Disneyland park can fit on the Florida property 72 times. Until you witness the vastness for yourself it just will not fully register. That said, bring broken in, proven comfortable shoes. Since a Florida downpour can soak your feet, bringing two or more pairs of shoes is a good idea. **Tip:** It is probably not a bad idea to physically prepare yourself for Walt Disney World®. Before your trip, I recommend walking or biking a little bit every day before you depart for your vacation.

What Should You Pack?

The climate is unpredictable these days. The weather changes quickly in Florida. In spring, summer, and fall you can expect warm (or downright hot) weather with regular bouts of rain. It is really only in the winter months where you might want to pack some warmer clothes when temperatures can drop down into the 40s F or even lower. Late spring right through to early fall is considered "Hurricane Season" in Florida. While these weather events are rare, it's good to know that they are possible and to plan accordingly with rain gear, travel insurance, or flexible plans.

Thankfully, most of the Disney Resort hotels have laundry facilities, which means you don't need to overpack or worry about running out of clean clothes.

Year-round, sunny mornings can turn quickly to afternoon rain and then back to sunshine again. This is Florida…it will likely rain at some point. A simple folding umbrella can keep you in the fun on rainy days when the crowds are much smaller. Don't dismay if it rains on your vacation – many of Disney's best attractions are fully enclosed and continue running during inclement weather!

More and more, your Disney experience is managed via your smartphone. But that means you need to keep your devices powered throughout your day. Bring an extra battery charger or two for your devices. Yes, there are places to charge your devices within the parks and hotels. But they are limited. Bringing battery packs will keep you connected to the necessary resources from park opening to park closing.

Protect your Technology

Smartphones and tablets are common sights these days at the parks, but turbulent rollercoasters, passing storms and soaking water rides can permanently damage your devices. Protective cases are highly recommended. **Tip!** Bring a simple zip lock bag that you can slip your phone into whenever you are about to get on a ride with the threat of some water. Capturing a little air in the bag can even add a layer of cushioning that can further protect your gadget. **Tip!** A tablet may have a camera on it, but if you are using a tablet as a camera there is a good chance you are blocking the view of many others behind you. Be courteous to others – use a phone or a regular point and shoot camera when you are watching a show with a crowd.

Getting to Orlando

This guide book will not recommend a specific airline or the best way for you to drive to Orlando. There are just too many variables. Some things you do need to do for yourself. But I will give you the information you need to make smart decisions. How you get to Orlando can simply depend on your distance from Florida and the time you want to spend on the road versus getting to your vacation destination fast and efficiently through the air. For some people, the journey is just part of the adventure. There might be plenty of beautiful sites to experience between your home and the Walt Disney World® Resort.

It might just boil down to some simple budgetary math. Compare the cost of driving (gas, time, hotel stops along the way, toll roads, hotel and theme park parking fees, etc) versus the cost of air travel (tickets, bag fees, rides to and from the airport) and you might come up with very clear answers for you and your family.

It should be noted that the global pandemic adds new twists to consider. Controlling exposure to extra people and unsure surfaces. If practical, you might want to consider driving your own car as a way to keep your family in a known safe sanitary bubble. But factor in how many stops you might need to make for fueling, restroom, and hotel breaks depending on the distance you are willing to travel. Plus driving comes with additional fees. Many hotels in Orlando charge a parking fee per night. Many parks charge a parking fee per visit. And let's not forget about toll roads and simple wear and tear on your vehicle. Those extra costs can really add up.

Air travel might bunch you up in a crowded jet. Depending on the airline you fly, some carriers are very vigilant about the health threats and take your personal safety very seriously. Some, not so much. Learning how an air carrier promises to keep you and your family safe should be a priority as you make your plans. Remember masks may be required (and eye protection might be a good additional precaution) while on a flight. Most airlines do cycle in outside fresh air constantly while filtering out stale cabin air. In most cases, the air within an airplane is kept cleaner than you might find in your neighborhood grocery store.

For the most part, airports have been very good about implementing heightened cleaning procedures and ways to socially distant travelers. There are ways to do contactless ticketing and payment for little amenities along the way. Rules are in flux but I suggest you wear a mask whenever around other people and wash your hands obsessively. Airports are probably more safe than most public areas in your life. But the pandemic is not over everywhere and airports and airplanes cater to people from all over the world.

Do the math. See what saves you the most money or provides you with the best possible experience.

Get your park admission in advance

There have been some very big changes to how Disney handles access to the parks. Walt Disney World® has recently enhanced its ticket structures. You must now purchase advance tickets for the specific dates you intent to visit the parks. And now park admission does indeed expire.

During the global pandemic, Disney may limit the amount of guests who may enter a park on any given day. You will need to reserve the specific day you wish to visit a park. This makes working closely with a qualified Disney travel planner more important than ever.

On the downside, this means you might need to plan your vacation a little more than you might during normal times. Look at how much time you will have at the Walt Disney World® Resort and make smart decisions about purchasing admission to the parks. For example, let's say you have planned a whole week at Walt Disney World®. Will you have time to visit a park on your travel days? Maybe, maybe not. Don't buy more admission than you might really need. You can always add tickets later. If you work with Customer Service or a ticketing agent, Disney will give you the package price for additional tickets if you add to a multiple ticket package.

That said, you should buy admission for all the days you know you are going to spend in the Disney Parks. The cost of Disney admission actually goes down the longer you stay. For example, a one-day admission to Magic Kingdom® is roughly $120, but if you buy a five-day admission, it will cost you about $80 a day. Even less beyond that.

With the Magic Kingdom®, Epcot®, Disney's Hollywood Studios®, and Disney's Animal Kingdom® all waiting to be explored, you might want to buy at least a four-day admission to experience all four parks.

If you plan to experience any of Disney's wonderful water parks, bundle those tickets in with your main park admissions to save money over buying the water park tickets separately. The true savings seem to come if you plan more than one day in the water parks.

Park Hopping

Park hopping allows you to visit two or more different Disney Parks on the same day. It is an option you can purchase if you have a multi-day pass to Walt Disney World®. While Disney is stepping back many of their pandemic rules, Disney might still control access to individual parks to keep them from overcrowding. You can check to see if the other parks are reaching capacity by calling 407-560-5000 before you choose to hop.

As a Park Hopper, you can start your day at Disney's Animal Kingdom® to take in the Festival of *The Lion King* and then use Disney's transportation options to "hop" over to Disney's Hollywood Studios® to ride Tower of Terror. Then you might decide to grab a Minnie-Van ride on over to Epcot® for an amazing lunch somewhere within the World Showcase. Then you may hop onto the monorail to the Magic Kingdom® to get dinner and catch the fireworks over the castle at the end of the night.

That was a somewhat extreme example, but it gives you an idea of how park hopping can really let you orchestrate an incredible day if you know where everything is and how best to get there.

If you are new to the Walt Disney World® experience it may be wise not to choose park hopping, as it adds a layer of time consumption and logistics you may not want to take on until you become a more seasoned Disney visitor.

Beware of third-party discounts and special offers
I strongly advise you to buy your admission passes only from Disney's phone reservationists at 407-W-Disney, the official MyDisneyExperience app, waltdisneyworld.com, or a Disney Certified Travel Expert.

The internet is jammed with discount tickets and special offers. Many of these are outright scams, or bait offers to get you to attend a real estate seminar or some other sales pitch. Don't waste your time. Don't risk purchasing bogus admission passes.

In most cases Disney admission is non-transferable, which makes it very difficult for third parties to obtain real tickets to sell. The best way to be sure you have real admission passes is to buy them directly from Disney or a Disney Certified Travel Expert. During these days of restricted attendance in all the parks it is more important than ever to work directly with registered Disney experts.

Official Disney Special Offers and Packages

Disney does offer special deals and packages throughout the year. Sometimes its significant discounts on Disney hotel room rates. Sometimes its free dining when you book a Disney hotel package. Sometimes it is a discount on park admission bundled with a hotel stay. It's not always boldly posted on the Walt Disney World® site or their app. You can usually find deals by scrolling to the very bottom of the website in fine print under "Vacation Packages". Be sure to ask your certified Disney vacation planner about special deals too. Check in with them often before your trip. Ask if any new deals have been offered. They can often apply some deals even if they appear after you already booked your vacation!

MagicBands

In 2014 the Walt Disney World® Resort began transitioning away from paper and credit card-like tickets to its MagicBand system. MagicBands are plastic wristbands with an embedded RFID (radio frequency) chip.

Basic MagicBands were complementary when you booked your vacation with a stay in a Disney Resort hotel. They are no longer free. But they can be purchased through the MyDisneyExperience app or website. **Tip!** Old Magic Bands from previous trips can be reactivated and used again. While the MagicBands are certainly nifty and convenient. A lot of the same functions can be accomplished on a smart phone you probably already have. Plus the phone will allow you to make changes to your plans (Genie choices, dining reservations, etc) where the MagicBands cannot. That said, the bands are undeniably cool and can grant some independence to members of your family who might not want to spend vacation time on their smart phones.

This band securely references your park admission, your Disney hotel room key, your dining plan points and restaurant reservations. It can even link charging privileges to a credit card or to your hotel room if you wish. MagicBands can be purchased with your hotel reservation or admission to the theme parks via the Disney app or website.

One cool service you can add to your MagicBands is Memory Maker. With Memory Maker, Disney's pro photographers and ride cameras will snap your photos and automatically send them to a website for you to download later. Disney is working on special features that will enhance moments on certain rides and character greetings by reading your MagicBand to personalize your experiences. We'll talk more about Memory Maker in a moment.

Don't panic if you lose your MagicBand. Go to any park's Guest Services station or your Disney hotel concierge desk and they will outfit you with a new one and deactivate your missing one.

One of the things I love most about MagicBands is their excellent built-in security. Your band is matched to your biometric information (a finger print or a facial scan), so even if someone gets ahold of your lost MagicBand, they can't use it to gain access to a park. They can't make any purchases on it either since that requires a PIN, and your hotel room number is not printed or stored anywhere on it. In fact, none of your personal information is stored on the MagicBand at all – the chip only holds a number, which matches you to your information on Disney's secure computers.

If you lose a MagicBand, Guest Services can replace it in minutes and deactivate the missing band, making it nothing more than a piece of plastic. The "magic" is gone from the missing band. Your information always remains safe.

During the global pandemic, Disney was not requiring the finger print scan. You may be asked to verify your admission against a government issued ID in some rare cases. Disney is phasing in touch-less facial recognition technology that may one day soon replace the finger print scan.

MagicMobile!

Honestly having a smart phone during your vacation is becoming more and more important. Disney is reducing its emphasis on the MagicBands and moving many of those capabilities to smart phones. Either device or a combination of both can make your Disney vacation really convenient. Even if you resist technology, you may want to adopt a smart phone before visiting Disney Parks.

Introducing Disney Genie, Disney Genie+, and Lightning Lane!

This is something brand new being offered for the first time in the fall of 2021. Disney has retired the FastPass system and replaced it with a comprehensive, day planning assistant, built right into the MyDisneyExperience app called **Disney Genie**. Basically, Disney has automated the entire process of visiting the parks if you choose to use it. I really recommend you use it! More than just for reserving rides, the Disney Genie assistant will help you plan your day by taking a quick questionnaire to measure your family's interests and tastes. You can pick characters, thrill rides, DoleWhips, or select them all. The automation considers your choices then helps plan your day before you arrive. It adjusts on-the-fly to get you into the shortest lines and appropriate dining choices. Disney Genie is complimentary and available for everyone with a smart device.

Disney Genie+ is a $15 up-charge per ticket, per day, but this up-charge allows you access to Lightning Lanes at select attractions. This is the replacement to FastPasses. You choose one attraction reservation at a time for Disney's most popular attractions (for yourself or your whole travel party if they too have Genie+ and are linked together with you in the app). As soon as you use one of these **Lightning Lane** entrances, you can create another in your app. One by one, throughout your entire day. Unlike the old FastPass system, the Genie+ system should continue to feed you Lightning Lane options all day and it should know when you park-hop and offer up the appropriate ride options for the park you are actually in at any given moment.

For an additional charge, you can purchase access to premium Lightning Lane attractions. Limit two per day and prices for this privilege might vary widely depending on the crowd levels in the park. These premium attractions may include Disney's blockbuster rides like *Star Wars*-Rise of the Resistance, *Ratatouille*, *Guardians of the Galaxy:* Cosmic Rewind, and the *TRON* coaster. These premium attractions will not be offered on the selection of Genie + attractions for Lightning Lane access. However, these premium attractions will continue to have regular free standby lines or free boarding groups every day.

PhotoPass will now be part of Disney Genie and will offer special filters and special effects only available through the app. Disney visiting pros know the Disney PhotoPass photographers offer magical surprises when you let them take your picture. However, now some new magic augmented reality photos and videos will appear through the app on your smartphone! Memory Maker is the way you can pre-pay for all the special photos shot by Disney Photographers and on-ride photos and videos

Disney Genie can provide audio offerings as you wander through the parks giving you some of the insider information, park history, and secrets throughout your day.

You can ask the Disney Genie questions throughout your day via the app's text capability.

It is yet to be seen if this new offering is going to be the amazing service Disney hopes it will be. But I have to admit, if this service delivers what it promises, this really could expedite lines, minimize confusion, and maximize your fun. The pandemic and the ever-growing popularity of the parks have admittedly made visiting the parks more complicated than ever before. Though throwing a technology solution at these challenges might not always be the right answer, and tech-challenged guests might really suffer, I think this could be a great innovation that will only get better with time.

At the time of writing this book, folks on social media are concerned with these changes. But honestly, Disney is late to this pay-for-access way of running amusement parks. Other parks, including Universal Studios, have had this sort of ticketing up-charge for quite some time. And since we really won't know how this affects everyone until it is fully implemented this fall, griping about it might be very premature.

Everyone is focused on the pay-per-access for some premium rides aspect of the announcement. But they are overlooking how this might actually benefit the folks who choose not to pay for special access at all. Free stand-by lines and boarding groups are still going to be available for every attraction. Premium or not. Disney has hinted that they will greatly boost the price of the two paid premium access choices people can make on any given day if the demand for the attraction is great. Which will deter most people for paying for that option. The fewer people using the premium paid options benefits the folks who are waiting for free access.

Since Disney Genie and Genie+ no longer allow for advanced ride reservations like the old FastPass system did, something that has been missing at Disney World for a while might return: Spontaneity. Guests actually complained a lot about the idea of choosing rides and restaurants months before their vacation even began. And though reservations are still recommended for many of Disney's dining venues, Disney Genie might bring back the simple joy of choosing what you want to do in the moment or at least on the same day as your visit. In this new system, paid option or not, no one gets a real head start at anything in the parks. Choices for all the Genie options have to be made same day or in the moment. The system is meant to put regular guests into the shortest queues and open them up to possibly finding a dining option during the time they actually feel hungry. Not months before.

With better managed free options, a good assortment of Genie+ Lightning Lane choices, and a very limited amount of pay-for-premium ride options, it is possible that this new approach to running the parks could make visiting the parks better for everyone. We shall see in the coming years if this is the case!

Memory Maker and PhotoPass

Disney offers two amazing photography/video services. PhotoPass and Memory Maker.

PhotoPass includes literally hundreds of Disney photographers placed strategically throughout the parks (and some resorts) readily standing by to snap pictures of you. They will scan your Magic Band and you will be able to go back and view and purchase your favorite pictures later.

The Memory Maker service costs around $200. It's a way of pre-purchasing all the PhotoPass photos in advance. It is a great way to ensure you go home with amazing vacation photos. It lets you and your family actually be in those family photographs together, rather than always missing one family member who is stuck handling the camera.

You can add Memory Maker to your Disney vacation package well in advance (usually discounted with an advanced purchase) or add it to your MagicBand's capabilities anytime during your vacation.

Disney photographers are located just about everywhere throughout the parks. They just scan your MagicBand and take your photo whenever you want to capture a moment. During the global pandemic, Disney's photographers cannot take pictures with your cameras. For your health and safety, they are required to only handle their own camera gear. Hopefully when things return to normal, Disney's shooters can go back to helping you get great shots with your own phones and cameras. But for now, please understand their need to stick to their own gear.

The Memory Maker service also includes those special photos that are automatically snapped from the precipice of Splash Mountain, or just before you are dropped down the Tower of Terror's elevator shaft. This service really does provide images and videos that you could not take yourself!

If you opt-into the Memory Maker service, be sure to use it often! Have those Disney photographers photograph you, family, and friends at every opportunity. The service costs the same whether you barely use it or you use it a lot, so use it a lot!

Capture the Moment

You can hire a Disney PhotoPass photographer for a private session around the castle at Magic Kingdom. One 20 minute session costs $50 but you can book a double session if you want more time and more keepsake images for $100. Call 407-939-7758 to reserve your time if you want studio quality images of you and your loved ones on your next visit to Magic Kingdom (not yet offered in other parks).

Keep Track of your Plans

The MyDisneyExperience.com website, app, and Disney Genie are great for keeping track of your plans. However, there are times when you might not have a good Wi-Fi connection, or it may not be practical to access your device.

Here is a simple spreadsheet I use when I plan my Disney vacations. In fact, here is an example of how I recently used it. You can use it as a template or print up a few copies on good old-fashioned paper. Sure, it's low tech, but it will allow you to keep your plans in order even if your devices are unavailable.

Example:

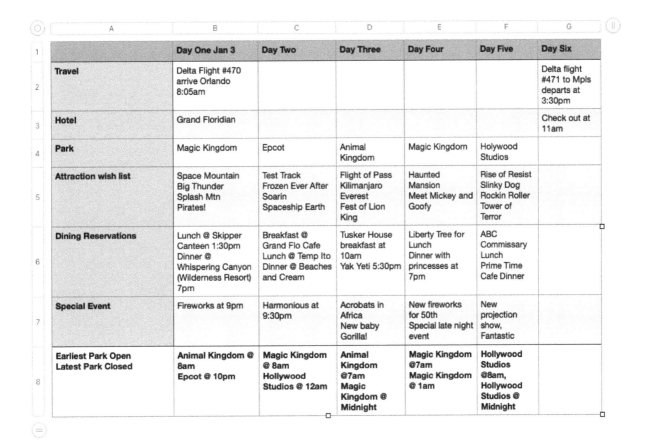

	Day One Jan 3	Day Two	Day Three	Day Four	Day Five	Day Six
Travel	Delta Flight #470 arrive Orlando 8:05am					Delta flight #471 to Mpls departs at 3:30pm
Hotel	Grand Floridian					Check out at 11am
Park	Magic Kingdom	Epcot	Animal Kingdom	Magic Kingdom	Holywood Studios	
Attraction wish list	Space Mountain Big Thunder Splash Mtn Pirates!	Test Track Frozen Ever After Soarin Spaceship Earth	Flight of Pass Kilimanjaro Everest Fest of Lion King	Haunted Mansion Meet Mickey and Goofy	Rise of Resist Slinky Dog Rockin Roller Tower of Terror	
Dining Reservations	Lunch @ Skipper Canteen 1:30pm Dinner @ Whispering Canyon (Wilderness Resort) 7pm	Breakfast @ Grand Flo Cafe Lunch @ Temp Ito Dinner @ Beaches and Cream	Tusker House breakfast at 10am Yak Yeti 5:30pm	Liberty Tree for Lunch Dinner with princesses at 7pm	ABC Commissary Lunch Prime Time Cafe Dinner	
Special Event	Fireworks at 9pm	Harmonious at 9:30pm	Acrobats in Africa New baby Gorilla!	New fireworks for 50th Special late night event	New projection show, Fantastic	
Earliest Park Open Latest Park Closed	**Animal Kingdom @ 8am Epcot @ 10pm**	**Magic Kingdom @ 8am Hollywood Studios @ 12am**	**Animal Kingdom @7am Magic Kingdom @ Midnight**	**Magic Kingdom @7am Magic Kingdom @ 1am**	**Hollywood Studios @8am, Hollywood Studios @ Midnight**	

Here's a blank template you can use for your own planning. Or make one of your own.

	Day One Jan 3	Day Two	Day Three	Day Four	Day Five	Day Six
Travel						
Hotel						
Park Pass						
Attraction wish list						
Special Event						
Dining Reservations						

Make Wise Hotel Choices

Perhaps, the biggest decision you will need to make well in advance of your vacation will be where you will stay.

Do you want to stay at a Disney Resort hotel?
Or do you want to stay at a hotel outside the Disney property?

Many people assume that off-campus, non-Disney-run hotels must be less expensive than the famous Disney Resort hotels. That may be true at first glance, but remember — you may be able to skip the added costs of a rental car, gas, and parking while staying at a Disney Resort hotel.

Factor in the complementary shuttling between attractions and other advantages Disney hotels offer – including preferential reservations at Disney's finer dining spots, time saved traveling to and from the parks, as well as early admission into the parks. Suddenly, staying at a Walt Disney World® Resort hotel becomes more and more attractive.

You may be surprised to learn that along with their famously luxurious themed resort hotels, Disney also offers many options for budget-conscious travelers without sacrificing the quality or service you would expect from a Disney-branded hotel. You may also be surprised to learn that Disney now has many family suites available within their Value Resort hotel options.

Okay. Let's dive a little deeper into this topic...

Non-Disney Hotels

The area surrounding Disney's campus is packed with all types of hotels: ranging from the budget-minded to the downright ritzy. You can find most major national chains here.

As a rule, stick to the hotel brands that you know. Read online reviews. Find out what extra services these hotels might offer in an effort to compete with the considerable perks offered by the official Disney hotels. That said, there are some really wonderful resort hotels in the surrounding area that might be less expensive than the famous Disney hotels.

Most area hotels will provide basic amenities like pools, family suites, and shuttles to many of the area's major attractions (but not always for free), and many will offer special rates and meals for children traveling with their parents.

If you have a large family or a bigger than average group, you might want to consider renting an area vacation home. Travel agencies keep listings of privately-owned houses that can accommodate larger numbers of people. Sometimes these vacation home rentals can be more affordable than some of Disney's bigger lodging offerings.

Do the math. You could save some serious money staying at a non-Disney hotel. But you need to consider the extras to complete the picture. How much is the shuttle service offered by the hotel? How much will a rental car, fuel, parking, and tolls add to your vacation? How much time might be wasted in traffic between your hotel and the parks?

If the numbers line up for you, and the math works out to be similar for a Disney and a non-Disney lodging, I strongly recommend you consider staying "on property" at a real Walt Disney World® Resort hotel. Here's why…

Walt Disney World® Resort Hotels

Staying in a Disney Resort hotel can make a good vacation even better because the Disney magic is with you throughout your entire stay. Disney offers a range of incredible resort hotels that could easily be standalone vacation locations even without the theme parks nearby. The fact that these amazing places happen to be in the middle of the largest vacation destination on the planet just expands your vacation experience.

The Perks of Staying at a Walt Disney World® Resort Hotel:

Time

I can't stress this one enough. Your vacation time is precious, right? Consider how much time you will spend commuting to and from the parks every day of your vacation if you decide to stay off campus. If you stay in a Disney hotel, you are literally in the middle of it all.

Depending on which Disney hotel you choose, there will be buses, cable cars, boats, and/or monorails departing for every corner of the Disney property every 15 to 20 minutes – you are never more than a half hour from another Disney Park or resort hotel. By comparison, many Orlando hotels are about an hour drive from the Disney campus in traffic.

Disney's Complementary Magical Express

When you book a stay at any Walt Disney World® Resort hotel, you can enjoy Disney's complementary Magical Express service that takes you from the Orlando International Airport to your Disney hotel in a comfortable air-conditioned motor coach, and then back to the airport at the end of your vacation.

Disney will be phasing out the Magical Express bus service sometime during 2021. Take advantage of it while you can! Mears Connect (the current contracted provider of Magical Express) will take over the resort shuttle service in 2022. This will no longer be a complimentary service but it will offer expanded coverage to the Universal Resorts too. Mears Connect will charge $32 per person, round trip service between the airport and the Disney Resorts.

The city of Orlando and the Walt Disney World® Resort complex is building a high-speed rail system between the airport and Disney Springs®. This cool new transportation choice is estimated to become available before 2024. We assume this rail system is the reason why Disney is phasing out their complimentary bus service from the airport. This streamlined new rail option will likely become the preferred (and perhaps most cost-effective) way to shuttle between the Disney Resort and the Orlando Airport once the Disney Springs® station opens in a few years.

The Walt Disney World® Transportation System

Disney Resort hotel guests enjoy free and unlimited use of the well-designed system of buses, ferries, and monorails that crisscross the massive property in a swift, intuitive and convenient way. No need to hassle with traffic or parking. No need to rent a car. No getting lost or stressed out. Imagine a vacation without these pitfalls, and the transportation advantages of staying at a Disney hotel become obvious!

Parking Advantages

If you choose to drive to the Disney Resort or rent a car once you arrive in Orlando, you need to know that Disney Resort hotel guests do pay a fee to park at the resorts (between $15 and $25 per night depending on the resort you choose) but they enjoy free standard parking at all the Disney theme parks during their stay. If you need closer access to the parks from the parking lot, you can pay the difference for premium parking in the theme parks.

Minnie-Vans

Only Disney Resort guests can summon a red and white polka dot SUV through the Lyft® car service app. Disney charges the same rates as a premium Lyft® and may vary depending on the time of day and the demand of the season. This is not a free service but it is a great option when you need to park hop across the resort to make it to a dinner reservation, or you just don't want to wait for the other more crowded complementary transportation options. This service was halted during the pandemic shutdown but we expect it to return soon.

Extra Magic Hours... Kind of

During the pandemic, Disney discontinued a major perk for Disney Resort Hotel guests called Extra Magic Hours. This offered either an early hour admission into a select park before it opened for the rest of the park guests or two extra hours of fun after closing (limited only to guests of Disney's hotels). According to the official Disney website, a slightly altered version of this perk might be coming back. The new version of Extra Magic Hours would keep select attractions open in a select park during these extended hours limited to select Disney Resort hotels. More details to come, but keep your eyes open for more on this much beloved Disney perk's return.

Early Entry to the Parks

Though it is not the perk it used to be, Disney Resort hotel guests will now enjoy a half hour head start at all the theme parks. This early entrance means you and your family can knock out at least one, maybe two, of the most popular attractions at any park by arriving before the posted park opening times. Disney Resort guests also get a slight head start each morning on the Disney Genie app to plan and select or purchase Lightning Lane choices.

Dining Options and Advantages

This is not an official perk, but more of an advantage many newcomers overlook. Anyone, whether they stay at a Disney hotel or not, can book dinner reservations throughout Walt Disney World® 180 days in advance (60 days in advance during pandemic times). Most people use this perk to book breakfast with Cinderella in the castle or with the Beast in his opulent dining room. While these are great choices, Disney pros know that some of the best dining experiences in all of Disney are outside of the parks in the resort hotels or at Disney Springs®. Depending where you choose to stay might put you just a few steps away from an amazing dining experience. Knowing that some of these special restaurants are located outside of the parks, it can provide a much needed break from the bustling theme parks. When you make your advanced reservations consider these incredible options that many people miss.

Concierge Services

Once your vacation is underway, as a Disney Resort hotel guest, you also have access to the hotel's concierge service to plan additional spur-of-the-moment dining options, tours, and events.

The Disney Dining Plans

Disney Resort hotel guests can opt-into one of Disney's special dining plans, which can provide guests with an all-inclusive feel to their vacation. Guests can choose from a variety of options including table-service, quick counter-service, or a combination of the two.

When you purchase a dining plan, everyone in your travel party is allotted points to cover a certain number of meals and snacks every day of your stay, and you can use the points at whatever pace you choose. When you do the math and know the variety of dining options available and consider what you get for your money, the dining plan can be a real value to vacationers with big appetites. The plans offer a lot of food.

I think of these plans as more of a convenience. What you might get with a dining plan is similar to the value you might pay out-of-pocket meal to a meal.

No doubt, food can be a wild fluctuation on your vacation budget. Some folks love the dining plans as it locks down the cost of food during their trip.

During slower times of the year, Disney will even offer the dining plan for free! Keep an eye out for these packages! Free Dining at Disney can be one of the best bargains they offer. For more details on the Disney dining plans, check out the Dining section of this book.

Disney's dining plan offerings are not currently available at the time of this writing as a measure to reduce capacity in restaurants to preserve guest safety. I assume this perk of staying within the Disney Resorts will return when normal operations can resume.

Golf Privileges

Walt Disney World® contains some of the country's finest fairways and greens. Disney Resort hotel guests get preferential tee times. Even so, these courses are so popular you will want to make your arrangements as far in advance as possible. As a Disney Resort hotel guest, you can reserve your tee time as soon as you book your room.

Recreational Options

Besides the wonderfully themed pools, shops, and restaurants at any Disney Resort hotel, you have an array of other recreational opportunities available to you while staying at a Disney hotel. Kid's pool parties daily, nightly complementary movies, Boating, fishing, waterskiing, surf lessons at Typhoon Lagoon®, behind-the-scenes tours, nighttime safaris at Disney's Animal Kingdom Lodge, horseback riding at Fort Wilderness... the list goes on and on!

Disney's Cast and Crew

Honestly, the reason all of us at *Actual Factual Magic* keep returning to Disney time and again is because they hire such extraordinary people. There are lots of other good amusement parks out there, but if they aren't staffed with friendly, bright, service-minded people, then they're just a collection of rides. Disney hires the cream of the crop. In polls, 80% of travelers have cited Disney's Cast Members as being their favorite part of their Disney vacation. I wholeheartedly agree.

If you decide to stay at a Disney Resort hotel, make your reservations as early as possible because these wonderful places have very high occupancy rates all year round. Not booking your room early could mean you'll be looking for lodging elsewhere.

Let's take a look at all of Disney's official lodging options...

The Walt Disney World® Resort Hotels

The Disney Resort hotels fall into three categories: deluxe, moderate, and value. Deluxe Resorts offer the highest level of luxury, amenities, and services. Moderate Resorts offer many of those quality services and amenities but at a more moderate cost. Value Resorts offer lots of Disney magic at more affordable prices. Let's start with the biggest and best and work our way down.

Deluxe Villas

Disney offers guests traveling with larger families the opportunity to enjoy the best of a Disney Resort experience while having roomier accommodations and special features like multiple bedrooms and bathrooms, full kitchens and dining areas. These villas and apartments are typically Disney Vacation Club member's lodging but anyone can book these villas. Disney offers these bigger accommodations as regular hotel rooms but **Tip!** With some extra planning you might find these rooms at a bargain by renting Disney Vacation Club points from DVC members who cannot use their points at that particular time. Check out Dave's Vacation Club Rental at dvcrequest.com and maybe save some big money on your family's next get-away.

Disney's Animal Kingdom Villas: Jambo and Kidani Houses

These special wings of the Animal Kingdom Lodge offer larger accommodations for bigger families to relax. Some rooms offer views onto wild grasslands populated by real giraffes and zebras. Adjacent to the main resort hotel pools you will find wonderful themed shops and restaurants.

Bay Lake Tower at Disney's Contemporary Resort

This new addition to the Walt Disney World® Resort collection offers larger rooms for bigger families and is only one walking bridge away from all the amenities and restaurants of the Contemporary Resort.

Disney's BoardWalk Villas

Waterfront cottages put guests in a prime location to enjoy the nightlife and excitement of the BoardWalk® entertainment area. Large, apartment-like accommodations allow bigger families or just weary travelers to stretch out and relax. Larger cottages for families and romantic studios for couples. These villas share the pools, shops and restaurants with Disney's BoardWalk Inn.

Disney's Old Key West Resort

Reminiscent of the classic resorts of the Florida Keys, this is a 760-room hotel community where you can choose between studio, villa, and one, two or three-bedroom accommodations. Located close to Disney's famous Lake Buena Vista golf course and downtown Disney Springs® for endless nighttime fun. There's not just one pool here...there are four! Guests can also enjoy beaches, two arcades, a basketball court, bike rentals, a fitness center, community hall, jogging trails and more.

Disney's Saratoga Springs Resort and Spa

Themed after an old Floridian estate with a touch of Victorian class, this is where you will find the famous Disney Treehouse Villas. Recently renovated to provide even more family comfort. This resort's suites and villas provide full kitchens and laundry facilities. The Grand Villas are big enough to sleep 12 guests. Enjoy a barbecue pavilion, community hall, basketball court, bike rentals, jogging trails and easy access to Disney's legendary golf courses.

Boulder Ridge Villas at Wilderness Lodge

Attached to the main lobby of the Wilderness Lodge Resort, a five-story tower houses larger accommodations for those who prefer more space when they travel. The villas share the pools, shops and restaurants of the main hotel.

The Polynesian Villas and Bungalows

Newly added to the famous Polynesian hotel property, these incredible accommodations include stilt houses built above the waves of the Seven Seas Lagoon. How cool is that?

Disney's Riviera Hotel

This brand new hotel will primarily host Disney Vacation Club members. But guests who need a little more space or prefer a hotel with a little more professional business feel can book rooms here too. The Riviera is connected to some other resorts, Epcot®, and Disney's Hollywood Studios® by the new Skyliner cable gondola system. Of course it is also a part of the normal Disney transportation system with buses running regularly to all the parks.

Deluxe Resort Hotels

The Contemporary

Set as the perfect backdrop to the Magic Kingdom's Tomorrowland, this futuristic A-frame structure was one of the original resort hotels when Walt Disney World® opened, and it is famous for the monorail that passes right through the middle of the main hotel. It has recently gone through a major renovation and expansion. Many of the rooms have incredible views of the Magic Kingdom® (fireworks!) and the Seven Seas Lagoon. Nestled on top of the Contemporary, the California Grill offers exceptional views and dining. Hotel amenities include shops, dining at Chef Mickey's, Steakhouse 71, and The Contempo Cafe in the lobby, a new pool area, white sand beach, a marina on the Bay Lake side, tennis and volleyball courts, and boat rentals. Transportation to the rest of the resort is by monorail, ferries, and buses. You can even walk to the Magic Kingdom®. It is only a few blocks away from the Contemporary grounds. **Tip:** If you dine at the California Grill or the adjacent lounge anytime during the same day, you can return with your receipt that evening to view Magic Kingdom's fireworks from the hotel's rooftop observation deck.

The Grand Floridian Resort and Spa

Meant to be an extension of turn-of-the-century Main Street USA, this is the finest official Walt Disney World® hotel and ranks as one of the top hotels in the world. This seaside Victorian giant occupies the western shore of the Seven Seas Lagoon. Taking design cues from the classic Hotel del Coronado in California, this iconic resort has some of the Walt Disney World® Resort's finest dining including Citrico, Narcoossee's, and Victoria and Albert's. You can find less formal dining at Gasparilla Grill and Games, and the Grand Floridian Café. Two restaurant lounges were recently combined into one gorgeous *Beauty and the Beast* themed lounge called the Enchanted Rose. Character dining opportunities can be found at 1900 Park Fare. This resort boasts two beautiful pools and full spa facilities, white sand beaches, watercraft rentals, preferred golf reservations, jogging trails and more. Transportation to the rest of Walt Disney World® is by monorail, ferries and buses. There is a newly opened walking path to the Magic Kingdom®.

Grand Floridian Lobby

The Polynesian Resort

One of the Walt Disney World's most iconic resorts, the Polynesian, was designed to extend the Adventureland experience with its South Seas theme. 'Ohana is the featured restaurant and Kona Cafe offers a more relaxed sit-down dining experience. This resort has two quick-service dining spots: Captain Cook's and Kona Island. Smaller food offerings are also available around the pool. The Polynesian regularly stages a dinner show featuring hula dancers in an outdoor tropical theater setting. Seek out the almost hidden Trader Sam's lounge for an unforgettable evening in a South Seas speakeasy kind of setting. There is a marina where guests can rent boats, a white sand beach, play volleyball, and enjoy a large themed pool. Transportation to the rest of the Walt Disney World® attractions is by monorail, ferries, and buses. The Polynesian is wrapping up an extensive resort-wide remodeling which will include lots of new *Moana* themes.

The Wilderness Lodge
The perfect continuation of your Frontierland experience, this Deluxe Resort was designed after the rustic lodges of America's great national parks, like Yosemite, complete with a geyser that erupts periodically in the courtyard. Artist Point is the featured restaurant, with other moderate and quick-service dining options including Territory Lodge, Roaring Fork, and the Whispering Canyon Café. There is a wonderful North Woods-themed pool, a boat marina, a beach on beautiful Bay Lake, jogging and hiking trails, bike rentals, and fishing. Transportation to the rest of the Walt Disney World® Resort is by ferries and buses.

The Animal Kingdom Lodge
Modeled after a South African safari lodge, some rooms have windows and balconies that literally look onto the hotel's own African savannah. You may find real giraffes and zebras browsing the grounds outside your room window. Jiko-The Cooking Place is the standout restaurant here, featuring an African and Middle Eastern menu. Sanaa and Boma Flavors of Africa provide more moderately priced dining. You can grab a drink at the Cape Town Lounge & Wine Bar or private dining rounding out the rest of your dining options. Other amenities include a wonderful gift shop and a massive safari-themed pool. Transportation to the rest of Walt Disney World® is by bus.

Disney's Beach Club Resort
Located between the Epcot® and Disney's Hollywood Studios® theme parks on beautiful Crescent Lake, directly across from Disney's BoardWalk® entertainment area, this resort was designed to resemble a classic New England seaside resort. Fantastic dining spots are shared between this and the connected Yacht Club Resort. Signature dining is at the Yachtsman Steakhouse, with additional dining at the recently expanded Beaches and Cream Soda Shop, Cape May Café, Beach Club Marketplace, and Ale & Compass lounge and restaurant. The Beach Club shares a massive white sand beach pool with its neighbor, Disney's Yacht Club Resort. There are bike and watercraft rentals, fishing, and a fitness center. Transportation to the rest of Walt Disney World® is by ferries and buses.

Disney's Yacht Club Resort
This lakeside resort evokes turn-of-the-century New England yachting luxury and shares a large nautically-themed pool and beach area with Disney's Beach Club Resort. Fantastic dining spots are shared between this and the connected Beach Club Resort. Featured dining is at the Yachtsman Steakhouse, with additional dining at newly expanded Beaches and Cream Soda Shop, Beach Club Marketplace, Cape May Café, Captain's Grille, Ale and Compass Lounge and the Crew's Cup Lounge. Enjoy the white sand beach on Crescent Lake or at the pool. You can bikes, go fishing. or rent a watercraft. Transportation to the rest of Walt Disney World® is by ferries and buses.

Disney's BoardWalk Inn

This hotel is literally a part of Disney's BoardWalk® entertainment district and features a carnival-themed pool with a large water slide. It has an elegant seaside feel, modeled after the classic turn-of-the-century boardwalks of Atlantic City and Coney Island. Featured dining is at the Chef Menu, the CoraNation Room or Flying Fish. Perhaps, the greatest draw of this resort is its direct connection to Disney's BoardWalk® area with its impressive array of dining and nightlife options. Transportation to the rest of the Walt Disney World® Resort is by ferries and buses.

Disney's Reflections Lakeside Lodge

Slated to open in late 2022, Reflections occupies the property where America's first water park, River Country, used to stand. This Deluxe Resort will offer stunning views of Bay Lake yet offer a secluded outdoorsy feel nestled between the Wilderness Lodge and Fort Wilderness Campgrounds. It will certainly offer signature dining, pools, and a full marina. Boat access to Magic Kingdom. Bus transportation to the other theme parks and Disney Springs®.

Walt Disney World Dolphin Resort

Drawing inspiration from the Italian Renaissance, award-winning architect Michael Graves designed the Dolphin Resort and her sister across the water, The Swan. These hotels are actually owned and operated by an outside company (Marriott) under special agreement with Disney. They offer many of the same perks as Disney-owned resorts, including full use of the Disney transportation system. Signature dining is at Shula's Steak House – rated one of the top steakhouses in the United States – and at Todd English's Bluezoo. You'll find lighter fare at The Fountain and Picabu's. Enjoy the grotto pool and beach, volleyball, watercraft rental, jogging paths, miniature golf, shops, special cruises and more. Transportation to the rest of the Walt Disney World® Resort is by ferries and buses.

Walt Disney World Swan Hotel

The sister hotel to the Dolphin, with the same style and class. The Swan offers some of the best upscale dining and accommodations on property. These hotels are actually owned and operated by Marriott under special agreement with Disney. They offer many of the same perks as Disney-owned resorts, including full use of the Disney transportation system. Try signature dining at Kimonos for some great sushi in Florida, or enjoy fine Italian fare at Il Mulino New York Trattoria. Lighter meals can be found at Splash Grille, and character meals can be found at Garden Grove. Enjoy the grotto pool and beach, volleyball, watercraft rental, jogging paths, miniature golf, tennis courts, shops, specialty cruises and more. Transportation to the rest of the Walt Disney World® Resort is by ferries and buses.

The Swan Reserve

This is one of the newest lodgings on property, in fact it is not even finished construction while I am writing this. However, they are starting to book rooms. This is a fourteen story hotel tower added to the Swan's property and will be sharing some of the amenities with Dolphin and Swan. This expansion is booking as a separate hotel from the Swan and is said to offer more spacious accommodations than its older sister hotel. Transportation to the parks is provided by buses, but you can also take a friendship boat to Disney's Hollywood Studios®, Disney's BoardWalk®,

Epcot® and some of the area Disney Resort hotels. Swan Reserve is owned and operated by Marriott.

The Four Seasons
For those who want the very best in accommodations, the legendary upscale Four Seasons hotel experience is now available at Walt Disney World®. Part of the Marriott portfolio, Four Seasons has a special partnership with Disney to provide the best of luxury with the best of Disney's magic, and guests receive special luxury motor coach service to the parks. There are six outstanding restaurants ranging from upscale to casual character breakfasts. Please check out their website for details. www.fourseasons.com/orlando.

Disney's *Star Wars* Galactic Starcruiser Hotel
Roaming the streets of Black Spire Outpost, flying the Millennium Falcon, hanging out with Chewbacca, and rebelling against the First Order on board one of their Star Destroyers not enough for you? In 2022, you can start booking passage abroad the Halcyon — the galaxy's sleekest star-liner. Two night cruise packages will allow total immersion into the realm of Star Wars. While onboard, you can visit the interactive bridge, gather for drinks at the onboard galleys for family dining experiences, sneak into hidden crew areas, learn the ancient mystical practices of the Jedis, and stumble upon adventures happening onboard while evading star battles outside the hull. Disembark for day excursions to the exotic outpost of Batuu. Check Disney's website and apps for more details as the Halcyon gets closer to lift-off sometime in 2022.

Moderate Resort Hotels

The Cabins at Disney's Fort Wilderness Resort
Nestled into 750 wooded acres, these cabins offer the perfect setting for a family vacation with all the comforts of home. Ideal for folks who would like a quiet setting to escape to within their Walt Disney World® vacation. Enjoy all the recreation possibilities of the Fort Wilderness Campgrounds without the hassles of actually camping. Dining options include Trail's End Restaurant, Crockett's Tavern, and Mickey's Backyard BBQ. Do not miss the Hoop-Dee-Doo Musical Revue dinner show! Transportation to the rest of Walt Disney World® is by bus and ferry.

Disney's Caribbean Beach Resort
This very large resort somehow manages to make things feel almost quaint buy grouping guest rooms into small "villages" scattered around a large lake surrounded by a white sand beach. Each village is named after Caribbean Islands. And each village has its own small pool, with a large pirate-themed main pool near the main lobby complex. This resort was beginning to fall out of favor with travel critics, but Disney fixed that. Oh boy, did they fix that! They gave Caribbean Beach Resort its own hub on the Skyliner cable transportation system. They completely revamped the dining offerings here. The stand out restaurant here is Sabastian's Bistro. A Latin/Island flavored sit-down featuring seafood and steaks. Lighter fare available poolside at the Spyglass Grill. Miscellaneous dining options have been added in an all new expanded food court area called Centertown Market. Many of the guest rooms have been upgraded too. Transportation

to the parks provided by the Skyliner or Disney's bus service. Buses run a circle route to pick you up and drop you off closer to your "village".

Disney's Coronado Springs Resort Featuring Gran Destino Tower

The edition of this towering center hotel building transforms what was once a mundane Disney Resort known most for business convention traffic into a destination resort nearly worthy of a Deluxe qualification. While the resort still have rooms sprawled out across its large property. Choice accommodations and amenities are located in the new tower. Spacious modern rooms are perfect for business travelers and modern vacationing families alike. There is a fantastic Mayan-themed central pool and three other smaller leisure pools. Dining options have been greatly expanded on the property. The Three Bridges Grill literally sits in the middle of the resort lake. The Maya Grill features authentic Mexican fare there is even a sports bar on property if you simply cannot miss your game. Other snack options are scattered throughout the expansive resort. Transportation to the rest of the Walt Disney World® fun is provided by Disney's buses.

Disney's Port Orleans Resort: French Quarter

Disney's architectural interpretation of Bourbon Street offers Southern-style fun, tucked along the Sassagoula River. The main pool has a Mardi Gras feel, and guests can also share the Ol' Man Island Pool at Port Orleans Riverside just down the river. Dining is at a quick-service food court that features pizza and burgers, but also has excellent muffaletta sandwiches, gumbo, and jambalaya. Rent a bike or take a horse-drawn carriage to the Port Orleans Riverside. There are jogging trails and fishing holes, and you can rent watercraft at the marina at Port Orleans Riverside or enjoy a special cruise. Transportation to the rest of Walt Disney World® is by boat to Disney Springs® and buses to everywhere else. **Tip!** Disney insiders come here just for the fresh Beignets; light powder sugar pastries made famous in New Orleans.

Disney's Port Orleans Resort: Riverside

The Old South has been beautifully recreated here, from a Louisiana bayou mill to old Georgia plantation mansions. The grounds, walkways and waterways are simply gorgeous. There is a large pool designed to feel like an old southern swimmin' hole, and guests can also enjoy the Mardi Gras-themed pool over at the Port Orleans-French Quarter Resort. Upgrade to one of the "Royal Guest Rooms" to treat your family a room themed after some of their favorite Disney movies. Boatwright's Dining Hall offers Louisiana flavors, the Riverside Mill Food Court has quick-service food offerings, and a New Orleans-style lounge called River Roost provides some grownup after-hours fun. Rent watercraft at the beautiful riverside marina, or enjoy the horse carriage rides, bike rentals, jogging trails, and arcade. Transportation to the rest of Walt Disney World® is by boat to Disney Springs® and buses to everywhere else.

Value Resort Hotels

Disney's Art of Animation Resort

One of Disney's newest hotel takes family resorts in an exciting new direction, featuring literally hundreds of family-sized suites. If you have a large family, there's no need to rent multiple rooms here – this hotel features many suites with two bedrooms, two bathrooms and a family area with additional foldout couches or wall beds. This four-winged resort also has some of the best Disney theming outside of the theme parks themselves. The *Lion King*, *Cars,* and *Finding Nemo* wings feature the family suites, while the *Little Mermaid* wing features smaller, more traditional rooms. Don't miss the *Finding Nemo*-themed main pool where you can hear your favorite aquatic characters talk to you underwater! Secondary pools have *Cars* and *Little Mermaid* themes. Dining is at a colorful food court called Landscape of Flavors, and transportation to the rest of Walt Disney World® is by bus and the new Skyliner. This cable gondola system connects this resort, the Pop Century Resort and the Caribbean Beach Resort with Disney's Hollywood Studios® and Epcot®.

Disney's All-Star Movies Resort
Second only to Disney's Art of Animation when it comes to immersive Disney theming, All Star Movies has just experienced a significant make-over. After all, you came to Disney to get the full Disney experience, right? This lower-cost resort delivers many features than more expensive non-Disney hotels would miss. Each section of the resort is themed after a classic Disney movie (our favorite is the *Toy Story* wing). Other popular sections include *The Love Bug, Fantasia,* and *One Hundred and One Dalmatians.* The big main pool has a *Fantasia* theme with Wizard Mickey as a centerpiece fountain; a secondary pool features a *Mighty Duck*s hockey theme. Dining is at a food court with a good counter-service selection. There is a poolside outdoor bar that stays open late, and an arcade and a nice gift shop located just off the lobby. Transportation to the rest of Walt Disney World® is by bus.

Disney's All-Star Music Resort
This resort has a musical theme, with each section of the hotel represented by large musical instruments and a different musical genre. They rang from Broadway, jazz, to country and rock. Some of the rooms have been upgraded to be more affordable family suites. The main pool is guitar-shaped, with a smaller pool shaped like a grand piano. Dining is at a large food court, and there is an arcade and gift shop just off the lobby. Transportation to the rest of Walt Disney World® is by bus.

Disney's All-Star Sports Resort
This resort has a sports theme, with each section of the hotel designated by different sports – giant footballs, soccer balls, basketballs, surfboards, etc. There is a large beach-themed surf pool, with a smaller pool shaped like a baseball diamond. Dining is at the End Zone Food Court, and there is a gift shop and an arcade next to the lobby. Transportation to the rest of Walt Disney World® is by bus.

Disney's Pop Century Resort
This resort salutes the fads and phases we went through during the past hundred years. Hotel sections are designed around the cultural contributions of the 1950s, 60s, 70s, and 80s. There are three swimming pools, including a 1960s-themed flower-shaped main pool. Dining is in the food court, with a gift shop and arcade near the lobby. The Pop Century Resort is my pick when I want a lower-cost place to rest my head. Transportation to the rest of Walt Disney World® is by bus. This resort shares a Skyliner gondola station with Disney's Art of Animation Resort. Mountain ski resort-style, the Skyliner will whisk guests to Hollywood Studios® and Epcot®.

Roughing it, Disney Style

Disney's Fort Wilderness Campgrounds

It's a little hard to explain the Fort Wilderness Campgrounds because they offer simultaneously more...and less...than the other Disney Resorts. There are campsites where you can pitch a tent, hookups for recreational vehicles and cabins you can rent, so the experience can be as rugged or as pampered as you prefer. The campgrounds offer recreational opportunities that you may not even find at some of the more expensive Disney Resorts – things like horseback riding, carriage rides, two pools, and a full marina. Plus, you have all the traditional trappings of camping, like outdoor grilling and BBQ, fishing, hiking, and campfires. They also have the famous Hoop-Dee-Doo Musical Revue western dinner show is located here. The rates for staying at the campgrounds and cabins vary widely from super affordable to about the cost of a Moderate Disney Resort room. Prices depend on whether you choose a spot for a tent, a hookup for a giant RV or a log cabin that can sleep six comfortably.

Good Neighbor Hotels

Disney has granted some of their perks to hotels located just outside the borders of the Disney Resort. Thus, they like to call them "Good Neighbor Hotels." These are usually national chain hotel brands. If you are looking for a good alternative to the expensive Disney hotels, check them out. They won't have all the perks of the Disney hotels but maybe just enough to make them more affordable alternatives.

To learn more or book a stay at one of these amazing Disney Resort hotels, call 407-W-DISNEY, visit www.waltdisneyworld.com, the MyDisneyExperience app, Disney's new Genie app or consult a Disney Certified Travel Expert.

Exclusively for Members of the U.S. Armed Forces

Shades of Green Resort

Shades of Green is a former Disney Resort complex that is now a full Armed Forces Recreation Center dedicated to current and former military personnel and their families. In appreciation of those serving our country, this resort offers the Disney experience at a discounted rate. Although this resort is on Disney property, it is not run by Disney. Reservations need to be made through authorized military travel professionals. Visit www.shadesofgreen.org for more details and eligibility information.

Walt Disney World® Planning Timeline

Sometimes we just need things laid out for us in the simplest way possible. What follows is a chronological digest of most of the things I have talked about so far. You can use this as a check list for getting things done if you like

200 days before your trip

Start narrowing down your plans. Gather your family together. Start talking about the special things you might want to do and where you might want to stay during your vacation. Choose the time period best for your family to take your vacation. If you feel confident in your plans, there is no downside to start booking your vacation lodging even this far out.

180 days before your trip

Make dining reservations for the special dining options you really want to lock down, like a character breakfast or one of the world-class dining options Walt Disney World® has to offer. Character meals and some of the resort's most popular dining spots do book up fast and many people who are 'in the know' pounce on this 180-day mark to lockdown the best options. Some advanced reservations will require a credit card deposit. Note: During the pandemic advanced reservation requests were shortened to 60 days before your arrival.

You do not have to have a Disney hotel reservation to make advanced dining reservations. You can book your choices via the MyDisneyExperience app, Disney Genie, or website, or by phone via 1-407-WDW-DINE. Of course, you can try to make reservations for any restaurant anytime, but the most popular venues will surely book up early.

Check back regularly on any booked venues you wanted to reserve – there will be occasional cancellations and thus reservations openings you can nab if you are lucky and diligent. Some third-party websites that track dining reservations may also be helpful here.

90 days before your trip

Choose and book your hotel. This is not a hard deadline, but it is a smart one because Disney's most popular resort options will start booking up well in advance. Popular non-Disney resorts will also start booking solid around this time, so try to make your hotel choices and book your stay by 90 days out.

Book your air travel. Airfares vary widely these days, and most travel professionals will tell you to start watching for deals 90 to 30 days from your vacation dates. Sure, there are sometimes bargains to be had traveling last minute, but unforeseen changes (like weather, cost of oil) might also bump up the cost of your tickets. Don't wait too long and get stuck with no bargains at all.

60 days before your trip

During the pandemic, 60 days is the mark for making special dining reservations. Do not miss your chance to book a dining experience you and your family might never forget.

For stays, hotel guests can make online reservation requests for their hotel rooms, like wanting to be closer to the pool, or closer to transportation. You can even opt for online check-in, allowing you to bypass the whole hotel lobby check-in process and go right to your room upon arrival.

35 days before your trip

You can customize your MagicBands through the MyDisneyExperience app, Disney Genie, or website. Everyone in your party can choose their favorite color and have their names printed on the inside of the band.

30 days before your trip

Make the final payment for your trip. Different resorts have different policies on when they expect payment in full for your stay. Check with your hotel for their policies.

Start planning your transport from the airport to your hotel and back again at the end of your trip. Magical Express is available for Disney Resort Guests up until the end of 2021. In January of 2022, this service becomes Mears Connect and will no longer be complimentary. Either way, arrange your transportation with your travel agent, Disney or Mears Connect online.

Go to the postal service website and have them hold or delay your mail for the span of your vacation. It's a little thing but this can protect your home from looking unoccupied while you are away.

14 days before your trip

Some hotels have kitchens and refrigerators. Most of Disney's hotels have at least a mini fridge. If you have special dietary needs or would just like to have a supply of snacks in your room, now would be a good time to make grocery delivery arrangements with an area grocery store like GardenGrocer.com on Instacart. Your Certified Disney Travel Expert can provide you with other options too.

Within 10 days of your trip

Your MagicBands and your Magical Express Packet will be delivered separately during these last few days before your vacation. Don't pack your MagicBands in your checked luggage – you will need them to check in at Disney's Magical Express bus station on the lower level of the Orlando airport. Keep them on your wrists, or at least in your carry-on bags. In 2022, check-in with Mears Connect to make sure your shuttle from the airport is reserved.

7 days before your trip

Start packing, you're almost there! Have your group make a list of all the things you will and won't need during your stay and remember that all the Disney Resorts have guest laundry facilities. You don't need to overpack, but be ready for seasonal weather such as cold nights in the winter and the occasional threat of rain. You can buy most toiletries and sun care needs at your hotel or in the parks. Remember that airport security limits the volume of lotions and fluids you can carry and pack! Airport friendly hand sanitizers and wipes are a must!

Just before your trip

This is a pro tip: Since Disney requires a deposit or advanced payment for some of their most popular dining options, some guests may cancel their dinner reservations at the last minute due to changing plans. This might open up some last minute reservations to these dream dining venues. Check each evening of your trip too as Disney as the deposits are non-refundable to no-shows. So guests are "encouraged" to cancel if they cannot make their reservation. Meaning there could be a small assortment of openings at popular venues overnight or even same day.

Call your bank and your credit cards to let them know you will be using their cards in another state soon. Many credit and debit cards have automatic safeguards meant to keep hackers and identity thieves from using your card without your permission. By alerting your card issuers in advance of your trip you will probably keep your cards from being shut down during your vacation.

Tip! Keep a change of clothes and a swimsuit in your carry-on bag so you are ready to get right into the fun when you arrive, just in case your luggage is delayed or lost.

Check to see if there have been any changes to your flight plans, particularly if you made your travel arrangements months ago. Most airlines will let you check the details of your flight online, or you can call and speak to a person. Alert your Certified Disney Travel Expert of any changes, but with a bit of luck there won't be any. You have an amazing vacation awaiting you!

Remember: The new Genie and Genie+ systems Disney being implementing to help you plan the perfect day does not really allow you more than just a few hours of advance planning before your actual time in the parks. Be ready to start each day with your smart phone working with Genie to make initial choices and book boarding groups if needed. Disney Resort guests get a slight one hour head start on these choices before the system is available to everyone else that day. Though Disney Resort guests only get a 30 minute head start on the crowds staying elsewhere when it comes to actual entry into the parks.

Have a magical vacation.

The Disney Theme Parks

Here are some thoughts that apply to all the parks. Considering these items before and during your vacation should help you prepare for a better experience.

How should you spend your time in the parks?

Walt Disney World® is so large that it is simply impossible to experience everything in the span of a typical vacation. The best you can hope for is to fit in as much of the truly good stuff within the time you have. Rest assured, you can come back again and again, year after year, and always find new things to do!

As a rule, try to spend at least one full day at each park. Four full days – and no, travel days don't count – This will give you time to see most of the main Disney Parks: The Magic Kingdom®, Epcot®, Disney's Hollywood Studios®, and Disney's Animal Kingdom®.

If you enjoy water parks or plan to golf or see other attractions in the area, add additional days for those. Trust us, no matter how much time you can spend at Walt Disney World®, it will never feel like enough!

Our Suggestions

I strongly recommend you plan on a full week to explore Walt Disney World® if you are able to – the longer, the better! Travel days can be unpredictable, so two of your days may be absorbed with the task of just getting to and from Orlando. When you book your flight, try to arrive in Orlando as early in the day as possible and schedule your departure as late in the evening as possible, so you can maximize your Disney vacation time enjoyment.

If you get the Park Hopper privileges attached to park admission for the full length of your stay, you can move freely throughout the entire resort. I love this, because it lets us see things at a less frantic pace and I don't feel guilty about taking time to enjoy the pool or other amenities at my hotel. Slow down and marvel at the incredible details Disney applies to everything they do. Relax. Enjoy. Vacations are supposed to be about leaving stress at home, not dashing from one place to the next on a strict schedule!

Orlando has many wonderful attractions besides Walt Disney World®. If you plan to spend time at Universal Studios®, Sea World®, LegoLand®, Kennedy Space Center, area beaches or any other world-class area attraction, plan ample time for those experiences too.

Shorter Visits

What if you can't spare a whole week? What if you only have a single day? What if you want to see Orlando's other attractions during your time?

Obviously, you would run yourself ragged if you tried to see everything in such a small amount of time. It is actually impossible. Stick to the idea of spending one day per park. If you have two days, you can take in two parks.

Visit the park that has the most appeal to you and save the other parks for another trip. You will still have a wonderful time.

Use this guidebook to help make your decisions about what not to miss – especially if you are a first-time Walt Disney World® visitor, haven't been in some time, or will be embarking on a shorter vacation with strict time restrictions.

Less Crowded Dates

If you have a little flexibility when you will be visiting Walt Disney World®, there are times of the year that are predictably less crowded, which means you can accomplish more and at a more relaxed pace.

Early September up until Thanksgiving are generally quieter times to visit, because kids are back in school and many families schedule their vacations around the school calendar. Crowds diminish again just after New Year's Day, and the parks stay relatively quiet from then until mid-March when the college spring break crowds arrive. Then there is another brief window between Easter and Memorial Day.

Keep in mind that these are general observations, and a special event or promotion in any of the parks (such as RunDisney® events) can spike attendance right back up. Generally speaking, your best odds at finding smaller crowds and shorter lines will be:

- Late winter (shortly after New Year's Day through the first part of March).
- Late spring (after college spring break and Easter weekend).
- Autumn (September to late November), except the days around Halloween and Thanksgiving.
- The first two weeks of December.

More Crowded Dates

On their busiest days, the theme parks can feel downright claustrophobic, but there is good news – you can avoid crowded times with some planning! Just as there are predictably quieter times of the year in the parks, there are also predictably busy times.

The parks are particularly busy during the summer vacation period between Memorial Day and Labor Day, with an attendance spike on July 4th for the Independence Day Fireworks. They will also be very busy on Halloween night, Thanksgiving week, Christmas weekend, and New Year's Day (plus the days right around them).

I cannot stress this enough! During busy times of the year, Disney Resort hotel guests should take full advantage of Early Entry. Only Disney Resort hotel guests can enjoy the parks during these select times, allowing for a rare uncrowded run-of-the-park 30 minutes before other park guests are allowed in. This is one of the best perks of staying at a Disney Resort hotel during peak season!

If you are not a fan of long lines but need to take your vacation during one of these busier times, consider going off the beaten path with one of the Walt Disney World® Resort's many recreation options outside of the parks. There are plenty of things to do that remain relatively uncrowded while the parks are jammed with people. Enjoy the amazing pools at your Disney hotel. Book a behind-the-scenes tour. Rent a boat for an hour...or for the whole day. Book a fishing expedition. Go waterskiing or parasailing. Dine at one of the Deluxe Resort restaurants. Go horseback riding at Fort Wilderness. Get a spa treatment at The Grand Floridian. Golf! Tennis! The list goes on and on.

It takes some planning and reservations, but there are plenty of things you can do that are usually just as much fun as a day spent in one of the amusement parks. In fact, Disney offers so many options outside the parks, you could really have an amazing vacation without ever even stepping foot in a theme park.

The different Disney Parks have different capacities for absorbing large crowds. In our opinion, Disney's Hollywood Studios® is the least well designed to accommodate extremely busy days, but the other parks actually do handle large crowds fairly well. Use Disney Genie+ to experience the most popular park attractions. On the busiest days, go explore attractions or activities outside the main parks that you might not otherwise have discovered.

If you still want to visit the main parks on the busiest days, be sure you are mentally prepared. It will be impossible to do everything you might want to do. Familiarize yourself with Disney Genie+. Make use of Single Rider Lines where available. Be patient. Be tolerant. Be polite to others, and be open to experiencing Disney in a different way. Visit attractions you might not normally check out. Enjoy the parks very early before they become crowded and then take a break midday when they are jammed up. On nights when the parks are open late, return just after dinner to close them down as other crowd-weary guests are starting to file out.

Tip! Take full advantage of Early Entry if you are a Disney hotel guest! Always take advantage of Early Entry whenever you can. It might not seem like much but this 30 minute head start while other guests are waiting to be let in means you can ride one, maybe two, of the parks best attractions with a minimal wait.

Tip! Keep refreshing the Disney app. The new Disney Genie and Disney Genie+ automated planners are fluid. They report the best options for you in the moment, but those options are constantly changing in the system. If you do not see an attraction you like for your Lightning Lane choice or your stand-by option, refresh the app and see what it might offer again. The system is like shuffling a giant deck of cards. There is no guarantee but each time you check in, it's going to present fresh offerings. A ride or restaurant you wanted to experience, might become available in a few moments.

Visiting with Young Children

Walt Disney World® can be sensory overload for many people, particularly children. Only you know how your own kids react to rides, crowds, costumed characters, or changes to their sleeping and dining routines.

If you are staying at a Disney Resort hotel, I suggest you break up your days in the parks to build in naps, lunch, and pool time back at the hotel – although not necessarily in that order. This is another good reason to consider staying at a Disney hotel – it provides a convenient escape out of the parks when the kids – or grownups – have hit their limits.

A day with some planned 'down time' can be the difference between having an unforgettable family experience and enduring a screaming toddler meltdown in the middle of a long, inescapable queue.

Disney allows children's snacks into the parks, so carry a supply of munchies that will keep your kids from getting overly hungry and cranky between meals.

Disney visits mean a lot of walking for adults. It can feel like a double marathon for little ones! Use strollers when appropriate for small children. You can rent strollers at the parks if you don't want to transport one from home. Disney manages strollers very well and provides stroller parking at rides, but be sure not to leave any valuables in parked strollers when you are visiting an attraction. Plan frequent rest breaks, meals and snacks to keep everyone energized.

For the safety of everyone, Disney restricts the size of strollers (baby prams, perambulators, baby buggies, push-chairs, etc.) they will let into the parks. Single seat and most double seat strollers are fine. But double strollers wider than 31 inches and longer than 52 inches are now banned from the parks. Also, Disney is now banning pull wagons. Plan accordingly. Strollers are available for rental at all the parks and there are independent rental services who will set you up with the appropriately sized stroller if you need one. Ask at your hotel concierge for assistance.

If your kids balk at something, please don't force them to go on an attraction, even if you are confident it's appropriate for them. Let them meter their own ride tolerances. Before the trip, review descriptions of the rides you think your children might enjoy. Go over them with your kids, so everyone has the proper expectations when they arrive at the park. That's where this guide can be particularly helpful.

For some children, Disney is more about the characters than the rides, and in recent years Disney has made 'meet and greet' character areas attractions in themselves. You may be surprised how much joy you will get from watching your children meet Disney Princesses and costumed characters like Mickey, Minnie, and Goofy. Something truly magical happens when a child gets to meet a character from their favorite stories.

Take lots of photos! Very young children might not remember everything about visiting Walt Disney World®, but you can bet the pictures you take will become cherished keepsakes as they get older.

Disney has very nicely equipped quiet areas called Baby Care Centers, generally located near the middle of each park. These centers can provide a space for nursing mothers, naps, and just simple quiet time when needed.

Disney for Older Kids and Teens

In some circles, Walt Disney World® is thought of as a "kid's park." However, Walt made sure there was plenty of fun to be had for everyone — even the hard to impress, smart phone addicted, teen kids these days. While *It's a Small World* and the princesses might make them roll their eyes, teens might prefer a guided tour of all of Disney's thrill rides (see the VIP treatment section just ahead), and time spent at Disney's two world-class water parks, Blizzard Beach® and Typhoon Lagoon®. Magic Kingdom® offers a really cool selection of interactive searches. *A Pirate's Adventure* in Magic Kingdom's Adventureland offers a series of treasure seeking challenges. Maybe book them into the *Wild Africa Trek* at Disney's Animal Kingdom®, or have them explore *Star Wars*-Galaxy's Edge (undeniably cool) at the Studios. Disney Imagineers have woven in an array of smart phone games and interactions into Batuu. They can spend an afternoon doing water sports (like mini speed boat rentals off the numerous marinas around the resort). Check out the new Cirque de Solei show at Disney Springs®. When the parks are open very late, they take on a whole new very cool feel that even a disaffected teen could not resist.

If your teen lives on their social media apps, I dare say there is no place that offers more Tik-tok-able or Instagramable settings that the Disney Parks and resorts.

Please do not just drop off kids without supervision. Disney strictly enforces their children supervision rules. Children 14 and under must be accompanied by an adult.

Date Night!

Sometimes even the most dedicated parents in the middle of the most magical family vacation need a break from their kids, or maybe you just want some time to enjoy the more adult nighttime offerings available around the resorts. Disney has a partnership with the local service Kid's Nite Out to provide qualified babysitting at fixed rates. This service is for children 6 months to 12 years old. Ask your hotel's concierge service for a referral. Several of Disney's bigger hotels are offering kids clubs which offer supervised childcare services for kids 3 to 12.

Disney for Adults without Children

Because Disney devotes so much marketing to families with kids, some people have it in their heads that Disney is just for children. This is so not true! Disney offers a whole world of decidedly grownup experiences – luxury hotels, spa treatments, golf courses, championship bass fishing, world-class dining, vibrant nightclubs and endless entertainment options that would not interest a child whatsoever.

In fact, it could be argued that Disney offers a lot more for adults than it does for children, which is why Disney has become the nation's number one honeymoon and wedding destination. It is one of the top destinations for young couples and is increasingly popular among single adult travelers for being one of the safest vacation destinations available. I promise adults without kids and single travelers, this could be the best vacation you ever had.

Character Dining

There are lots of opportunities in the parks and hotels for guests to meet their favorite Disney cartoon characters, pirates, and princesses. Character dining experiences require advanced reservations, and they tend to book up quickly as these venues are extraordinarily popular. Most of these restaurants offer table-service or buffet style dining; they are not always gourmet experiences, as the focus is sometimes more about meeting the characters than the meals.

These venues are more expensive than dining at similar restaurants without characters. Some character dining venues will cost two table-service credits per person if you are on a Disney Dining Plan, but character dining is one of the best ways to have truly special moments with your favorite characters.

Note: not all characters appear at every venue. Some will feature characters from Winnie the Pooh, some will favor princesses, and others will feature the classic Disney characters like Mickey and Goofy. Be sure to check with your reservationist if you want to meet a particular character. They will direct you to the right character dining experience. Make your reservations as far in advance of your trip as possible at 407-WDW-DINE, on the MyDisneyExperience app or website, and through your Disney Certified Vacation Planner.

The VIP Treatment

Want to visit the parks like a celebrity? Explore the parks with your own personal guide? Bypass long lines and skip advanced dining reservations? It is possible, but it certainly is not cheap.

Walt Disney World® now offers a limited number of VIP tour services each day, with several different options suited for guests who might want to spend more to get more out of their time in the parks. VIP tour packages include private transportation from your hotel in Central Florida to the park's front gates and a special Disney guide to take you on the most efficient path through the parks to the attractions you want to experience. These special tours include special entry to attractions and special seating for shows, events and even restaurants.

There is a Premium VIP tour that you help plan in advance with your Disney Guide. Ultimate Day tours highlight Epcot's Food and Wine Festival, and Ultimate Day of Thrills tours are for those wanting to focus on Disney's array of thrill rides. Ultimate Day for Young Families tours focus on the charming selection of children's attractions and character experiences.

These tours are expensive, and there are very strict minimum requirements of time and the number of guests per tour guide. For more information and reservations for this very special way to experience Walt Disney World®, call 407-560-4033 for the Premium tour service and 407-939-PLAY for the Ultimate Day tours.

The Best Tip of All…

Here at *Actual Factual Magic,* I talk a lot about magical moments; Those special interactions with characters or Cast Members that pop up out of nowhere to become some of our all-time favorite memories.

"How can I guarantee one of these moments happen for me or my family when I am at Walt Disney World®?"

I get this question a lot. And my answer is always the same…

There is no way to guarantee you might have one of these moments. But you can increase your chances by doing one simple thing everywhere you go within Disney property: Treat Cast Members with the respect they deserve.

Cast Members put in very long hours. They work in blazing hot sunshine, soupy humidity, monsoon-like rain, and yes even some pretty cold nights. They are up before sunrise and sometimes work into the next day. For many of them, service is in their DNA. They get a heart-felt joy out of making people happy. And many of them do so at (or only slightly above) minimum wage. Yet, without fail, they greet you with a smile. These are amazing people who have come from all over the world to create the magical environment you enjoy throughout Disney property.

Some things probably will go wrong on your vacation. You might not get exactly the room you wanted. Rules around pandemic safety might change. All your family's magic bands might not open your hotel door. An attraction might breakdown. You might be late for a virtual queue or a dinner reservation. You might miss a bus. Or have to wait for the next monorail. Your whole family might not fit in one ride vehicle. You might drop an ice cream cone. You might get sun burned. It might rain. You might not get into the restaurant everyone told you to get reservations for 180 days in advance. You might not use all your dining plan points. Your child's favorite character might not be available.

Lots of things can go wrong.

None of these things are the fault of the Cast Member you seek out for assistance.

Getting angry, being rude, demanding things, getting loud, getting obnoxious, flailing your arms around…. Some people think this is how you get a little extra something out of Cast Members. I am here to tell you this is dead wrong. The way to experience those special little extras is to be friendly, understanding, complimentary and grateful for the hard work Cast Members put in every day. That means ALL the Cast Members. From the ones who show you wear to park your car in the morning to the ones who wave giant Mickey gloved hands goodbye to you when you exit the park late at night. When you take a moment to think about it: each one of them play a role in your entire vacation. Each one of them set the mood for the rest of your day. Each one of them will try their hardest to provide you with the most amazing vacation they can. They will try just a little harder for people who treat them with the respect they deserve.

I know some Cast Members who have become life long friends. I can tell you, for them, service is a true calling. They go to work every day genuinely fired up knowing they are going to make thousands of people happy. You can ruin their day just as easily as they can ruin yours. So, cut them a little slack if you see them struggling — it can happen. Commend and recognize them when you see them go above and beyond. Here's the key: do not expect anything in return.

You may earn a smile. You might make a friend. And yes, sometimes something truly special might happen beyond that. You never know. *That's* what makes these moments truly magical.

Money Saving Tips

Walt Disney World® has a reputation for being expensive, and it certainly can be. But I see things a little differently. Have you been to a major concert or a professional sporting event lately? How much did you spend for maybe 90 minutes of entertainment at those venues? Considering what you get for your money at Disney – a consistently full day of non-stop magical fun – I believe you really do get good value for your dollars spent. Yet, everyone loves a bargain, so here are a few tips for your pocketbook:

Use a Disney Certified Travel Agent.

I know I have said this a few times now but it is important. A good Disney Certified Travel Agent will cost you nothing more than booking directly through Disney's phone reservation line, website, or app. Where they can save you significant money is if Disney offers a discount or promotion after your vacation is booked. A certified Disney vacation planner is going to monitor these changes and they will rework your reservation to take advantage of the better pricing (if they are able to). They can also help you book those special events you've been dreaming about as they become available during Disney's phased reopening as the pandemic subsides.

Use Disney's Magical Express while it is still complimentary.

In what I assume is an attempt to cutdown on congestion, Disney now charges $15 to $25 per day for parking at their resort hotels depending on which Disney Resort you are staying at. Before you get upset, remember that Disney offers complementary shuttle services to and from the Orlando Airport (Magical Express airport shuttle is ending in December 2021). A replacement is coming in 2022 from Mears Connect, the same resort shuttle service that was once Magical Express, which will now offer shuttle services to the Universal Resorts too). Mears Connect will not be a free service. Mears will cost $32 per person round trip.

Starting in 2022 Uber or Lyft to and from the Airport

While we are sorry to see the Magical Express complimentary service go away, we believe a better, low-cost option is on the horizon. Disney has announced a partnership with the City of Orlando and the Brightline high-speed rail service, which currently operates a north-south line in Florida. Train service prices for this existing line are very affordable. However, the estimated completion of the rails and the future Disney Springs® station might be a few years off. In the meanwhile the most cost-effective way to get from the airport to your Disney Resort destination might well be a car sharing service, like Uber® or Lyft®. Remember to request a bigger car if you have a larger family and a lot of luggage.

Use Disney's Free and Unlimited Internal Transportation Options.

Free and unlimited use of their system of clean, fun monorails, boats, buses, and even cable gondolas to get you wherever you need to go within their mammoth property. Leaving your car at home or not renting a car at all will save you money if you are staying on Disney property.

Food

Walt Disney World® has the reputation of having expensive food, but you have a myriad of choices. From fast food to fine dining. You can choose to eat exclusively from counter-service venues and save some money over the sit-down restaurant choices. In our opinion, you should treat yourself to some of the nicer dining options now and then during your vacation if you can work them into your budget.

A counter-service offering at the Magic Kingdom® costs about what you might pay at your local family chain restaurant – roughly $20 or less per person. A sit-down meal at a Disney restaurant will run about $20 to $40 per person, comparable to what you would pay at a nicer family restaurant elsewhere. Disney's special dining experiences are in line with what you would expect to pay anywhere at a fancy restaurant, or for dinner and a show ($20 to $80 per person). There are some five-star, world-class dining opportunities available that can be off the charts expensive. You can have amazing dining experiences though without breaking the bank.

In short, you have lots of options: You can eat as cheaply or as extravagantly as you wish. You can stick to a budget. Knowing that you can find really good food choices at some of Disney's counter-service venues means you can enjoy a really good meal at lower prices if you know where to find it. Our food writer, Kat, can help with that part. Check out her dining section of this book for details.

Disney's Dining Plans

Let me try to be clear here: When Disney Dining Plans are offered free during seasonal promotional times, it is a real bargain. If it is not being offered for free during your vacation stay, the cost of the dining plans is pretty close to that if you were to just purchase meals in the same restaurants paying out-of-pocket. If you cannot get the Disney Dining Plan for free, you will probably save more money using some of the following money saving dining tips…

Family Meals in your Hotel Room

This might be the biggest money saving tip of them all. If you are in a family suite, chances are you have a full-sized fridge. You can save a lot of money by stopping at a grocery store or even having one of the local stores deliver groceries to your vacation rental. Many family suites have kitchenettes or full kitchen facilities, and even Disney's Value Resorts have a small in-room fridge. Having a family meal or two every day back at your hotel can really add up to significant savings.

Bring your own snacks to the parks

You cannot bring coolers, ice, or glass containers, but Disney does allow you to bring your own snacks and sandwiches into the parks as well as empty water canisters. You can save some money by packing your own lunch rather than eating in park restaurants.

Eat dinner at lunchtime

Some of Disney's nicest dining spots offer less expensive lunch menus between 11a.m. and 4p.m. Planning to eat your main meal of the day a little earlier than traditional dinnertime can save you some money.

Get a few sandwiches

On my first travel day I like to go to Disney Springs®. Why waste a park ticket on a partial day, right? Before I leave Disney Springs® I stock up on the affordable and very delicious, Earl of Sandwich® sandwiches to keep in my hotel room fridge. This gives me a very less expensive dining option waiting in the hotel room when I feel like taking a break from the parks later in the week.

Opt-out of the refillable resort mugs

Unless you get this for free as part of your dining plan package, or you plan to spend a lot of time in the lobby area or main pool area of your resort, I suggest skipping this add-on option. Why? Because the refill stations are only offered in the food court area of your Disney hotel. And in most cases, it's a very long walk between your hotel room and the food court. The free refills only work at the resort hotels. You cannot refill them in the parks. I prefer to get a couple of 2-liter soda bottles from the food court/gift store at the beginning of our stay and keep those in our hotel room next to my ice bucket. I find this is more cost-effective and convenient.

Bring refillable water bottles

Florida is hot most of the year. It's important to stay hydrated while you're walking outside for long hours in the parks. Buying bottled water again and again during your day adds up fast, plus it's not the most environmentally sound choice. Bring your own refillable container or buy one water bottle early in your day and refill it at the numerous free drinking fountains around the parks to save yourself some cash.

Ice Water is FREE at Disney Parks

Most counter-service restaurants and snack stands will have cups, ice, and water available at no charge. Just ask! Why pay for those expensive bottles of water?

Bring your own toiletries

All the Disney hotels will provide you with the basics; Hand soap, bath soap, shampoo and conditioner. But if you need special items for whatever reason, bringing your own personal care products can save you money over trying to purchase them once you've arrived. With ever-changing airport security rules this may be easier said than done, but toiletries like sunscreen, shampoo, toothpaste, aspirin, bandages, mouthwash, diapers, baby essentials, etc. tend to be more expensive if you buy them at your hotel than if you get them at your hometown store and take them with you. Check your airline's current security rules before you pack so you know what is and is not allowed in your luggage.

Discounted Gift Cards

Big box retailers like Target and Walmart and membership-driven bulk stores like SAM's Club and Costco sometimes offer Disney gift cards and/or their own gift cards at a discount. Since Disney gift cards are accepted virtually everywhere in the parks and across the property it's like getting a discount everywhere in Disney on almost everything.

There is a slightly more complicated twist to this hack: If your big box store offers a discount in store for using their credit card (like Target offers 5% off on purchases within the store with their

Red Card) you can use their purchasing card discount to buy Disney gift cards at a discount too. There are some occasions around the holidays where store might offer a discount on the Disney gift cards. This gives you a chance to double-up on savings and then basically transfer the 5%-10% discount to nearly everything you purchase with Disney gift cards during your trip.

Ship some necessities from home
As long as the address label includes the dates and details of your stay, Disney Resort hotels will accept packages that arrive days before or during your stay for a small fee. Before you leave home, send yourself a box with the things you know you will need!

Buy park admission when you reserve your hotel room
There is no guarantee that this will save you money, but Disney admission costs are locked-in from the time of purchase until you use your passes. If you buy your passes months before your trip and ticket prices go up between then and your vacation, your passes will still be honored at the original price you paid. You will not be asked to pay the difference.

Opt-out of housekeeping
In an effort to be more eco-friendly, some Disney Resort hotels are offering a gift card to guests who choose to opt-out of daily housekeeping for their hotel room. This cuts down on water and energy consumption in a big way, while also putting a little extra money back in your pocket. Maid services will still provide fresh towels and whatnot by request. The amount of the gift card (or promotion) will vary due to length of stay and requests made to housekeeping during your stay.

Buy admission passes for the entire length of your stay
Walt Disney World® park admission operates on a downward sliding scale: the longer you stay, the less expensive your park passes become. For example, a one-day, one-park pass can cost around $120 or more, but if you buy a weeklong multi-park pass, the cost per day is cut nearly in half. Ask a Certified Disney Travel Expert for details.

Dollar Store rain ponchos & umbrellas
Hopefully you won't have to use them, but you can save yourself some money if you bring those little folded rain ponchos with you rather than buying them at the parks. You might want to bring rain ponchos just for the wetter rides like Kali River or Splash Mountain anyway, and then you will already be prepared if it happens to rain on you too.

Personally, I prefer to carry a small umbrella – it's easy to stow away in a bag, and unlike a raincoat, an umbrella doesn't become an uncomfortable piece of clothing to lug around later in the day when the rain stops and the sun gets hot again.

Vacation Bundles and Packages
Travel agencies and travel websites often offer packages combining air travel, hotel, and rental cars for a special bundled price. When booking these special deals, make sure you factor in any missing items such as park admission passes, where you are going to eat, and ground

transportation. If the package you choose includes a Disney Resort hotel, call it directly and they can help you fill in those missing pieces.

Check back frequently with your Certified Disney Travel Expert to see if any new promotions, discounts or offers have sprung up since you booked your vacation. Whenever possible they will gladly rebook your vacation to include the new offers.

Do try to work only with Certified Disney Vacation Experts or Planners – they have had special training and have earned access to the same offers as Disney's own experts.

Organizational Discounts

AARP and AAA offer their members special savings on park admission and vacation packages, and some employers offer corporate discounts. Disney offers discounts on vacation packages and admission tickets to members of the U.S. military. Ask your Disney travel professional for details, as offers can vary widely. Big box wholesalers like SAM's Club and Costco sometimes offer exclusive deals on tickets and hotel stays and even bundled vacations if booked through their travel services. Some of these savings can justify the cost of these membership fees.

Accessibility

Disney has made their beautiful parks as accessible as possible. In many cases, they have redesigned attraction entrances to make them more accessible to everyone, eliminating the need for special entrances for guests using wheelchairs or other assistive devices.

Guests with greater mobility challenges may request a DAS (Disabled Access Service) card. Due to runaway abuse of Disney's generous accessibility policies in the past, this is now a very limited service and there is a process for registering for it at any theme park's Guest Service Center. Guests in wheelchairs or mobility scooters do not need a DAS card. Both DAS cardholders and those in wheel chairs and scooters will be given a time to return to a given attraction similar to the posted standard wait times. At that given return time, they may come back and experience the attraction with the assistance of Cast Members with a minimal wait.

Attraction entrances and queues have clear warning signs posted, indicating who may ride and who may want to pass on an attraction. Cast Members are always available to answer questions.

At most shows and theater attractions, Disney may offer assistive devices or services to those who may need them. Check with the Cast Member stationed outside the attraction to see if they have special accommodations for your particular challenges.

Disney welcomes Seeing Eye® and other registered assist dogs or miniature horses and their human companions. They provide special areas where these animals can relieve themselves. Many attractions might be too intense for animals. Working dogs may use the Rider Switch program enjoyed by parents with small children. Be sure to bring the animal's certification paperwork or identification card with you. However, at Disney's discretion, emotional comfort animals might not be granted entrance into the parks. Check with Disney Guest Services before you attempt to bring an animal to the parks. For a complete overview of the Walt Disney World® Resort's accessibility practices, call Disney at 407-W-Disney.

Other Helpful Things to Know

Once you touch down in Orlando Airport (MCO), you are going to want to get right to the fun. If you made advance arrangements with Disney's Magical Express grab your luggage and then proceed directly to the Disney Magical Express station in the Orlando airport (Magical Express ended their luggage service during the pandemic). Friendly Cast Members will scan your MagicBand and point you toward the right bus heading to your Disney Resort hotel.

Please note: Magical Express is being phased out during the coming year. Mears Connect will be replacing Disney's branded shuttle service with a paid shuttle service. Disney and the city of Orlando will soon be offering a high-speed rail service from Orlando Airport's Terminal C running to Disney Springs®. This may eventually become the best car-less way to get to the Walt Disney World® Resort.

If you are renting a car or staying outside of Disney property, you'll find the Orlando International Airport has lots of clear signs and friendly staff who will help you find the baggage claim and ground transportation options.

Getting Around

Finding Walt Disney World® is easy. As I have pointed out, it's the size of a major city. But getting around the property can seem like a challenge all of its own. Knowing how to use all the transportation options that are available could make you a Disney navigating pro! There are certain advantages and disadvantages to everything here. Let's review your choices…

Driving Your Own Vehicle or Renting a Car

Having your own vehicle can give you an added element of freedom when you are visiting Walt Disney World®. However, that freedom comes with a price. Florida has toll roads, parks and resorts charge for parking, and of course, you have to keep that car fueled. Those things can really add up. You need to weigh the costs against the benefits and see what's right for you.

You can find Walt Disney World® nestled between I-4 and the Florida-429.

From the Orlando International Airport, take the South Exit (417 South) to Osceola Parkway West (Exit 3). Follow the signs to the Walt Disney World® Resort.

Driving West on I-4, Take Exit 68, 67 or 64B. Follow the signs to the Walt Disney World® Resort.

Driving East on I-4 take Exit 64B, 67, or 68. Follow the signs to the Walt Disney World® Resort.

Use your car's navigation system and smart phone guidance for more details and most recent construction detour information as things are changing fast around the property.

Using Disney's Internal Transportation System

I talk about this topic a lot in this book because it really is central to the Disney experience. Knowing how to use the selection of free buses, monorails, boats, and cable gondolas to your advantage can be key to your enjoyment of the parks — especially if you choose to do some park hopping.

Not all forms of transportation go everywhere you want to go.

For example, the monorails actually run in closed loops: one goes to most of the Magic Kingdom® area resorts, another runs a loop between the Magic Kingdom® to the Transportation and Ticket Center (near the Magic Kingdom's parking lots), and the third runs between the Transportation and Ticket Center to Epcot® and back.

The boats usually run to different destinations on smaller loops between parks and specific resorts.

The buses have by far the widest reach between your resort and the parks, as well as from park-to-park. But at this time, there are no direct bus routes between Disney's Resort hotels. You must use a theme park as a hub to go from a hotel to another hotel by bus.

Disney now has a cable car gondola system called Skyliner, which strings together certain parks with some resort hotels. At the moment, Skyliner runs between Disney's Hollywood Studios® and Epcot® with stops along the way at Pop Century, Art of Animation, Caribbean Beach, and Riviera Resorts. Basically, the Epcot® area hotels not served by friendship boats. Some stations are shared by two resorts and you might need to transfer cable lines to get exactly where you want to go.

The key to successfully navigating Disney's free transportation options is to give yourself enough time to get to your destination – especially if you are trying to make a dinner reservation or get to a Genie+ window of time. Give yourself at least an hour to get anywhere. Walt Disney World® is massive, and it takes time to get from point A to point B.

If you need to be somewhere fast, you can always use a taxi, Uber®, Lyft®, or Disney's option; The Minnie-Van. Disney has partnered with Lyft® to allow you to summon a Minnie Mouse-themed SUV that seats six people to take you to any destination within the Disney property for the cost of a premium Lyft® ride. Note: Lyft's pricing structure and schedules do vary due to demand and time of day. This is an awesome solution if you find yourself running late for an important dinner reservation! The Minnie-Van service is available everywhere within Disney's borders and can be requested through the Lyft® app.

In normal times, I highly recommend leaving your car at home and letting the Disney transportation network shuttle you around. As they navigate through pandemic restrictions, Disney may limit the amount of passengers on each bus or watercraft. This is bound to potentially slow down the process of getting from point A to point B around the property. If you are an impatient traveler or do not like the idea of sharing even limited space with strangers during a pandemic, renting, using a ride service, or bringing your own car might be worth the added expenses. It is something to consider if this gives you peace of mind.

Respect The Power of the Florida Sun

This is no joke. Sunburn can make your dream vacation a literal nightmare. If you do not bring sun screen, protective clothing, or a sun-smart hat, plan on purchasing these things soon after arriving in Orlando. Be generous when you apply sun screen and do not forget spots like the back of your neck and the back of your legs. The sun can burn you even through cloud cover and even when you are underwater at your hotel pool. Sweat and a water rides can remove your sun protection, so be prepared to re-apply throughout your day. You might want to show off all your hard earned muscles from the gym, but the sun doesn't care. Pool shirts are becoming more and more popular. Do not let your first sunny day be the cause of misery for the rest of your holiday.

Medical Emergencies

Disney Parks are exciting places. It's easy to get distracted and have a misstep or forget to take care of yourself the way you might in the routine of home. You can find a very well-equipped First Aid Station near the center of every Disney Park – just ask any Disney Cast Member for assistance if something goes wrong. They will be happy to help. For more dramatic emergencies it is comforting to know Disney has several community fire departments and a full complement of first responders standing by at all times.

Lockers and Disney Resort Package Services

It's easy for an impulse souvenir purchase or two to grow into shopping bags full of stuff that you probably don't want to carry onto attractions or lug around for the rest of your day. All Disney theme parks and water parks have lockers near the entrances available for same-day rental. Another option is to request your purchases be held for you to pick up at the end of the day at one of the package pickup centers near Guest Services at the park gate.

Tip! Walt Disney World® Resort hotel guests can also opt to have their souvenir purchases magically brought to their hotel's gift shop within 48 hours – just ask the shopkeeper for details.

Dealing with Long Lines

I confess. I kind of like the lines at Disney. I hate the lines at other amusement parks as much as anyone else, but at Disney, the queue areas are usually as much a part of the attraction as the ride itself. For example, Expedition Everest's queue is filled with mountain climbing artifacts. You actually design a car in the Test Track waiting area. The Seven Dwarfs have built all sorts of magical things to do while you wait for their mine train. See what I mean? Fun, right? You'd miss all that if you just did Lightning Lane all the time. That said, once you know the full queue experience you might consider skipping straight to the most exciting part the next time you ride – that's when Genie+ and Single Rider Lines can really pay off for you.

Single Rider Lines

This may be even better than Genie+. Many major attractions now have a Single Rider Line to help fill the extra seats on vehicles with an odd numbered party. Say a ride seats six and there is a family of five that wants to ride together – a single rider would fill in that one extra seat in the ride vehicle. If you want to experience a ride with a shorter wait and you are traveling alone or don't mind breaking up your group into single riders, this can be a great way to get on with a minimal wait. Plus, you might make a few new friends this way!

Height Restrictions

Disney is known for having attractions everyone can enjoy, but some of their more thrilling offerings do have size restrictions for riders to ensure they have a safe experience. There are different limitations for different attractions. 35 inches (89 cm) is the smallest height requirement in all of Walt Disney World® for the kid coaster, Goofy's Barnstormer, at Magic Kingdom®. Most restrictions for more adventurous rides are between 40 inches (102 cm) and 48 inches (122 cm).

Don't dismay if you have very small children – there are lots of rides, shows, and attractions that have no restrictions at all.

Rider Switch

For families that have squeamish kids and adults of all ages, Disney offers the rider switch service. If you have a child that is too young or too small to enjoy an attraction, simply ask the Cast Member at the entrance to help you do a rider switch. One adult in your party will remain with the child while the others enjoy the attraction. When the others return, the Cast Member will see that the remaining rider gets onto the ride with a minimal wait.

Lost People

Children and adults alike can get confused and end up separated from their groups. Before beginning your day at any Disney Park, make sure everyone knows that while it's not okay to talk to strangers, it *is* okay to talk to Disney Cast Members. Point out the uniforms and costumes, and the friendly name tags they all wear. Adults should also seek out Disney Cast Members when they become separated.

Disney has a very elaborate system to reunite families quickly. Most Disney Cast Members are connected to one another by radio or cell phone. They receive special training in the art of calming panicked children. Every Disney Park has a special area for lost children to wait for their families to collect them. This area is called The Baby Care Center/First Aid Center. Any Cast Member will direct you to these spots.

In this digital age where kids often have their own cell phones, it's not a bad idea to get a "find-a-friend" app, so even when you are not in sight of one another, you can still see where everyone is.

Agree on an impossible-to-miss landmark where you'll all meet if you become separated during the day (The statue of Mickey and Walt in front of the castle is an excellent example).

Most people become separated from their parties at the exits of major attractions. Make a pact with your group that nobody will move on to the next attraction until everyone has been accounted for at the exit and keep your group together.

Lost Items

With all the distractions of a Disney vacation, it is easy to leave a set of keys, a camera, a phone or a purse in a ride vehicle or a restaurant. Luckily, the Walt Disney World® Resort's lost and found department has an amazing record of reuniting people with their stuff. If you notice you lost something in the moment, go to Guest Relations usually located near the entrance in any park, items are collected here before being sent on to a central Lost and Found office for the entire resort. Some restaurants will hold things for a short while before they get collected to Guest Relations. If you realize you're missing something a day later, go to the Disney app or website, search "lost and found" and fill out a claim form. Disney will do their best to reunite you with your lost item.

Do it all with your Smart Phone

Just like out in the real world, Disney is starting to incorporate most of its magical services into their smart phone apps. Everything your MagicBand can do can also be done with your phone now. Disney was the first large organization to adopt ApplePay and other forms of touch-less payment. Park admission can be scanned off your phone. Your hotel room can be opened by your phone. Plus, you are able to amend and adjust plans on your smart phone, something a MagicBand cannot do.

The Play Disney App

Perhaps the ultimate distraction for killing time in a long line, Disney has developed a smart phone app that challenges you and your whole family to a variety of trivia games, charades, and eye-spy type games that are location aware. For example, if you are in the queue for the Seven Dwarfs Mine Train, the game might challenge you to Snow White trivia. Or, it may urge you to be the first to spot the hidden Mickey on the adjacent wall. So much fun! The Play Disney app plays a major role in the *Star Wars* Galaxy's Edge immersive experience so charge up your phone completely before setting out to the parks!

Device Charging

No one wants to keep your cameras and smart devices up and running more than Disney. You can customize and adjust so much of your Disney experience on the fly using Disney's special apps, but it's easier to spot a Hidden Mickey than it is to find an open electrical outlet in a Disney Park! There are a few, but by the time you locate one, chances are someone else will have gotten there first.

Your favorite hometown gadget store will have some great, device-charging, backup batteries that you can carry with you to keep your cameras and phones capturing memories all day and all night. If you forget your backup chargers or prefer not to carry the extra weight all day, Disney has come up with a clever alternative. Located throughout the parks – usually in the larger souvenir shops – you will find "Fuel Rod" vending machines. The starter kit costs about $30 and consists of a battery and an assortment of connector cables. The Fuel Rod battery is good for two to three charges, depending on the battery size of your device, but you can swap a drained one for a fully charged one at any Fuel Rod kiosk for $3. Pretty cool! If you take one home with you at the end of your vacation, it's just like any other rechargeable battery – you can charge it from any USB connection and keep using it as a battery backup.

Disney Park Planning Smart Phone Apps

Disney is on the cutting edge of the technology revolution. All Disney parks and resorts now have good (but not always great) Wi-Fi. During the global pandemic, use of the Disney app is downright vital. Contactless purchases, tickets and making reservations for most Disney's dining spots is now mostly handled on the app. Use of the app can literally help keep you safe.

The official MyDisneyExperience (and soon Disney Genie) app will carry all your personalized vacation information, but I also like the unofficial app Magic Guide, which has quick access to general park information like maps, wait times, dining options, events, and park hours. Disney's new ShopDisneyParks app is a revolutionary way to obtain those must-have souvenirs. When you see an item you want to purchase while visiting the parks, you can scan its barcode and it will be shipped directly to your home (U.S. only at the moment). No more need to lug those treasures around all day! No more overstuffed suitcases at the end of your vacation!

Mobile Food Ordering

Many of the counter-service restaurants in the parks now offer mobile food ordering via the MyDisneyExperience app. Place your order through the app and they will message you when your order is ready. Mobile ordering signs are posted on the side of most service counters. During the health crisis, mastering mobile ordering will be a big plus to your vacation. Most counter-service and food stands now use Mobile Ordering to keep everyone safe. Sit-down restaurants have begun offering a walk up waitlist feature to their portion of the app. This might be a way to snag a last second reservation at one of Disney's popular dining spots!

Hidden Mickeys

Want something fun to do that does not eat up smart phone batteries while you are waiting in a long line? Challenge yourself or your family to find Hidden Mickeys! Disney Imagineers and designers have a lot of fun working the image of Mickey Mouse into just about everything. Look for the three circles that represent Mickey's head and ears, and you will start to see Hidden Mickeys everywhere. You'll find them often in very clever ways — patterns in carpeting, emblems in wallpaper, stacks of barrels, etc. If you do an online search for Hidden Mickeys you will see hundreds of examples.

Park Maps and Literature

When you first arrive at any park, you can pick up a souvenir map and a complementary schedule of the day's shows, parades, and fireworks. Knowing what events you want to see and when they happen is critical to planning your day. If there is a show or parade you are not interested in, use that time to check out some major attractions. Crowds will be drawn away from the rides to the event that you're skipping. Event schedules vary way too much to be included in a printed book. You never know if a third-party website or app is up-to-date, but you can always count on Disney's own park apps, maps, and literature to be correct. Be sure to pick those up right away when you arrive.

Traveling with your Dog

Recently, four Walt Disney World® Resort hotels began welcoming dogs in certain rooms. The resorts that allow dogs are Disney's Art of Animation, The Cabins at Fort Wilderness Campgrounds, Disney's Port Orleans Riverside, and Disney's Yacht Club Resort. A limited number of pet-friendly rooms are available at each hotel, for an additional charge of roughly $50 to $75 per night, depending on the resort. With this special reservation comes a package for your pup, including mats and bowls, an ID tag, plastic disposable bags, and even puppy pads.

To be clear, while some hotels are now dog-friendly, only registered working dogs such as Seeing Eye® dogs are allowed in all of Disney Resort hotels and theme parks. Disney reserves the right to allow or decline the admittance of comfort assistance dogs on a case-by-case basis. There is a kennel located near the Port Orleans Resort called Best Friends Pet Care. It is not a Disney-operated facility and is not associated with Disney Resort hotels, so reservations for your pets must be made separately. For details, call 407-209-3126.

No Straws or Covers

In an effort to minimize unnecessary waste and protect their animals, Disney is phasing out straws and cup lids for fountain drinks in some of their parks. You might want to consider bringing a set of reusable straws or lids with you if you prefer to drink through a straw.

Tipping and Celebrating Great Service

The Walt Disney World® Resort is not one of those snooty places where bellhops will hold out their hands until you grease their palms with cash. No one employed by Disney seems to expect – let alone solicit – a gratuity, but I strongly encourage you to reward great service whenever it is appropriate. Disney's restaurant staffs work so dang hard to make sure your experience is top-notch. Make sure they know you appreciate their service by tipping well. If "Mouse-keeping" does a great job keeping you in clean sheets and towels, leave them a little something with a note expressing your gratitude. When a hotel worker nearly breaks his/her back getting all your family's luggage to your room, show them that you care.

For workers who are not in positions where a tip is appropriate, take the time to make note of their name and where they were working. Ask to fill out a Cast Member Appreciation Card at the park's Guest Services or your hotel's front desk. Disney has a system in place to get these comments back to the right Cast Member, and the company recognizes the outstanding employees who receive these cards.

There is an even easier way to show your love of Disney's great customer service – just log in to Twitter and tell everyone about your amazing experience using the hashtag #CastCompliment. I will be using this hashtag a lot on my next trip!

Smoking is not permitted in the parks or resort hotels

As of May 1, 2019, Disney is restricting smoking of any kind to designated areas outside of the park entrances and outside of the main resort hotel grounds. This ban includes vaping.

Don't Be Afraid to Ask!

If you find yourself with a question while you are at Walt Disney World®, ask a Cast Member. If they don't know the answer, they will try to find it for you. Ask things like, "Where is the best place to watch the fireworks?" or "Did anyone cancel their reservation, so we can get in?" You never know what the answer will be unless you ask! It might be no. But when it's yes, doors can open to some really amazing experiences. Many of the details found in this guide were obtained simply by asking a Disney Cast Member.

Of all the Disney Cast Members, your Disney Resort hotel concierge and the Guest Relations hosts at the parks are the very best equipped to answer your questions. Even better, these specific Cast Members are in a position to make things actually happen for you!

Another Favorite Tip…

Of course, you should bring your cameras and try to capture lots of wonderful family moments, but when it comes to the big live shows, fireworks and parades, put your camera away and enjoy the moment in the moment with your friends and family. These big shows have all been videotaped and documented scores of times on YouTube. If you want to show your friends these spectacles after your vacation, look them up later on *ActualFactualMagic.com* or many other Disney fan websites.

The one thing your camera cannot capture is the emotion of just being together with your loved ones as the magic unveils itself. These mammoth extravaganzas are best experienced without shrinking them down to the size of a smartphone screen. They are meant to be experienced in the moment, live, in all their wide-ranging majesty. Put your camera down and enjoy these moments with your own eyes at least once before you try to document them. I promise you will thank me later for this.

What are Boarding Groups?

For very popular attractions, Disney has been trying out different ways to manage long lines. One method is to create a system that allows people to log into Disney Genie at the beginning of the day and perhaps again later in the afternoon to enter a lottery. The app will assign you to a group that will be called later in the day to access the attraction. Boarding Group #1 will be the first group called to the attraction via a text from the app. You will have 30 minutes to 1 hour to enter the attraction (these access windows of time may vary). Once most of the first group has experienced the attraction, then Boarding Group # 2 will be texted through the app to enter the attraction. Then Boarding Group #3, then #4, then #5…You get the idea. Disney tested this system with *Star Wars*-Rise of the Resistance. But it has been dropped in favor of the pay-for-Lightning Lane access now available in Disney Genie. Boarding Groups will probably return to help Disney manage access to very popular rides. Keep an eye out for more Boarding Groups in the future when the *TRON* coaster and *Guardians of the Galaxy*-Cosmic Rewind open in the coming months.

The *Actual Factual Magic* Rating System

I wanted to make this book as simple as possible. There is something to love in every Disney attraction, so I've left the final decisions up to you. However, there are some signature attractions that really take things to the next level. I call these "Do Not Miss" attractions. If you try to experience as many "Do Not Miss" attractions as possible and sprinkle in anything else that sparks your interest, you will come away with a Disney vacation unique to you and what you love.

Other attractions or experiences are not necessarily bad– it's hard to find a truly bad experience at Disney – but they may not have aged as well as newer attractions, or they may be aimed at very young audiences. Go ahead and experience any other attractions that appeal to you. What I love might be very different from something you might care about.

When it comes to food choices, we've listed as many dining venues as possible within the park or resort hotel descriptions, along with some general information about what is served at each venue. The Disney Dining section of this book is hosted by our own foodie, Kat Garbis, who will provide more detailed raves and recommendations. This way you can find food venues that are around you at any particular moment and make plans in advance for some truly special dining choices based on Kat's recommendations.

Let's get to the fun stuff!

The Magic Kingdom®

Magic Kingdom® Overview

When Walt Disney experienced the runaway success of Disneyland® in California, he was dismayed to see all the businesses and billboards that built up less-charming structures on the border of his "happiest place on earth." You can hear the street noise of Harbor Boulevard from Tomorrowland and see towering competing hotels jutting up over park walls. They are constant reminders that the real world is just a few feet away, making it difficult to preserve the magic he created within his original park.

Walt vowed this would not be the case when he began planning his massive Florida project. Florida's Magic Kingdom® is very purposely placed near the center of the massive property. There is no chance the outside world can encroach upon this park. Ever.

No matter how you plan to visit, you actually have to take a little journey to get to the Magic Kingdom®. This was very intentional. Guests must leave their cars in a massive lot on the other end of a large lake and take a monorail, ferry, or bus the rest of the way to the gates of the park.

And yes, the very intentional effect of traveling to a far-off magical place holds up beautifully! You do feel like you are leaving the regular world behind.

Getting to the Magic Kingdom®

Disney Resort hotel guests can take buses right to the gates of the Magic Kingdom®. Some Disney hotels also offer monorail and ferry access to the theme park's shores – check with your hotel for details. If you are coming from outside the Disney property, the parking lot and bus drop-off is at the Transportation and Ticket Center on the southern end of the Seven Seas Lagoon. You can get your admission passes here if you don't already have them (though you can also get your admission at any of the theme park entrances as well) and then hop onto either the monorail or the ferry to the park gates.

The monorail moves faster, but it will take you around the entire lagoon and its queue can sometimes be long. The ferry looks like it should be slower, but it goes straight across the lagoon and can carry a lot more people in one load than the monorail. I suggest you choose the ferry at the beginning of your day to get you there faster, and then take the monorail back at the end. Both offer unique experiences, so try to ride both modes of transportation during your vacation. **Tip!** On very busy mornings buses serve the Transportation and Ticket Center to the Magic Kingdom too. While lines are backed up for the ferry and the monorail, the buses will be relatively uncrowded.

Almost There!

Have your admission pass or MagicBand ready when you arrive at the gates of the Magic Kingdom®. Disney has heightened park security by matching your admission pass or MagicBand with a scan of your fingerprint. They will soon be rolling out facial recognition technology too.

Remember, during the health crisis, admission to every park is restricted and you must have an advance reservation for the day you are visiting in addition to having an admission ticket. These restrictions should lift when things return to normal, but quite necessary to allow safe distancing within the park. During the time of writing this book, this has been in effect.

All bags must be checked before entering the park. You can speed this process along by opening all zippered compartments on your purse or backpack for the security officer before you get to their inspection table. Make sure you re-zip and seal everything back up before you get underway – you don't want to leave a trail of personal items behind you as you proceed into the park! **Tip!** As a frequent visitor to the parks, I put all metal objects and electronic gear in a big see-thru zip-lock bag so that I can easily remove them to go through metal detectors and officers can easily see the contents.

Put your admission pass in a VERY safe place. Double check that your MagicBand is securely snapped on your wrist. You will need it throughout the day to redeem meal plans, engage PhotoPass Photographers, access to Disney Genie and Lightning Lane queues. In many cases your admission pass or MagicBand is also your hotel room key, so make sure you know where it is at all times.

Our Magic Kingdom® Strategy

The Magic Kingdom® is designed like a wheel, with Cinderella's Castle at its center and the "Lands" circling it. Because it is a right-handed world, most people run directly to the thrills of Tomorrowland or directly past the castle into Fantasyland, following the wheel to the right. I suggest you start your day instead by moving to the LEFT into Adventureland and then working your way clockwise, land to land around the castle, saving Tomorrowland for last. Why? Because – at least during the morning hours – this approach will give you noticeably smaller lines at popular attractions like Pirates of the Caribbean, Splash Mountain, Big Thunder Mountain and the Haunted Mansion while the bigger crowds are all trying to get onto Seven Dwarfs Mine Train or Space Mountain at the same time.

This guide follows this recommendation and will take you land to land in a clockwise circle around the castle.

Main Street U.S.A.

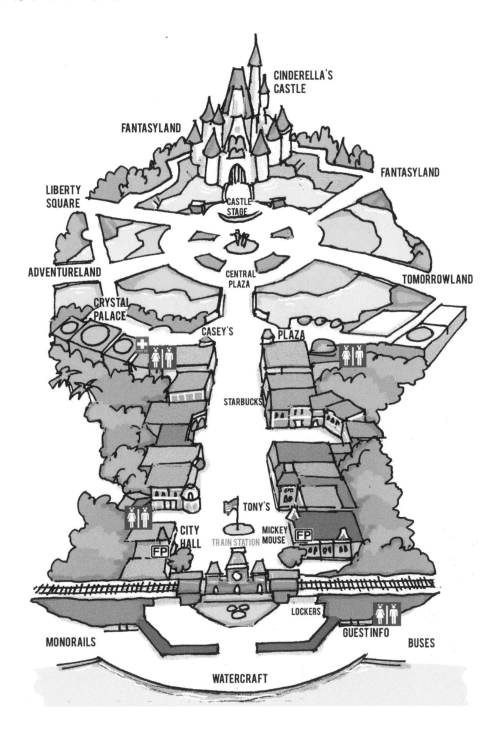

Intro to Main Street USA

Walt Disney wanted to welcome everyone to the Magic Kingdom® with a quaint turn-of-the-century street modeled after his childhood hometown. Main Street is pure Americana. You will immediately notice how clean the street is – not only here but throughout all of the parks. Walt

Disney personally made sure no guest was ever more than 25 steps away from a garbage receptacle. Legend has it, Walt himself would purchase a hotdog and meter how far he had to walk before he was finished and needed to discard the wrapper. That is how they came up with 25 steps. Main Street is primarily about amenities, shops and restaurants, but there are a few other things you might want to check out here as well.

It's nearly impossible not to gasp in awe when you first see Cinderella's Castle from the base of Main Street. This is the main route for the daily parades, and it's not uncommon to see old-fashioned vehicles moving along the street. Yes, you can ride in them. Vehicles pick up and drop off in the flag plaza and at the hub at the base of the castle.

Lockers

Rental lockers are available just inside the turnstiles and to your right. If you plan to do any shopping along Main Street, it can be a good idea to have a secure place to stash your treasures

before venturing out into the rest of the park. Wheelchairs and strollers are also available for rent near this location.

City Hall

This is where you will find the Magic Kingdom's Guest Services desk. There is also a Guest Services station just inside the turnstiles as you enter the park, where you can pick up maps and schedules. Get your questions answered and your concerns addressed here.

Main Street Chamber of Commerce

On your way out, this is where you pick up the packages and souvenirs you acquired throughout your day if you chose to have the store forward your purchases for you. Stores throughout the Magic Kingdom® can have your purchases sent over to the Chamber of Commerce for easy pickup at the end of your day.

Tip! Some of Disney's most popular princesses have moved to their new meet and greet home in Fantasyland's Fantasy Faire, but Mickey and Tinkerbell still call Main Street home – you will find them in the Main Street Theatre. Sleeping Beauty and other princesses have been appearing in the alcove between Town Hall and the Main Street Fire House. Many people miss them there.

Shopping and Snacking on Main Street

Main Street's souvenir shop runs the entire length of the street. From the outside it looks like many small storefronts, but inside, all the stores along this side of the street are interconnected. If you need to move along Main Street during a parade or fireworks show, know that you can move the entire length of Main Street inside the souvenir shops. The other side of Main Street is more about food, candy, treats and restaurants, and for the most part, only some of these stores are interconnected.

Since it's kind of a hassle to lug your souvenirs around all day, have the shop clerk hold your purchases for you at Chamber of Commerce until the end of your day or delay shopping until you're leaving the park. Main Street stays open a while after regular park closing for last minute shopping.

Baby Care Center/First Aid Station

Between Casey's Hotdogs and the Crystal Palace restaurant at the castle-end of Main Street, you will find a quiet little corner perfect for breast feeding mothers, midday napping, and attention to whatever ails you from cuts, bruises, sunburns, upset stomachs, bug bites, and allergy care. This site is being modified at the time of this writing. A temporary location for Baby Care Center/First Aid is in Tomorrowland near Space Mountain.

Do Not Miss…

Mickey, Minnie, and Tinkerbell at the Main Street Theatre

Mickey Mouse appears at different meet and greet venues in all four theme parks but this spot at the base of Main Street USA is one of our favorites. Within the walls of the Main Street Theatre you can queue up to meet two of Disney's character rock stars; Mickey Mouse and Tinkerbell!

Meet Sleeping Beauty and Snow White

One at a time on varying schedules throughout the day, Aurora and Snow White meet guests at a meet-and-greet station right next to Town Hall. This space may also host other characters throughout the day.

Meet More Disney Characters

The flag plaza at the base of Main Street, U.S.A. is a prime place to randomly run into an assortment of Disney characters. Keep your eyes open for your favorites!

Other Attractions...

The Walt Disney World® Railroad

Authentic classic steam locomotives and passenger cars take guests on a tour of train stations all around the park. The train stops at Frontierland and Fantasyland before returning full circle to Main Street Station. This is more of a transportation system than a ride, but I love this railroad – you should step aboard! Note: Operation of the railroad may be interrupted due to the construction of the *TRON* coaster in Tomorrowland. **Tip!** If there is not too much of a wait, the Walt Disney World® Railroad can be a great way to get to the other end of the park while giving your feet a rest.

Main Street, U.S.A. Dining...

Tony's Town Square Restaurant

Table-service. Pastas, seafood and salads. Themed after the Italian restaurant from Disney's *Lady and the Tramp*. Reservations recommended. Check the Disney App for the walk-up waiting list.

Plaza Restaurant

Table-service. One of our favorite little corners of the Kingdom. Sandwiches, burgers, and ice cream treats. Reservations recommended. Check the Disney App for the walk-up waiting list.

Crystal Palace

Table-service. Buffet-style dining with Winnie the Pooh and friends. Reservations recommended. Check the Disney App for the walk-up waiting list.

Main Street, U.S.A. Snacks...

Casey's Corner

Quick-service and snacks. Gourmet hot dogs, French fries and nachos with a fun baseball theme. Newly remodeled and expanded. Check for Mobile Ordering.

Starbucks

Quick-service and snacks, formerly the Main Street Bakery. Coffee, pastries, and sandwiches. Get your daily jolt of caffeine here! Check for Mobile Ordering.

Plaza Ice Cream Parlor

Snacks. Wonderful hand-dipped ice cream, sundaes, floats, shakes and other treats. Check for Mobile Ordering.

Main Street U.S.A. Restrooms

The restrooms at Disney can be a little hard to locate amongst all the theming. The restrooms on Main Street are located just to the side of the Town Hall. Not far from the entrance plaza before you even get to Main Street. There is another set of restrooms located at the end of Main Street, just between Casey's Hotdog shop and the Crystal Palace restaurant. Here you will also find the Kingdom's First Aid and Baby Care Center.

Main Street Patriotism

Every day just before sunset, the Magic Kingdom marching band and honor guard host an official United States flag retreat ceremony. Daily, Cast Members will seek out a guest who is a veteran of service to the U.S. Military and typically a war veteran. This veteran and their family will participate in the ceremony and be gifted the very flag that flew that day over Main Street, a certificate, and commemorative photo of the event. It is a very emotional moment that should be witnessed if you can fit it into your day.

Adventureland

Intro to Adventureland

This part of the Magic Kingdom® is inspired by stories of pirates, South Seas castaways, jungle natives, and enchanted tiki birds. You will find many of Disney's classic adventures here. **Tip!** There is quick access between Adventureland and Frontierland via passages by the restrooms near Aloha Isle and behind Aladdin's Magic Carpets.

Do Not Miss...

Pirates of the Caribbean

One of the best attractions in all of the Magic Kingdom®, this ride is a family favorite for young and old. Drop-in on the secret coastal keeps of the world's most famous pirates. Marvel at the details of each massive scene, populated by hundreds of scalawags. See how many times you can spot Captain Jack Sparrow as he moves from each scene!

The Jungle Cruise

Newly renovated with impressive new features, this light-hearted-campy-adventure takes brave explorers on a river journey deep into the jungles of South America, Africa, and Asia. You will see animated jungle cats, zebras, giraffes, elephants, hippos, and crocodiles. This ride is family-friendly, fun, and your boat captain's comic delivery will make the trip even more enjoyable. Great for younger explorers.

Different Kinds of Adventures
Pirates League. Become a pirate, empress or mermaid!
Ever dream of becoming the cutthroat scourge of the seas? Or maybe you would rather resemble a sea-worthy siren? The Pirate's League allows the kids – or you – to really become a pirate or mermaid for the day! For a fee, professional makeup and purchasable costume pieces will transform you into your inner pirate.

A Pirate's Adventures: Treasures of the Seven Seas
Even more pirate fun! Not a ride or a show, this real pirate treasure hunt follows a secret path around Pirates of the Caribbean and the Jungle Cruise. Treasure seekers are given a map and set off on their own to follow clues and solve mysteries. It's very fun, and an entirely different sort of interactive experience.

Other Attractions
The Magic Carpets of Aladdin
A Dumbo-style circular flight around this corner of Adventureland. **Tip!** Beware of the spitting camel and the nearby idol figures but be sure to watch them catch others by surprise!

The Enchanted Tiki Room
This classic Disney attraction is very family-friendly, featuring tropical birds and enchanted South Sea Tiki idols that come to life and sing.

Swiss Family Treehouse
Inspired by the classic Disney movie *Swiss Family Robinson*, this inventive home is cleverly suspended in a massive tree. Families can climb up into the highest branches and see how those clever castaways turned a giant jungle tree into a comfortable home. There are some amazing views of Cinderella's Castle and other parts of the Magic Kingdom® from the tree's lofty perches. It's particularly stunning after dark. This is an old school attraction. There is no elevator. There are lots and lots of stairs. You have been warned.

Adventureland Dining...
Tortuga Tavern
Quick-service. Pirate-themed on the outside; serving up tacos, taco salads, and burritos on the inside. Check for Mobile Ordering.

The Skipper Canteen
This Jungle Cruise-themed sit-down dining spot may surprise you. The tongue-in-cheek silliness of the ride carries over into a surprisingly good restaurant with a menu influenced by the ride's South American, African, and Asian themes. I especially love the giant heads-on shrimp. Reservations suggested. Check the walk-up waiting list on the Disney App.

Adventureland Snacks
Aloha Isle
The new and bigger home of the Pineapple Dole Whip and other frozen concoctions. The Pineapple Dole Whip is by far our favorite treat in all of Walt Disney World®. You can get this cup of wonderfulness at a few other venues around Disney, but for some reason the portions

73

seem much bigger here. They also offer orange whips and other flavors, and you can choose to have them as floats – but the plain old classic Pineapple Dole Whip is what I recommend you order! **Tip!** New this year, they have added the Pineapple Dole Whip Upside Down Cake, which is soooo good! Check for Mobile Ordering.

Sunshine Tree Terrace

Soft serve ice cream treats. Home of the popular Citrus Swirl. Check for Mobile Ordering.

Adventureland Restrooms

The restrooms are tucked away in the passthrough corridor to Frontierland located just between Aloha Isle and the Sunglass shop. There is a almost hidden set of restrooms inside the large Pirate of the Caribbean gift store. There is a set of restrooms also tucked inside the Tortuga Tavern.

Frontierland

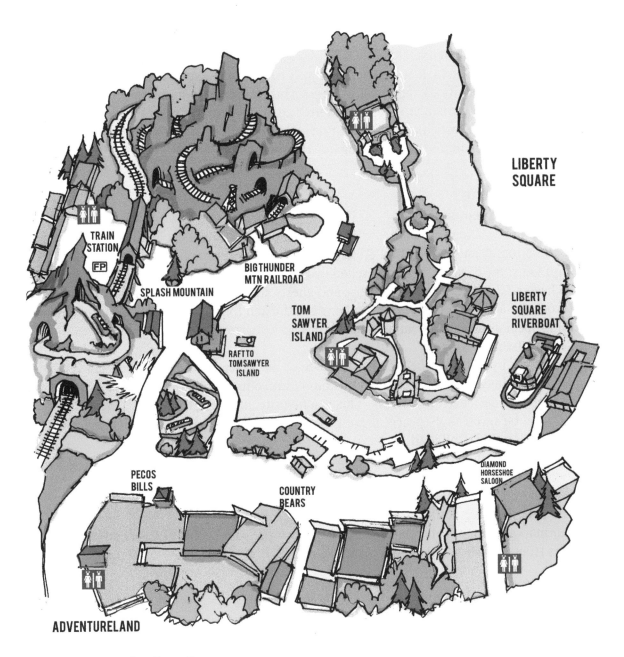

Intro to Frontierland

This section of the Magic Kingdom® feels like you just stepped into the Old West and America's pioneering past. This land is home to many of our all-time favorite attractions.

Do Not Miss...

Splash Mountain

This Magic Kingdom favorite is soon going to be transformed from its *Song of the South* theme to a new brighter *Princess and the Frog* setting. We expect a lengthy downtime for this changeover so if the attraction is running make sure you experience it because it might be unavailable for a while. Whichever version you experience, expect whimsical musical characters to lull you into a false sense of security before some significant drops and splashes occur. Height requirement: 40 inches (102 cm). There is a good chance you might get wet so plan accordingly.

The Big Thunder Mountain Railroad

Now featuring a fun interactive queue area! If you ask any roller coaster enthusiast where they first learned to love coasters, their answer may well be this runaway train ride. This is a thrill ride that everyone in the family can appreciate – it goes just fast enough to produce real squeals of joy without quite ever crossing over into the terror zone. The coaster passes through funny western scenery, and it feels like a different ride altogether after dark. It's so much fun you're likely to get right back in line and ride it again! Height requirement: 40 inches (102 cm).

Other Attractions

The Country Bear Jamboree

An outstanding attraction for families with smaller kids. Even skeptical adults are usually won over by these funny, musically gifted grizzlies. The Bears perform on a regular schedule all day long. **Tip!** On some days there is an unscheduled square dance in the streets, right outside of the Bear's Theater. Characters, Cast Members, and guests are all invited to join this impromptu street dance. Look for a cluster of characters gathering and listen for the atmospheric music to change. Something special might be about to happen.

Tom Sawyer Island

Accessible only by raft from the Frontierland side of the River of America, Tom Sawyer Island is a frontier-style playground where kids can explore, run, climb and blow off some extra steam. The island closes each evening at dusk. This is a favorite attraction for some visitors simply because it can be surprisingly peaceful even when the rest of the park is loud and crowded.

Walt Disney World® Railroad

The Frontierland Station is one of three stops along the train tracks encircling the entire Magic Kingdom®. This is a good way to rest your feet while steaming your way to the New Fantasyland Station and then on to the Main Street, U.S.A. Station.

Frontierland Shooting Gallery

Test your marksmanship with coin-operated rifles that fire safe beams of light and cause humorous frontier-style targets to jump and move.

Frontierland Dining...

The Diamond Horseshoe

Buffet-style. This Western dance hall is now open year-round and offers a wider selection in an "all you can enjoy" setting. Reservations suggested. Check the walk-up waiting list on the Disney App.

Pecos Bill's Tall Tale Inn and Café

Quick-service. Some claim this is the best burger in the Magic Kingdom®. If it is, it's tied with Cosmic Ray's over in Tomorrowland – both have very large condiment bars, so you can build your burger (or sandwich or salad) any way you want it and then some! Check for Mobile Ordering.

Frontierland Snacks

Westward Ho

Corn dogs and cool drinks. Check for Mobile Ordering.

Golden Oak Outpost

Quick-service. Chicken strips, nuggets and snacks. Open seasonally. Check for Mobile Ordering.

Aunt Polly's

This is the lunch spot open seasonally on Tom Sawyer's Island. Lunch sandwiches and ice cream treats. Limited operating hours. Check for Mobile Ordering.

Frontierland Restrooms

There are restrooms near the exit of Splash Mountain. There is a small set of restrooms near Aunt Polly's on Tom Sawyer Island. There are restrooms located within Pecos Bill's restaurant. The Adventureland restrooms are easily accessed through the passthrough located near the Diamond Horseshoe restaurant. But you do have to walk down the corridor towards Adventureland.

Liberty Square

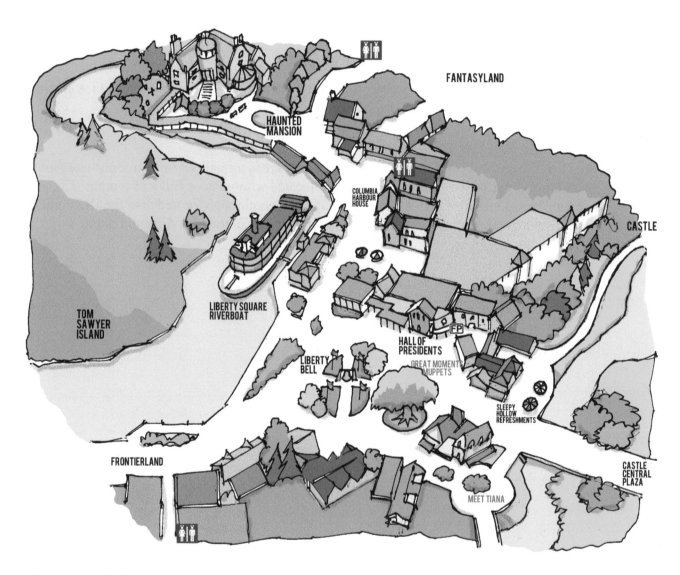

Intro to Liberty Square

Take a stroll through colonial America. This little slice of the Kingdom is meant to bring out your patriotic pride. Where else can you see all the American Presidents just down the street from 99 mischievous ghosts?

The 1700 style lanes are paved with a path through simulated "muddy" ground. Brown pavement depicts the lack of proper sewage disposal during colonial days. To stay true to the times, the only public restroom available in Liberty Square is hidden inside Columbia Harbour House, far enough back that it is technically a part of Fantasyland. Now *that's* an attention to detail!

Do Not Miss...

The Haunted Mansion

Truly one of the Magic Kingdom's premiere attractions, the Haunted Mansion is more whimsical than horrifying. This attraction was recently upgraded with some amazing new special effects and is an absolute marvel with all its creepy details. Pay especially close attention to the set of hitchhiking ghosts near the end of the attraction – these ghosts alone are likely to make you want to get right back into line to ride through the mansion again.

The Muppets Present Great Moments in American History

Your favorite Muppet characters tell the tale of a pivotal moment of the American Revolution using musical comedy. The show is presented across the windows spanning the upper level of the Hall of Presidents building. Showtimes vary seasonally and day-to-day, we recommend to check park schedules!

Other Attractions

The Hall of Presidents

Current and former audio-animatronic presidents appear in very realistic form. History buffs and American patriots will love this attraction, but it's no roller coaster. People with short attention spans or fidgety kids might want to pass on this one.

Liberty Square Riverboat

Take a real turn-of-the-century steam paddleboat on a tour around Tom Sawyer Island. The decks provide great people watching and photo opportunities.

Liberty Bell Replica

Of course, the Liberty Bell located in the middle of Liberty Square isn't real, but it is a close representation! This replica was made from the very same mold as the real Liberty Bell in the same foundry in France.

Liberty Square Dining...

Liberty Square Tavern

Table-service. History buffs, take note! This spot does a nice job of taking you back in time to an early American tavern with warm ambiance and hearty fare, including pot roast (seasonally) and a full turkey meal fit for a Pilgrim. One of the Kingdom's best sit-down restaurants. Check the walk-up waiting list on the Disney App.

Columbia Harbour House

Quick-service. This is one of our favorite counter-service dining places in the Magic Kingdom®. Chicken and fish, but with a real New England flair – you can get real lobster rolls here (seasonally)! Be sure to say hello to the Town Crier, especially if you are celebrating a special occasion. Complete your meal with the warm apple cobbler. **Tip!** There is a second floor to this restaurant that can sometimes provide a quieter experience. Check for Mobile Ordering.

Sleepy Hollow

Quick-service and snacks. Light lunch fare features waffles, waffle sandwiches, funnel cakes and ice cream. Everything is better on a fresh warm waffle. Check for Mobile Ordering. **Tip!** The strawberries and whipped cream waffle is a delight!

Liberty Square Snacks
Liberty Square Market
Quick-service and snacks. Assorted sandwiches, baked potatoes, ice cold beverages. Check for Mobile Ordering.

Liberty Square Restrooms
Finding relief in Liberty Square is a little tricky. Imagineers wanted to maintain a feeling of authenticity with this part of the park. The brown-embedded walkways are meant to symbolize the lack of proper sewers during the 1700s. They took this one step further by not offering a modern restroom in the area either. Not in plain view anyway. You can find a public restroom upstairs in the Columbia Harbour House. Patrons of the Liberty Tree Inn have access to a restroom in the restaurant.

Fantasyland

Intro to Fantasyland

In 2014 Disney completed a massive expansion of the Fantasyland section of the Magic Kingdom®. It's now by far the largest part of the park. Here you will find all the whimsical magical characters and attractions for which the kingdom is known.

Do Not Miss...

The Seven Dwarfs Mine Train

This family-friendly roller coaster delivers Big Thunder Mountain caliber thrills, with swinging barrel cars that are unique to this ride and not to be found on any other roller coaster in the world. It's a fun ride almost everyone can enjoy. Height requirement: 38 inches (97 cm).

Mickey's PhilharMagic

State-of-the-art widescreen 3D projection takes Donald Duck through Disney's most memorable musical moments. This is a surprisingly great show that often has a short wait!

Under the Sea – Voyage of The Little Mermaid
This slow musical ride-through attraction takes you on a journey through Ariel's famous story. A big hit with princess lovers.

Meet Ariel!
Mermaid Ariel receives visitors daily in the little cove next to her attraction.

Meet Gaston!
The princesses are pretty, the costumed characters are cute. If you want to experience a truly hilarious character meeting, Gaston is one of the only Disney characters who seems unrestricted to say whatever he wants and do whatever he chooses – often with funny results. He appears next to his tavern each day at designated times. Check park schedules for details.

Meet Merida!
The redheaded star of *Brave* has her own fun meet and greet area on the side of the castle across from the Tea Cups. You can find her lively stage area in the shadow of the castle.

Meet Princesses! Princess Fairytale Hall
Two separate meet-and-greet areas fit for royalty. This is a great place for little ones and fans of the classic Disney movies to have a photo opportunity with some of their favorite princesses! There are two queues here: One side features Cinderella and new favorite, Princess Elena. The other queue features Rapunzel and Tiana. Princess selection can vary from day to day.

Meet various characters!
The courtyard on the New Fantasyland side of the castle is a prime spot for random Disney characters. Keep your eyes open around this area for Peter Pan, Cinderella's hilarious stepsisters, and the Fairy Godmother.

Pull the sword from the stone!
The famous Sword in the Stone is located near the carousel facing the castle. Once a day, the sword is magically released by the stone!

NOTE: Character meetings are on hold during the pandemic. Meet-and-greets have been replaced with surprise character appearances in mini-parades called Character Cavalcades. Characters will also appear on upper levels of the castle, Frontierland forts, Tomorrowland stages and the Train Station randomly throughout the day. I expect character meetings and parades to be resuming soon.

Other Attractions

Fantasyland's attractions are great for all ages. Everything is charming and family friendly. It is okay for adults to enjoy the fairytale rides here and it's a good place for youngsters to fall in love with their first roller coaster. Any of these attractions could be considered Do Not Miss attractions. All of them have an undeniable charm and may represent your favorite childhood story. By all means check out any of these attractions to appease your inner child!

The Barnstormer
We're convinced this is the best "kiddie-coaster" ever made. If you want your youngster to love thrill rides, this is the perfect one to start them on. Height requirement: 35 inches (89 cm).

Enchanted Tales with Belle
A truly magical experience for small children and their parents. Visit the Beast's enchanted castle and have a storytelling session with the real Belle! There are some incredible audio-animatronic characters...and one really amazing mirror.

It's a Small World
Hundreds of animated dolls represent all the nations of the world and then some. The song will be stuck in your head for weeks, but when you go to the Magic Kingdom®, you kind of have to ride this ride, right?

Dumbo the Flying Elephant
Updated in 2012, the Dumbo ride is now twice as big with two flying elephant carousels to accommodate more people. The modifications have made this fairly straightforward ride into something truly beautiful – especially after dark. The new waiting area gives kids a playground to explore while waiting for their turn on the flying elephants.

Casey Jr.'s Splash 'N Soak Station
A welcome distraction for little ones who would rather play in a fountain then wait in a boring line. This train yard is a fun fountain splash area, perfect for cooling down kids on hot Florida days.

Peter Pan's Flight
This adventure will have you sailing through nighttime scenes from Peter Pan in a small flying ship. It's designed to appeal primarily to children. This attraction's queue area just got a wonderful upgrade.

Prince Charming's Regal Carousel
This carousel rivals the beauty of any in the world and riding a merry-go-round in the shadow of Cinderella's Castle has a charm all its own. One of the very best photo opportunities is on or near this beautiful attraction.

The Many Adventures of Winnie the Pooh
A ride through famous whimsical scenes from your favorite Winnie the Pooh adventures. Pooh fans will love this classic-style ride.

Mad Tea Party
Another classic Disney attraction. Yes, it's been copied by most amusement parks around the world by now, but this is the original spinning teacup ride! You just can't beat the original!

Special Moments
Princess for a Day
Bibbidi Bobbidi Boutique turns little girls into princesses for a day, with full costuming available for purchase with professionally done hair and makeup (for ages 3 to 12). Call for reservations: 407- WDW-STYLE (407-939-7895). This experience is an extra cost and is not included with park admission. **Tip!** There is another Bibbidi Bobbidi Boutique at Disney Springs®. If the Kingdom's castle boutique is booked, perhaps your little one can get an appointment at the other location! **Tip!** An adult version of this boutique is available at The Grand Floridian Resort. No, grown-ups cannot get fully costumed as a Disney Princess, but they *can* get Princess inspired hair, nail treatments and find Princess inspired casual wear to get a little closer to the magic. These Character Couture make-overs can be booked up to six months in advance by calling 407-939-7727. This is a paid experience. These salon experiences may not be offered, or are limited, during pandemic restrictions.

Fantasyland Dining...

Be Our Guest restaurant

Quick-service at breakfast and lunch, table-service at dinner. Breakfast, lunch or dinner, this is definitely one of those do not miss dining experiences in Walt Disney World®. Long lines form early for the chance to have lunch inside the Beast's castle, but it's well worth the wait. Evening dinner reservations are very hard to get – book yours as early as possible. The quick-service lunch features French-themed fare including sandwiches, soups, salads, and it is our favorite counter-service meal in all of the Magic Kingdom®. The dinner menu features finer French cuisine. **Tip!** I prefer the lunch experience over both the breakfast and the sit-down dinner experiences. Breakfast here is notoriously overpriced. Lunch is a much better value. The more upscale sit-down dining experience has recently improved their menu and they're getting better reviews. The gorgeous surroundings are the same no matter which experience you choose. Check the Disney app to reserve your spot for whichever experience you would like. Reservations strongly suggested. You can try the Walk Up Wait List feature in the app to see if you can snag a rare last minute opening. **Tip!** The Beast (without Belle) appears during the Dinner seating hours for a photo opportunity.

Cinderella's Royal Table

Table-service with special event pricing, this is generally the single hardest reservation to get in all of the Magic Kingdom®. It's without a doubt the most special way to meet the Disney Princesses, and a dream come true for most little girls. It may also be the most romantic dining spot in all of Walt Disney World®, judging from the number of guests who choose this ornate banquet hall within Cinderella's Castle to propose marriage or celebrate wedding anniversaries. Book your reservations months in advance if you want to experience this magical place. Please check with reservationist if the Disney Princesses will be at the dining service. At this time of writing, they are not visiting tables due to social distancing. Reservations required. Check walk-up waiting list on the Disney app for long shot last minute reservations.

Pinocchio's Village House

Quick-service. Features sandwiches, pizza, pasta and other quick bites. Great views of the Small World's boarding area from the windows in this dining hall. Check for Mobile Ordering.

The Friar's Nook

Quick-service and snacks. Open seasonally, with lots of kid-friendly choices. Check for Mobile Ordering.

Gaston's Tavern

Features large baked goods and snacks, including the specialty drink LeFou's Brew. Get your photo taken in Gaston's famous antler chair. Check for Mobile Ordering.

Fantasyland Snacks

Storybook Treats

Snacks, ice cream, treats, and sweets. Check for Mobile Ordering.

Cheshire Café

Quick-service and snacks. Famous for an extravagant pastry known as the Cheshire Cat's Tail. Check for Mobile Ordering.

Fantasyland Restrooms

Perhaps the most ornate restrooms in all of the Kingdom, just up the path from the Haunted Mansion and Columbia Harbour House, under Rapunzel's Tower, you will find restrooms and a really charming outdoor, quiet, chill zone. There is another set of restrooms near Pinocchio Village Haus. More restrooms can be found next to Gaston's Tavern. The Fantasyland Railroad Station also contains restrooms. On your way out of Fantasyland near the Mad Tea Party tea cups ride you will find more restrooms.

Tomorrowland

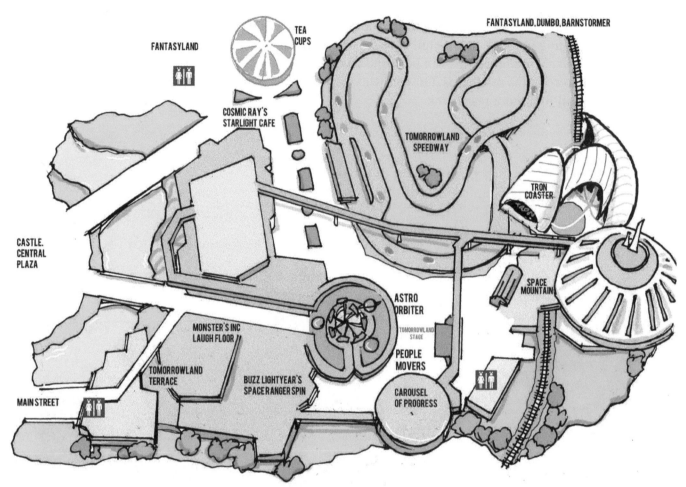

Intro to Tomorrowland

This section of the park is meant to give visitors a taste of the future. Sometimes it's silly and sometimes it's scary, but it's always fun. You will find some of the Magic Kingdom's most innovative attractions here.

Do Not Miss...

Space Mountain

Space Mountain is decades old, but it is still one of the most thrilling roller coasters you will find anywhere. Why? Because the whole thing plays out in the near complete darkness of space, which cleverly messes with your senses along the way. Even with all the mega coasters popping up around the world, roller coaster enthusiasts still have fond respect for Space Mountain. Height requirement: 44 inches (113 cm). **Tip!** You need to sit where Cast Members place you, but if you can get the front row of the front car, you will experience a whole new level of thrills. It does not hurt to ask.

Monster's Inc **Laugh Floor**

It makes me so happy to note that this attraction, closed during the pandemic, is opening back up again. The clever interactive comedy club features the characters from Disney/Pixar's *Monster's Inc*. Audience members are encouraged to contribute jokes and participate in the live show. The show follows a hard framework but the live interactions between Monsters and the audience can be very funny.

Buzz Lightyear's Space Ranger Spin

A ride through an interactive arcade inspired by Disney/Pixar's *Toy Story*. Riders compete for high scores through a series of laser shooting gallery-type challenges. Lots of fun!

***TRON* Coaster — Coming Soon**

Construction continues between Space Mountain and the Speedway. Soon, Florida's Magic Kingdom® will have an attraction that has been thrilling riders at Shanghai's Disneyland® for years. This super techno *TRON*-themed roller coaster is sure to add real excitement to Tomorrowland!

Tomorrowland's Transit Authority PeopleMover

A relaxing ride through some of Tomorrowland's best attractions. This is a very tame ride, but it uses some interesting electromagnetic technology to make it all run. **Tip!** This ride is great for folks who might want to have a peek into Space Mountain before deciding if they're up to actually riding it.

Other Attractions

Astro Orbiter

I enjoy this ride the most after dark, but even in the daylight, this grownup version of a Dumbo-style ride gives breathtaking views of the whole Kingdom. Riders have some control of the up and down motion of their rocket, but for the most part, it is a fast spin around the skies above Tomorrowland. **Tip!** I think this is a Do Not Miss attraction if the line is not too long at night. It's a beautiful experience after dark!

Tomorrowland Speedway

These real cars are always a hit with kids too young to have their own drivers licenses, but others might find the lack of speed and control a little frustrating. Two-seat gas-powered vehicles sputter around a track ruled by a guide rail. Height requirement: 32 inches (82 cm).

Walt Disney's Carousel of Progress

This attraction dates back to Walt Disney's contributions to world fairs of the 1950s and 1960s. The seating platform moves through decades of household innovations from the early 1900s right up to today. If you love nostalgia, this is your show!

Tomorrowland Dining...

Cosmic Ray's Starlight Café

Quick-service. Another of our favorite quick-service spots in the Magic Kingdom®. It looks like a futuristic assembly line, but this is an incredibly efficient way to serve a lot of food to a lot of people. Choices are segmented into different delivery bays, where you can choose from burgers, ribs, chicken, sandwiches, salads, and an endless array of condiments. Sit in the upper section for good views of Tomorrowland. Or, sit below and be entertained by an alien lounge singer. Check for Mobile Ordering.

The Lunching Pad

Quick-service and snacks. Hotdogs and other munchies. Check for Mobile Ordering.

Tomorrowland Terrace Restaurant

Quick-service, open seasonally. Pasta, chicken and even lobster rolls. Check from Mobile Ordering.

Tomorrowland Snacks
Auntie Gravity's Galactic Goodies
Snacks. Ice cream and other frozen treats. Check for Mobile Ordering.

Tomorrowland Restrooms
There is a set of restrooms near Auntie Gravity's Ice Cream Shop. There are restrooms adjacent to the Tomorrowland Stage, just south of the Space Mountain entrance. There is another restroom right on the border between Tomorrowland and Main Street. You need to walk down the corridor towards Tomorrowland Terrace to find them. These restrooms are adjacent to the Plaza Restaurant on Main Street.

Magic Kingdom® Final Thoughts
The Magic Kingdom® begins each day with a big welcome celebration and features shows and parades throughout the day. On evenings when the Magic Kingdom® is open later, you can expect a nighttime transformational castle show, and of course, fireworks. In the center of the Kingdom you will certainly encounter street performances and character appearances.

The best places to watch the parades are curbside along Main Street, U.S.A., particularly around the circle near Cinderella's Castle or the circle at the train station end of the street. Many people will camp out along Main Street hours in advance, but you can usually find good viewing areas on the curb closer to parade time along the parade route in Frontierland and Liberty Square. They're not always open, but there are special viewing spots from the stairs and second floor perches at the Main Street train station and from the bridges and elevated walkways leading into Cinderella's Castle.

The best places to watch the fireworks are anywhere along Main Street, U.S.A. If possible, find a spot somewhere in the plaza area in front of the castle. You can see the fireworks from almost anywhere in the park, but you might want to avoid Tomorrowland, which has some of the most obstructed views. I like those places where you can see Cinderella's Castle and the fireworks together at the same time – it's just a little more magical that way! If you are not a fan of the firework crowds, try watching the fireworks from the Fantasyland side of the castle.

Be a kid at heart. Be brave and ride up front. Don't worry about getting wet. Be curious. Ask questions and be sure to let Cast Members know if you are celebrating something.

In the weeks leading up to Halloween on October 31, Magic Kingdom® offers a very special ticketed event on select nights called Mickey's Not So Scary Halloween Party (due to the pandemic in 2021 they are offering a scaled back celebration called the Boo Bash). The park closes down to normal visitors, allowing ticket holders a truly special experience. Many rare Disney villain characters come out of hiding for this event to greet guests, and Disney offers up special party treats and trick-or-treat trails throughout the entire park. Most attractions in the park continue to run but only a few restaurants remain open, and some turn into special dance party venues. The night features special stage shows, the wonderful Mickey's Not-So-Scary Halloween

Parade and a stunning villain-themed firework spectacular! It is one of our favorite special events at Walt Disney World®!

Right after clearing out all the Halloween decorations, the Magic Kingdom® very quickly transforms into a holiday wonderland. On select nights in November and December, building up to Christmas week, the Magic Kingdom® offers Mickey's Very Merry Christmas Party. This too, is a special ticketed event. Unique holiday treats are served, and Disney's favorite characters come out in droves dressed in holiday costumes. There is a special Frozen-themed castle lighting ceremony, a wonderful holiday parade and a spectacular Christmas-themed fireworks show.

Although the parks become uncomfortably crowded, there is no more festive place to ring in the New Year than Disney Parks and Disney Springs®.

If you want to experience any of these amazing special events, plan way ahead. Lodging for the holidays books up well in advance of these special dates.

Epcot®

Epcot® Overview

Walt Disney's original vision was for Epcot® to be a real, working, futuristic city – a place where state-of-the-art technology was combined with Disney creativity to provide a safe, clean, comfortable community for people to live. In fact, Epcot® stands for Experimental Prototype Community of Tomorrow. Walt's idea eventually became a giant showcase for cultural and technological achievements, which sounds a bit stuffy, but it actually turned out to be a whole lot of fun.

Epcot® is currently going through a major transformation: The new vision for Epcot® is to divide what used to be Future World into three unique "lands."

World Discovery will be the current side of the park that hosts Test Track and Mission Space. It will soon be joined by a brand new Play Pavilion, a space themed restaurant called Space 220, and a massive new indoor coaster called *Guardians of the Galaxy* Cosmic Rewind.

World Celebration will be the new central core area of the park which will include new shopping and dining opportunities incorporated in a large structure that will provide a multi-tier viewing platform overlooking the World Showcase Lagoon for the new night time fireworks extravaganza. Spaceship Earth is slated for a major overhaul too.

World Nature which includes The Land Pavilion, Imagination, and The Seas will gain a *Moana* themed water attraction.

The World Showcase remains the 11 nation celebration of world cultures it has always been, but it will gain new attractions in France and United Kingdom.

Please forgive the construction. Disney is working on something that will be special for generations to come. But your visit in the coming years might be impacted by the work being done.

Getting to Epcot®

Disney Resort hotel guests can take buses from their hotels right to Epcot's front gates. If you are staying at a Disney hotel on the monorail system, you can take the monorail to Epcot® via the Transportation and Ticket Center near Magic Kingdom®, and there is ferry service between Disney's Hollywood Studios® and Epcot®. Hotels along the way, like Disney's Yacht and Beach Club and the Disney BoardWalk®, can also reach Epcot® by these ferry boats or by pleasant walking paths. Ferries arrive and depart at the International Gateway near France in the World Showcase. Disney now has a cable-suspended gondola system called the Skyliner which links some of the resort hotels to Epcot® and Hollywood Studios®.

Our Strategy for Visiting Epcot®

Epcot® now has two active entrances: The main entrance from the parking lot side where cars, buses, and monorails unload. The second is in the middle of the park (between United Kingdom and France on that side of the World Showcase) where friendship boats and the new Skyliner drops off guests. With two functional entrances and the park's construction building towards an all new layout, I don't know that there is a better way to start your day at Epcot® than just enthusiastically jumping in and trying things out as you encounter them. Don't miss the stand out attractions here; Test Track, Mission Space, Soarin', Spaceship Earth, The Seas, *Frozen* Ever After, and the new rides *Ratatouille,* and *Guardians of the Galaxy.* Epcot® is kind of a passive park, especially the World Showcase side of the property. Explore at your own pace.

Make dining reservations as far in advance as possible!

You can start making dining reservations months in advance of your trip. For some of Epcot's prime dining spots, this is a very smart thing to do. If you did not make your reservations well in advance, you can try to make same-day reservations at your Disney hotel's concierge desk, or you can use your own phone to make dining reservations on a whim by calling 407-W-DINE (407-939-3463). This is your best option for dining reservations if you are staying outside of the Disney property. Of course, you can use The Genie smartphone feature to make reservations too including the walk-up waiting list feature now offered for many popular restaurants.

Let's begin...

Your Epcot® experience can vary depending which entrance path you choose, the main entrance and the International Gateway on the side of the park located between United Kingdom and France in the World Showcase. For the sake of this book we are going to work our way left to right across the map to work through the new "land" divisions of what used to be Future World but now are World Discovery, World Celebration and World Nature... then work our way around the lagoon to Explore the World Showcase by pavilion. Let's dive in...

World Discovery, World Celebration, World Nature

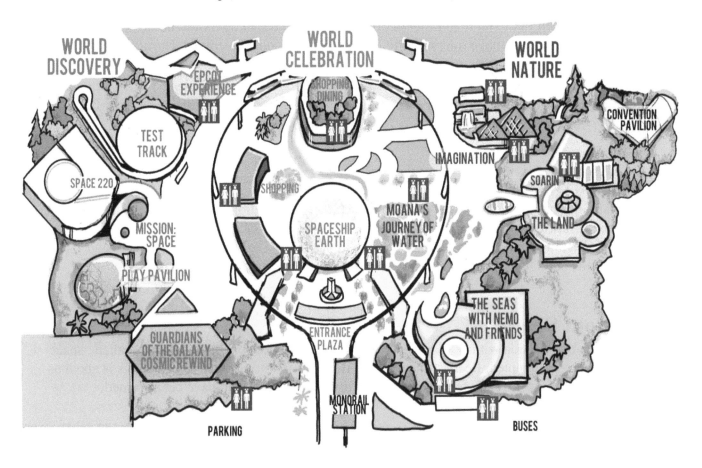

Intro to World Discovery, World Celebration, and World Nature

The massive front of Epcot® area is changing from Future World to new, more cohesive, theming. Future World is being segmented into three parts, each with its own vibrant identity.

World Discovery

Epcot® puts many of the park's hardcore thrills on this futuristic side of the park. World Discovery is a peek into our fantastic future.

Guardians of the Galaxy-Cosmic Rewind

This is the largest indoor roller coaster ever conceived. The queue area wanders through what used to be old Epcot's Universe of Energy building. Completely re-themed to introduce visitors to Marvel Comic's weird and wild Guardian's universe.

Do Not Miss...

Guardians of the Galaxy - Cosmic Rewind

Unlike other thrill rides you might find in other parks, this coaster spins and pivots its cars and slows and speeds up to make riders a part of a crazy comic book adventure. The actual show building that houses the main portion of the coaster is said to be big enough to cover three Spaceship Earth geospheres. That's really *really* big. With the spinning and speed, this attraction might not be for folks who do not appreciate big roller coaster thrills. Height requirement expected to be at least 48 inches (122 cm).

Play Pavilion

This hall once housed Epcot's spectacular Wonders of Life Pavilion. In the following years, it was used as an event center for Epcot's many festivals. Disney has recently announced this site will soon become home to a whimsical Play Pavilion. It's sure to engage all our senses and childhood wonder. Look for this new pavilion coming in the next year.

Mission: Space

Working in conjunction with NASA, Disney imagineers wanted to create the most realistic space simulation ever attempted. Real astronauts have ridden Mission: Space and agree, this is about as close as you can get to really feeling the thrill of a rocket launch. You have been warned.

Do Not Miss...

Mission: Space

This ride actually comes in two flavors: mild and wild. The milder journey offers a fairly tame ride through a simulated space mission into earth's orbit, while the wild one takes you on a startlingly realistic journey to Mars using the same sort of centrifuge simulators NASA uses to train real astronauts. You will be shocked at how powerful the launch sequence feels when real G-forces press you into your seat, followed by the sensation of floating when you finally reach orbit. This ride gives real roller coaster thrills and is not for those who are sensitive to simulations, spinning or thrill rides. All others will be amazed – and a little wobbly – as they disembark. Mission: Space recently got a complete upgrade with better visuals on both versions of the ride! Height requirement: 40 inches (102 cm).

Other Attractions

Advanced Training Lab

Younger space travelers will enjoy this space-themed play area. It's a waiting area for those who prefer not to go on the space simulator adventure. This section might not be fully available during the pandemic as it is a high touch area.

Dining In Space
Space 220
This brand new dining experience is located next to Mission: Space. It uses giant screens as windows out onto a breathtaking orbital view of the earth's surface as if the restaurant was a wing of a new Space Station. Diners take gentle launch vehicles (themed elevators) up to the restaurant and back. Hopefully not as jarring as the very realistic space simulator Mission: Space ride. Featuring a contemporary American menu, including breakfast, lunch, and dinner. Reservations required. Targeted to open in 2021. Check walk-up waiting list on the Disney app for long shot last minute reservations.

Test Track
Test Track takes guests on a fun exploration of the technology that goes into designing today's most advanced road vehicles. Design it and then ride it.

Do Not Miss...
Test Track
Enter the development labs at Chevrolet Motor Corporation. The queue area is an interactive design studio that lets you actually create a vehicle in a digital lab. Then, see how your design measures up to others in your ride vehicle. Once the design phase is complete, you board a test vehicle and take it out on the course. Test Track is actually one of the fastest moving rides in all of Walt Disney World® — cars get up to speeds exceeding 65 MPH! Height requirement: 40 inches (102 cm).

Other Attractions
Chevrolet® Showroom
This is one of the only attractions at Disney that does not exit into a gift shop. Instead you walk into a glorious Chevy showroom. Kick the tires on some of the hottest new cars and trucks. You'll find lots of photo opportunities and fun hands-on games here. Who doesn't want to get a photo with the new Corvette? *Then* you'll walk into a gift shop.

The Epcot® Experience
While Epcot® is undergoing the biggest transformation since its opening in 1982. You can visit this section of the park, which was originally the Odyssey Restaurant, to check out a presentation which previews all the amazing things coming in the near future to this park.

Do Not Miss...
Walt Disney Imagineering Presents the Epcot® Experience
A stunning on-going, walk-in presentation that completely surrounds you in 3D mapped imagery. No special glasses needed. This is the same wrap-around image technology that Disney uses to illuminate the castle during fireworks shows, brought indoors to a much smaller venue. It is an incredible way to see what Disney has planned for the near future of this park.

World Discovery Restrooms

Epcot's restroom situation is influx as major construction is bringing major changes to what used to be known as the Future World side of the park. There are restrooms in the corridor leading away from the Spaceship Earth entrance plaza towards what will soon be the access way to Guardians of the Galaxy Cosmic Rewind. There is a restroom located across the way from Mission: Space towards Spaceship Earth. There are restrooms located within the old Odyssey building (that now houses the Epcot Experience). Here you will also find Epcot's First Aid Station and Baby Care Center.

World Celebration

This center slice of Epcot® is being completely redone. Here you will find a welcoming park, playful fountains, and assorted shops and restaurants all in the shadow of Spaceship Earth. A large three-level platform will be added to the shores of the World Showcase Lagoon that will house new dining and shopping opportunities, along with improved viewing of Epcot's famous night time fireworks spectaculars. Please forgive the construction walls. Amazing things are coming to this section of the park. As dining spots open up again, be sure to check walk-up waiting list on the Disney app for long shot last minute reservations. Use Mobile Ordering in the app for counter-service restaurants.

Oh Beverly, We Missed You!

With both the pandemic and heavy reconstruction still underway, we are happy to announce long time favorite Club Cool will be returning to this park. Once it reopens, guests can taste the wide range of CocaCola® products offered all over the world. Including the grimace inducing, Beverly, an Italian soda drink. Have your camera ready when your friends try this one!

Spaceship Earth

Often referred to as the "giant golf ball," Epcot's amazing spherical centerpiece is an architectural marvel. It is almost as iconic as Cinderella's Castle. This giant globe encases a pretty neat attraction, Spaceship Earth.

Do Not Miss...

Spaceship Earth

Due for a major refurbishment and a whole new story to be told inside, Spaceship Earth might be closed during your visit. The pandemic has delayed many of Disney's ambitious construction projects and this attraction was one of them. Enjoy this classic Epcot attraction if you can. I can't wait to see what an infusion of Disney magic will do when the refurbishment commences. In its current state, the giant geosphere houses a ride through the history a human communication. The ride deposits guests in a fun interactive activity gallery (which might not be open during pandemic guidance). The update of Spaceship Earth will focus on the long shared human tradition of story telling.

World Celebration Restrooms

This central plaza to Epcot contains the main entrance to the park, thus there are a lot of rest facilities located in this area. With Epcot's major transformation underway, the location of these restrooms might change. There are restrooms on either side the entrance turnstiles to the park on the walk in from the parking lots. There are restrooms on either side of the base of Spaceship Earth. Though construction has not yet begun, there are likely to be restrooms located in the new multi-tiered observation platform near the shores of the lagoon.

World Nature

The new theme of this side of the park is a celebration of the environment and conservation. A section of this area will be reworked to include some pretty amazing water fountains and effects.

The Seas with Nemo and Friends

The Seas is a massive celebration of earth's aquatic life. You can enter the pavilion via a clamshell ride that introduces you to some of your favorite *Finding Nemo* characters, or you can just stroll in through the front entrance.

Do Not Miss...

The Seas with Nemo and Friends

There is a lot going on within this massive pavilion. First there is an optional clamshell Nemo themed ride that combines remarkable Pixar/Disney animation with views of real living sea life. The ride drops visitors off inside a giant sea lab that kind of exists within one of the world's largest aquariums. There are panoramic views of coral, fish, sharks, rays, and even dolphins. Inside the base there are numerous other displays including a close up look at rescued manatees.

Turtle Talk with Crush

Kids should not miss the side attraction Turtle Talk with Crush. A live interactive q&a with the coolest turtle in the ocean.

Dining Under the Sea

Coral Reef Restaurant

This unique-tiered restaurant features panoramic views into the Sea's massive aquarium. Of course the menu offers a unique seafood experience. Reservations required. Check the app for the Walk Up Wait List for your chance to dine with the fishes.

Moana's Journey of Water

A winding pathway through lush tropical foliage engulfs enchanted tumbling waterfalls and peaceful pools.

Do Not Miss...

Moana's Journey of Water

Finally an attraction worthy of the Polynesian Princess! The area between The Seas and The Land will soon be transformed into a tropical interactive playground of magical water features. No doubt this area will include a special *Moana* character meet-and-greet location too.

The Land

This pavilion contains two of Epcot's best attractions: One awe inspiring flight around the world and one relaxing educational boat ride. No visit to Epcot® would be complete without taking flight on the highly innovative Soarin'.

Do Not Miss...

SOARIN'

A breathtaking virtual hang-gliding ride over some of the world's most awe-inspiring views. This ride is extremely smooth, but if you are sensitive to simulated heights and motion, you may want to sit this one out. Recently upgraded with new digital projection and an all-new journey, they even built a whole new flying theater to increase ride capacity. Height requirement: 40 inches (102 cm).

Living with the Land

A leisurely boat trip through cutting-edge advances in agriculture, gardening, and aquaculture. If you love gardening, this boat journey is for you – you'll go right through real agricultural experiments being conducted by some of this country's leading universities.

The Land Dining

Sunshine Seasons

Quick-service. More like a food court than a single restaurant, this is our favorite quick-service dining this side of the park. There is lots to choose from, and some of the ingredients even come right from the Land's experimental gardens! Mobile Order.

The Garden Grill

Table-service. All-you-can-enjoy, buffet-style, character dining, with Chip & Dale, Mickey Mouse, and Pluto. Reservations recommended. Check Walk Up Wait List in the app for a spontaneous chance to dine with your favorite Disney characters.

Imagination!

A pavilion dedicated entirely to celebrating inspiration, including many of the elements that drive our dreams into reality. Disney Imagineers are planning some major upgrades to this pavilion in the coming years, which explains the temporary feeling of the current attractions. Expect attractions here to change.

Do Not Miss...

Pixar Film Festival

This is a seasonal attraction while Imagineers work on new plans for the pavilion. It is a collection of Pixar's rarely seen short films, and it is very entertaining.

Other Attractions

Journey into Imagination with Figment

It is good to see magical little Figment appearing in this watered-down version of what used to be a major attraction. Some clever moments. Good for small children.

ImageWorks

A large interactive playground that is both fascinating and fun.

World Nature Restrooms

There are restrooms almost hidden in the back of the Seas with Nemo and Friends near the Coral Reef Restaurant. Larger restrooms are located across the plaza from The Land near what will be the new Moana-inspired section of the park. Inside the Land Pavilion, there are restrooms on the second floor. There are companion restrooms outside the exit of the Soarin' attraction. To the side of the Imagination Pavilion, you can find another set of restrooms. A much needed brand new set of restrooms have been added to the park, just before entering the World Showcase on the way into Canada.

The World Showcase

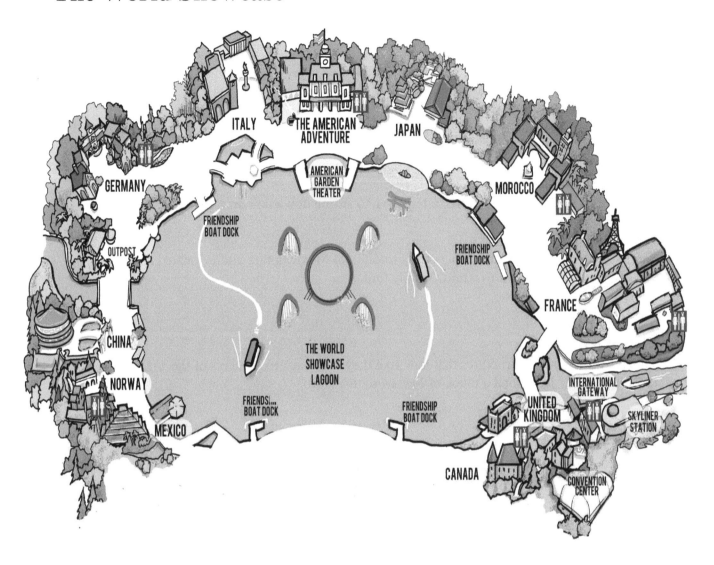

Intro to World Showcase

Around the World Showcase Lagoon, you will find one of the best collections of culture and cuisine gathered anywhere in one place. A smart visitor to the World Showcase will make time to dine here, but there are also some fun attractions and shows. Because so much of the World Showcase experience is focused on food, making some advanced reservations is a must! Use the smart phone app frequently.

Mexico

Discover Mexico's treasures in the shadows of an authentic-looking Aztec pyramid. Inside, discover a quaint, moonlit Mexican village marketplace.

Do Not Miss...
Gran Fiesta Tour Starring the Three Caballeros
This boat ride is similar to It's A Small World, but this journey takes you on a trip through Mexico's cultural history.

Dining in Mexico
San Angel Inn Restaurante
Table-service. This is Mexico's premier dining spot, located within the pavilion itself and overlooking the Gran Fiesta Tour ride. Fine Mexican dining, reservations recommended. Walk Up Wait List in the app might find you an open table.
La Hacienda de San Angel
Quick-service. The counter-service alternative to sitting down and dining in the main restaurant. Check for Mobile Ordering.
La Cantina Restaurant
Quick-service. This outdoor setting offers traditional Mexican fare and is located across the promenade from the main pyramid. Mobile Order.

Norway
This pavilion features structures that look like they date back to the days of the Vikings. More recently, Disney has added a touch of *Frozen* to this land.

Do Not Miss...
Frozen Ever After.
Fans of the *Frozen* sisters will be thrilled to experience their world in this fun boat adventure. The attraction is quite beautiful, and the queue area walks you through a whimsical Norwegian village.
Meet Anna and Elsa
The *Frozen* sisters now have a place to call their very own in the heart of Norway. This is one of the most popular character meet-and-greet opportunities in all of Walt Disney World®! Confession: Anna is one of our favorite princesses! Spoiler: She's not a princess anymore.

Dining in Norway
Akershus Royal Banquet Hall
If you can't dine with the princesses in Cinderella's Castle at the Magic Kingdom®, this Norwegian castle-themed restaurant is the next best thing. An assortment of princesses greet visitors here every day. Table-service, reservations recommended well in advance. Check Walk Up Wait List in the Disney app for a rare, spontaneous chance at dining with princesses.
Kringla Bakeri Og Kafe
Quick-service. Hearty sandwiches and pastries fit for a Viking. Try the school bread – it's so good! Check for Mobile Ordering.

Norway's Restrooms

Located between the entrance to the Anna and Elsa meet and greet and the Bakery you will find a set of restrooms.

The Outpost

The African continent is not officially in the World Showcase. This little spot between China and Germany perhaps serves as a placeholder for some future additions. Get a drink or a snack. Make a stop here and pose for some world traveler-style photos, then, move on with your day. If you crave African flavors, check out Animal Kingdom and the Animal Kingdom Resort!

China

An eye-catching ornate temple beckons you inside, where you will marvel at beautiful structures and gardens. Within the main pavilion is a collection of Chinese cultural treasures.

Do Not Miss...

Reflections of China

Using Disney's patented Circle-Vision 360° film format, you will experience China wrapped all around you.

Meet Mulan

Chinese heroine Mulan – and sometimes Mushu the dragon – periodically appear outside this pavilion. Check park schedules for details.

Acrobats

Often Chinese acrobats will perform shows throughout the day in the entrance courtyard near the ornate arch. See daily event schedule.

Dining in China

Nine Dragons Restaurant

Table-service. This is the China Pavilion's signature dining experience, with both modern and traditional Chinese fare. Reservations are recommended. Walk Up Wait List in the Disney app might find you an open table.

Lotus Blossom Café

Quick-service. Authentic Chinese choices delivered at the speed of takeout. Try Mobile Ordering.

Germany

An ongoing Oktoberfest celebration of German spirit, food, and music. There is a festive feeling throughout this old-world village setting.

Meet Snow White

Snow White makes scheduled appearances near her famous wishing well just outside this pavilion.

Dining in Germany

Biergarten

Table-service. All-you-can-enjoy authentic biergarten favorites, served up with a festive German atmosphere. Reservations recommended. Walk Up Wait List in the Disney app might get you into this polka party hall!

Sommerfest

Quick-service. A way to quickly grab a taste of Germany. Brats, pretzels, and an out-of-this-world strudel. Try Mobile Ordering.

Karamell Kuche

Wonderful caramel candies and baked goods. Mobile Ordering might be available.

Germany Restrooms

Located just across from the Friendship Boat docks, on the Italy side of the German Pavilion you will find restrooms nestled in just behind the model railroad village.

Italy

Drawing influences from Rome, Florence, and Venice, the Italian pavilion captures the flavors of Italy. It is a wonderful experience to pass some time in the pavilion's open square – get a glass of wine and soak in the culture!

Dining in Italy

Tutto Italia Ristorante

Table-service. This is Italy's premium dining experience, with a wide selection of pasta and other traditional dishes. Reservations recommended. Check for an opening in Walk Up Wait List in the Disney app.

Tutto Gusto Wine Cellar

Table-service. Sample meats and cheeses in a traditional Sicilian setting. Reservations recommended. Walk Up Wait List might get you in.

Via Napoli Ristorante e Pizzeria

Table-service. The aroma of wood-fire-baked pizza brings people in, along with other classic Italian fare. Reservations recommended. Check the Disney app for Walk Up Wait List. **Tip!** If you cannot get a reservation you can still sample their amazing pizza by the slice from a take out window. Note: The pizza offered in the sit down restaurant is better.

Italian Treats

Gelateria Toscana

Quick-service cart. Enjoy scoops on authentic Italian gelato. Perfect for cooling down on a hot Florida afternoon.

The American Adventure

This Colonial pavilion serves as the centerpiece and host to all of the World Showcase.

Do Not Miss...

The American Adventure Show

This moving and highly patriotic multimedia presentation combines period artwork, classic film footage, and Disney's remarkable audio-animatronic characters. The pre-show often includes live music by Disney's legendary vocal group "Voices of Liberty." If you have never heard the Voices (also known as Voctave), you're in for a real taste of choral wizardry. They are jaw-droppingly good.

American Heritage Gallery

This is the waiting area for the American Adventure Show, but it is home to some surprising national treasures in its own right.

American Garden Theater

This theater often hosts great live entertainment, especially during Epcot's amazing Food & Wine or Flower & Garden festivals. Check park schedules for details during your visit. This theater hosts some amazing musical acts!

Dining in America

Regal Eagle Smoke House

Quick-service. The famous Muppet, Sam the Eagle, hosts a BBQ contest here. A good place to try different styles of BBQ sauces and rubs on chicken, beef and pork. Mobile Order available.

Fife and Drum Tavern

Snacks. The tavern is known for its roasted turkey legs, but also offers lighter fare. Mobile Order.

American Adventure Restrooms

Located to the Japan side of the American Pavilion. Tucked back behind Fife and Drum. This might be the nicest rest area in all of Epcot®.

Japan

This pavilion showcases precisely manicured Japanese gardens and a five-story pagoda. Wander the paths that take you up into the back portions of this marvelous pavilion. Beautiful gardens and ponds lie around every corner.

Do Not Miss...

Mitsukoshi Department Store

It's not a ride or a show, but this branch of one of Japan's oldest and most popular department stores really is a great attraction. It carries a fascinating mix of traditional Japanese wares along with treats and whimsical pop culture items – I love this store! Don't miss its incredible pearl harvesting station.

Dining in Japan

Takumi-Tei

One of the finest dining experiences in all of Walt Disney World®. If you would like to experience the very best in Japanese cuisine, this is the place. Reservations required. Check Walk Up Wait List in the Disney app for a rare last moment opening.

Teppan Edo

Table-service. Chefs prepare, chop and grill your meal right before your eyes in an entertaining dinner show. Reservations recommended. Check for last-minute openings in Disney app's Walk Up Wait List.

Tokyo Dining

Table-service. A nice selection of fresh sushi and extremely good tempura and teriyaki. The menu is not large, but everything is terrific!

Katsura Grill

Quick-service. Sushi bar in a beautiful setting. Check for Mobile Ordering

Kabuki Café

Quick-service and snacks. Green tea and light Japanese snack items. Check for Mobile Ordering.

Morocco

As you wander through this pavilion, you really feel like you're passing through the streets of exotic Marrakesh. Morocco's royal craftsmen hand crafted the gorgeous tile work here. I recommend you take some time to explore inside this impressive collection of North African culture and cuisine.

Meet Aladdin and Jasmine

One or both of these famous characters often appear in the back of Morocco. A great photo opportunity!

Dining in Morocco

Restaurant Marrakesh
Table-service. Authentic North African cuisine...and belly dancers! Yes, Disney is full of surprises. Reservations recommended. Check for openings in the Walk Up Wait List in the Disney app.

Tangerine Café
Quick-service. Mediterranean fare served fast.

Spice Road Table
This lagoon-side Mediterranean café is Morocco's newest dining option, and is a great place to sit back, relax, and take in the views. Small plate appetizers, wines, beers, ice cream, and slushies for the kids. Table-service. No reservations accepted.

Morocco's Restrooms

Located between Morocco and France you'll find nice, clean, recently renovated restrooms across from the friendship boat docks.

France

This pavilion could easily get by just on its food and wine, but it also has some amazing sites and attractions.

Do Not Miss...

Ratatouille the ride!
It is official – Remy the lovable gourmet rat will be joining Epcot®'s attraction lineup in October of 2021. No doubt this will be a Do Not Miss ride, as it is very popular at Disneyland Paris!

Impressions de France
A film celebration of the beautiful French countryside and the breathtaking sights of Paris, the City of Light!

Beauty and the Beast Sing Along
The success of the *Frozen* sing-a-long at Hollywood Studios® has led Disney to craft another interactive musical number at the World Showcase.

Meet Belle
Belle often greets visitors in the shade of a tree near the water. For fans of *Beauty and the Beast*, this is the best spot in Walt Disney World® to meet their favorite bookworm.

Dining in France

Chefs de France
Table-service. This French restaurant offers perhaps the most traditional Parisian dining experience. But we think some of the other dining spots in France offer more culinary creativity. Reservations recommended. Walk Up Wait List in the Disney app might get you a last second seating here.

Monsieur Paul
Table-service. Just a few steps away from Chefs de France is another exquisite and one-of-a-kind culinary experience. The chefs here strive to uphold the standards of world renowned Master Chef Paul Bocuse. Reservations strongly recommended. Don't forget Walk Up Wait List in the Disney app if gourmet hunger pangs hit in the moment.

L'Artisan De Glaces
Snacks. Artisanal ice creams and sorbets. Quick-service.

Boulangerie Patisserie
Quick-service and snacks. Lots of delicious choices, including sandwiches, quiches, and French pastries. This might be the most affordable counter-service location in all of Epcot and it is fantastic.

La Crêperie de Paris
Table-service indoors, Quick-service outdoors. Unique French offerings off a special menu for the sit-down restaurant. A nice selection of crêpes can be ordered on-the-go through a counter window. More variations on this famous French treat than you can imagine. Check for Mobile Ordering.

France Restrooms
Near the exit to the new Ratatouille ride, there is a brand new set of restrooms overlooking the International Gateway canal.

International Gateway
Located on the side of the World Showcase between United Kingdom and France, this is Epcot's second entry point. This is where the Friendship boats shuttle guests between BoardWalk, Yacht Club, Beach Club, Swan and Dolphin Resorts, the Boardwalk® Entertainment area, and Disney's Hollywood Studios® theme park. This is also the location of Epcot's Skyliner station. Cable transport to Disney's Hollywood Studios® and several other resort destinations.

International Gateway Restrooms
There are restrooms located at the International Gateway, however they are outside of the park admission turnstiles intended for those just arriving via the Skyliner cable gondolas or by the resort friendship boats.

United Kingdom

Walking into this pavilion, you'll feel like you just stepped into an old London downtown neighborhood, complete with a friendly pub. There are beautiful English gardens to wander through and a courtyard in the back that often features great live music. If the British rock cover band is playing, find a comfortable spot to enjoy them—they're a favorite of ours!

Do Not Miss...

Live Music in the garden area.
Often, Disney brings in very talented cover bands who focus on the amazing array of rock music that comes from the British Isle, singing tunes from the Beatles to Queen.

Meet Mary Poppins and Alice in Wonderland
These famous Englishwomen are known to hang out in the gardens in front of and behind the U.K. pavilion.

Dining in the United Kingdom

Rose and Crown Pub and Dining Room
Table-service. This upscale British pub features traditional British fare like fish and chips or bangers and mash in its bar area, with additional menu items available in the dining area. Reservations recommended. Try Walk Up Wait List in the app to try to get a last minute opening.
Tip! If you time your visit to the pub well, the outdoor seating along the lagoon is a great spot to watch Illuminations!
Tip! The steaks here come from the same source that provides steak to the famous Le Cellier in Canada, where it is often difficult to acquire a reservation.

Yorkshire County Fish Shop
Quick-service. This is primarily a fish and chips stand, but it also carries snacks and British beers. I love this spot for a quick satisfying serving of fish and chips! Check for Mobile Ordering.

United Kingdom's Restrooms

There is a handy set of restrooms located just across from the Rose & Crown.

Canada

This pavilion accurately captures the architectural feel of British Columbia. Be sure to explore the waterfall passageway in the back of the pavilion that leads to a gorgeous garden area.

Do Not Miss...

Canada — Far and Wide
A beautiful Circle-Vision 360° film showcases the rugged beauty of the great, snowy, north.

Canadian Gardens

Most visitors walk right past this beautiful peaceful garden, complete with waterfall and babbling brook. This is one of our very favorite rare quiet spots in all of Walt Disney World®.

Dining in Canada

Le Cellier Steakhouse

Table-service. Carnivores, take note! This is one of the best places to get a steak in all of Walt Disney World®. Trust us on this. Because of its reputation, Le Cellier is one of the hardest reservations to acquire—you may need to plan months ahead to secure a reservation. Do not forget Walk Up Wait List in the Disney app as a last chance for a last moment seating here.

Canada's Restrooms

Not really located within the boundaries of the Canadian Pavilion, but, you can find restrooms nearby. Just up the walkway, a bit towards to the entrance of World Nature's Imagination Pavilion, there is a brand new set of restrooms.

Some Final Thoughts on Experiencing Epcot®

All of Epcot® teems with live shows, impromptu street performances, and entertainment representing the many countries of the World Showcase. Be sure to pick up a show schedule when you first enter the park so you can plan your day around some of these shows.

Do Not Miss...

Harmonious!

After dark on most nights, Epcot® puts on the most amazing collection of music, fireworks, lights, and colors. This is a show that's well worth keeping the kids up past their bedtime. No Walt Disney World® vacation is complete without taking in this incredible spectacle that you won't be able to experience anywhere else!

The best views are anywhere along the shores of the World Showcase Lagoon where you have an unobstructed view of both the sky and water. People will stake out sections of the walkways around the lagoon hours before the show, but because so much of the show happens high in the sky, you don't need to spend half of your evening waiting to be sure you have a prime vantage point.

Tip! After the night's fireworks spectacular ends, linger behind in the World Showcase while the crowds push toward the park exits. You'll enjoy a peaceful stroll through the park.

Epcot® is in the middle of a major facelift! The hope? All these massive changes would be done by the resort's 50th anniversary celebration. Then came the pandemic, which put many of these projects behind schedule. There will be construction going on well into the next few years. However, this park is still offering a lot, making it worth your time. I cannot wait to see what is on the horizon for Epcot®.

Disney's Hollywood Studios®

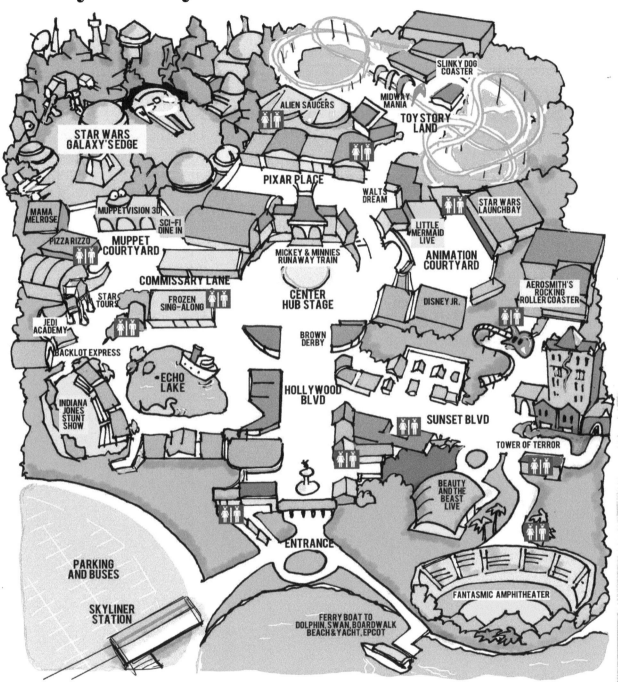

Overview of Disney's Hollywood Studios

Disney has been at the leading edge of moviemaking since the first days of cinema. Disney's Hollywood Studios® is a tribute to the best of movies, music, and television. In the summer of 2018, Disney opened *Toy Story* Land. In late 2019, it introduced the massive addition of *Star Wars*: Galaxy's Edge. And in 2021, Mickey and Minnie's Runaway Railway opened. Lots of brand new experiences are now open and ready to be enjoyed here!

Getting to Disney's Hollywood Studios®

All Disney Resort hotel guests can take buses straight to the front gate. Some Epcot® area Disney hotels, like the Yacht and Beach Club Resort and the BoardWalk Resort hotels, also offer ferry transport. If you have a Park Hopper Pass, you can get from Epcot® to Hollywood Studios® via ferry from the International Gateway Plaza near France. The Studios are also connected to other parts of the property via the new Skyliner gondola.

Our Strategy for Visiting Hollywood Studios®

There are a lot of exciting things happening at Disney's Hollywood Studios®. In just the last few years, the Studios have opened *Toy Story* Land and Mickey and Minnie's Runaway Railway. But, of course, the biggest news in the whole solar system is that *Star Wars*-Galaxy's Edge is now open. There is no doubt that this land is going to be the focal point of everyone's vacation coming to Walt Disney World® for the foreseeable months. There is no doubt this "land" is going to be packed every day. Our best advice is to make sure you stay at a Disney Resort so you can take advantage of Early Access. That precious time before the park opens to the general public is going to be the best possible time to live out your *Star Wars* adventures. The rush of fans to Galaxy's Edge might create a vacuum effect elsewhere in the park. Early in the day, other sections of the park could be clear of crowds.

When you arrive, grab the daily schedule for the big shows like the *Indiana Jones* Stunt Spectacular, the *Beauty and the Beast* musical, Fantasmic evening shows, and of course the *Star Wars* fireworks extravaganza. There will be special nighttime offerings during the 50th Anniversary celebration too. Plan your visit around these spectacles so you know when to head over for a show, and then fill the rest of the day with continuously operating rides. Knowing where everything is and when shows begin, will help you get a good seat. That is especially important at this park.

Hollywood Blvd, Echo Lake, Commissary Lane

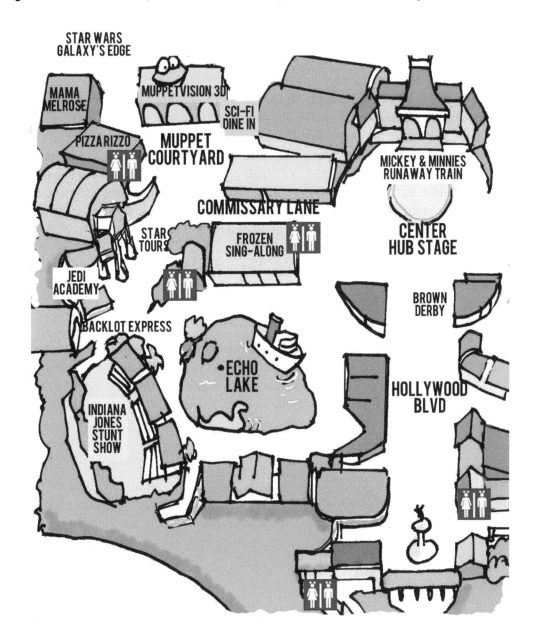

Intro to Hollywood Blvd, Echo Lake, and Commissary Lane

This is essentially the Main Street, U.S.A. of Disney's Hollywood Studios®, ending at the replica of the famous Chinese Theater. There are shops filled with movie memorabilia, souvenirs, and snacks, as well as some great attractions and dining.

Do Not Miss!

Mickey and Minnie's Runaway Railway

This unique, family thrill ride combines something Imagineers call a "Disney 2 ½ D" experience (no special glasses required) with simulation and roller coaster elements. This is the first ride to feature Mickey Mouse in Disney Parks. Guests will step through the movie screen into one of Mickey's hilarious animated short films! This ride incorporates unique, trackless ride vehicles. The Railway replaces the old classic Great Movie Ride. I think it is a worthy successor.

Dining Along Hollywood Boulevard
The Hollywood Brown Derby
Table-service. One of the nicer dining spots in Disney's Hollywood Studios®. There's a good selection of American favorites, and a world-renowned Cobb salad. Reservations recommended. You can try to get a last moment reservation through the walk up waiting list offered in the Disney app. **Tip!** The Hollywood Brown Derby offers an otherwise unpublicized dining experience called the Brown Derby Lounge—a small collection of outdoor tables that offer a walk up, no reservations, first come, first serve treat for people looking for exceptional cuisine. Here you have access to the full Hollywood Brown Derby menu, as well as a special lounge menu. Just ask to be seated in the outdoor lounge to experience this secret treat.
The Trolley Car Café
This is the park's main Starbucks coffee location. The current home of the famous Carrot Cake Cookie amongst other delicious pastry treats. Check for Mobile Ordering.

Hollywood Boulevard Restrooms
There are restrooms located just outside the entrance turnstiles for the park near the customer service windows. Once inside, you will find restrooms next to the Gas Station stroller rental spot inside to the right of the entrance. There is another set of restrooms on the corner of the Frozen Sing-a-long Theater facing the Chinese Theater.

Echo Lake
This is a small lake is just off of Hollywood Boulevard with attractions scattered along the lakeshore, including the seasonally-opened, Dinosaur Gerdy's Ice Cream Stand.

Do Not Miss!
Frozen **Sing-Along**
Some folks might think this movie is suffering a little from overexposure, but it's really special to experience the sheer joy of a thousand kids and adults singing along with the characters during scenes from the movie.
The *Indiana Jones* Stunt Spectacular
Fans of the popular adventure movies will love seeing how some of the epic stunt sequences were shot. Boulders tumble, stunt fights break out, characters jump from high buildings — and there are a lot of explosions! **Tip!** Stunt actors are usually available at the end of the show for photos.
Star Tours
This simulated turbulent *Star Wars* space journey was recently improved with high definition 3D video. There are so many different versions that it's slightly different every time you ride. Height

requirement: 40 inches (102 cm). **Tip!** It's not always possible, but try to sit in the middle of the back two rows of the Star Speeder—the motion and 3D visuals are optimized for that area.

Other Attractions

Mickey's Vacation Fun

A very cute new addition to the park. A small Mickey-themed movie theater plays a rotation of a new Mickey Mouse short film. A fun excuse to sit down and get some air conditioning for a little while.

Dining Along Echo Lake

Hollywood and Vine

Table-service. This all-you-can-enjoy buffet features Disney Junior characters at breakfast and lunch, but not during the dinner hours. Reservations recommended. Rare last minute openings might be available via the Walk Up Wait List in the Disney app.

50's Prime Time Café

Table-service. This classic diner features traditional comfort food options served with a fun 1950s attitude. Reservations recommended. In the moment openings might be found in the Walk Up Wait List feature in the Disney app.

Min and Bill's Dockside Diner

Quick-service. Light lunch fare and snacks. Check for Mobile Ordering.

Oasis Canteen

Snacks. Best known for funnel cakes, but it also serves ice cream treats. Check for Mobile Ordering.

Backlot Express

Quick-service. The Backlot Express is designed to look like a Hollywood prop shop, and features vegetarian sandwiches, chicken, and salads. Look closely and you may spot props from some of your favorite movies. Mobile Order if you can!

Echo Lake Restrooms

Restrooms located across from Star Tours and around the corner from the new Mickey's Vacation Fun theater.

Muppet Courtyard

I love this attraction and all the Muppet-inspired visuals you will encounter here. Keep an eye out for many fun details worked into the surroundings. There is a sign out front of the queue area that says "Back in five minutes-Key under mat!" And, if you look, there is indeed a key hidden under the nearby welcome mat. The Miss Piggy Fountain: the paint accident that meanders from outside to inside a store as if you could see the mischievous muppet bumbling through the area. Maybe you'll see a few hidden Mickeys too.

Do Not Miss!
MuppetVision 3D
A family-friendly experience that combines wonderful Muppet characters "live" in the theater with those in the 3D movie. **Tip!** Linger a little behind at the end of the show to watch how the theater magically repairs itself.

Muppet Courtyard Dining
Mama Melrose's Ristorante Italiano
Table-service. Italian food delivered with a little New York attitude. Lots of fun, and a favorite stop for many of us at *Actual Factual Magic*. Reservations recommended. Check for openings in the Walk Up Wait List feature in the Disney app.
PizzeRizzo
A Muppet-themed pizza place. Counter-service, with lots of seating upstairs. Not our favorite choice for dining in this park. Disney needs to tweak its machine-made individual pizzas. However oddly other things on the menu here are really good. Try the meatball sub. Check for Mobile Ordering.

BaseLine Tap

Craving a cold beer to cool off on a hot day, or a relaxing glass of wine? This is your place. Sample a selection of California's best craft beers and wines. Beverages are complemented with breads and cheeses. No full menu dining choices here. Check for Mobile Ordering.

Muppet Courtyard Restrooms

Whimsically called the "Royal Flush Restrooms" are located just outside of Pizza Rizzo's restaurant.

Commissary Lane

This is a back street that connects the center of the park to the Muppets and *Star Wars* side of things, but there are some fun dining spots along the lane.

Dining on Commissary Lane

Sci-Fi Dine-In Restaurant

Table-service. A fun drive-in-themed diner where people load into car-style booths and watch campy old sci-fi movies on a big screen as they eat. Reservations suggested. Check the Walk Up Wait List in the Disney app for last moment openings.

ABC Commissary

Quick-service. This is one of our favorite quick-service spots in the Studios because it is seldom loud or busy. It's a little off the main path, and from the outside, it looks like a sit-down restaurant. As a result, many people miss it. It can sometimes be a quiet, air-conditioned haven from the hubbub of the rest of the park, and they serve up a good burger, chicken sandwich, and a newly expanded menu. Check for Mobile Ordering.

Commissary Lane Restrooms

At the very end of Commissary Lane, near the Chinese Theater, you can find restrooms on the corner of the *Frozen* Sing-a-long Theater.

Star Wars: Galaxy's Edge

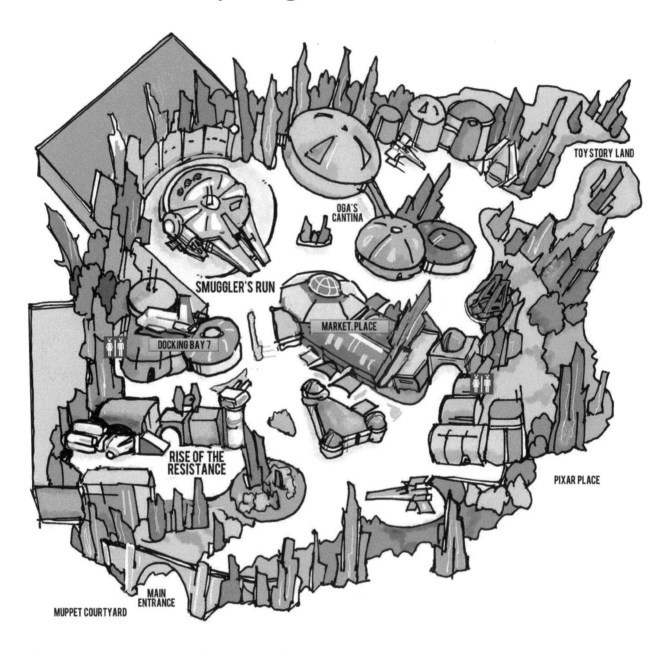

Intro to *Star Wars* Galaxy's Edge

Welcome to the star port of Black Spire on the planet Batuu. As the story goes, this far corner of *Star Wars*-Galaxy's Edge is the largest single expansion in Disney's park history (14 acres). This is nirvana for *Star Wars* fans around the world and sure to be one of the most popular (and populated) theme park sections on this planet. Plan accordingly! **Tip!** Take advantage of the Disney Resort hotel's perk, Early Access. Lookout for special limited-ticketed event nights (if Disney offers any in the foreseeable future) and try to go on rainy stormy days to take advantage of possibly reduced crowds.

Do Not Miss!

Rise of the Resistance

This is no ordinary theme park ride. *Star Wars*-Rise of the Resistance is a revolution in theme park entertainment. This attraction takes guests on a very realistic, completely immersive, *Star Wars* adventure. From being recruited to join the Rebellion, to being transported off for training, to being captured by the evil First Order and forced to escape from the passageways of a giant star cruiser. The attraction makes every moment of the ride, queue, pre-show, pre-ride, and actual ride, so seamless that its difficult to know where the adventure begins and ends. Imagineers used every trick in their magical book to design this one. There are literally three ride components baked into this one adventure. Countless audio-animatronic characters populate every section of the experience. No spoilers here. Just be prepared to be blown away. This is the most popular ride in all of the theme parks. Recent changes to the queues means there are no longer boarding pass lotteries to experience Rise. You can either line up in the stand by queue or opt to pay the variable price to access the Lightning Lane to enjoy this amazing attraction.

Smugglers Run (Fly the Millennium Falcon)

A cutting-edge interactive flight adventure that puts you in the cockpit of the fastest hunk of junk in the galaxy. Take note of the damage you inflicted on the Falcon when you leave the cockpit. Must be 38 inches to ride. **Tip!** Pilot is definitely the best role on this ride, but the right side pilot is the one that controls the jump to light speed!

Dining In Galaxy's Edge

Oga's Cantina

This is Black Spire's immersive cantina experience. To quote a Jedi master, "You may never find a more wretched hive of scum and villainy…but the drinks are pretty tasty." Fashioned after all the seedy bars ever featured in the *Star Wars* movies, Oga's is the place to rub elbows with alien travelers and more than a few galactic smugglers. Not much food here, but plenty of crazy beverages (alcohol and otherwise) that can only be found in a galaxy far, far away. Reservations are a must. Check Walk Up Wait List in the Disney app for a rare opening.

Docking Bay 7

This large enclosure houses loads of memorabilia and props from the *Star Wars* universe mixed in with a good assortment of galactic quick-service food choices. Mobile Order.

Ronto Roasters

This is emerging as the favorite quick-service stand in the Black Spire. Meats cooked in what appears to be the heat of a re-purposed pod racer engine. The standout here is the Ronto Wrap. It appears to be a glorified hotdog, but it is in fact, a sausage matched with roast beet and a spicy coleslaw wrapped in warm pita bread. It's delicious. Mobile Order.

Blue Milk Stand

This counter-service shop serves up Blue Milk, Green Milk and other treats. The official drinks of the galaxy far, far away. Mobile Order.

Shopping in Galaxy's Edge

I am purposely being vague about the location of some experiences. Discovery and interaction with the citizens of Black Spire is definitely part of the fun here. You will encounter a galactic pet shop, a droid workshop, a large interstellar antiquities museum. If you're lucky, you might even find the secret contraband lightsaber maker who hides his wares behind the guise of a scrap metal collector. Ask the locals where you can find "scrap metal" and they might direct you to the right place. But shhh! Don't tell any storm troopers!

Use Your Smart Phone!

Galaxy's Edge is connected closely with the MyDisneyExperience app and the PlayDisney app. You will be able to mobile order at a few of the spots within Black Spire. The PlayDisney app features translators and fun hacks of droids, ships, and interactive panels scattered throughout the land. Keep your phone handy for an otherworldly experience.

Galaxy's Edge Restrooms

Known by the local residents of Batuu as "refreshers", you can find restrooms at the Rise of the Resistance end of the Marketplace.

Toy Story Land

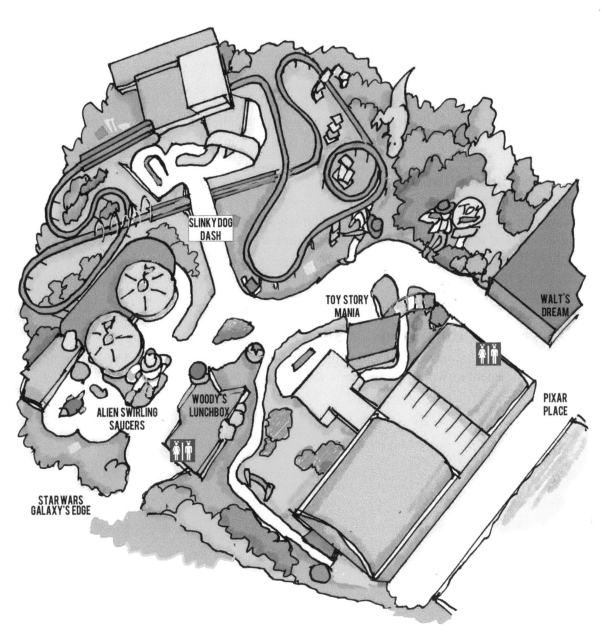

Intro to *Toy Story* Land
Dedicated to Disney's famed partnership with the computer animation geniuses at Pixar, this is the first major expansion to Disney's Hollywood Studios® since its gates opened in 1989. *Toy Story* Land is very popular – let's take a closer look!

Do Not Miss!
Slinky Dog Dash
A wonderful, family-friendly coaster with just enough thrills to make everyone happy, but especially good for younger riders wanting to experience a slightly more advanced coaster. **Tip!**

This is one of the park's newest coasters. You can bet it is going to be worthy of Genie+ Lightning Lane choice! Height requirement: 38 inches (97 cm).

Toy Story Mania

All your favorite _Toy Story_ characters join in on this ride-through a game-filled carnival midway —it's fun for everyone!

Other Attractions

Alien Swirling Saucers

This is a well-themed, twister-type attraction hosted by the alien squeeze toys from _Toy Story_. Great for smaller kids. Height requirement: 32 inches (81 cm).

Toy Story Land Dining

Woody's Lunchbox

Quick-service. Sandwiches, salads, soups, and treats set in a friendly outdoor picnic setting. The grilled cheese and tomato soup combo is a lunchtime treat. Mobile Order.

Round Up Rodeo BBQ

The _Toy Story_ characters are hosting a rodeo themed BBQ and you are invited. Coming soon. Reservations expected.

Toy Story Land Restrooms

There are restrooms before you get to the main entrance of Toy Story Land. There is another set of restrooms adjacent to Woody's Lunchbox Restaurant.

Animation Courtyard, Sunset Boulevard

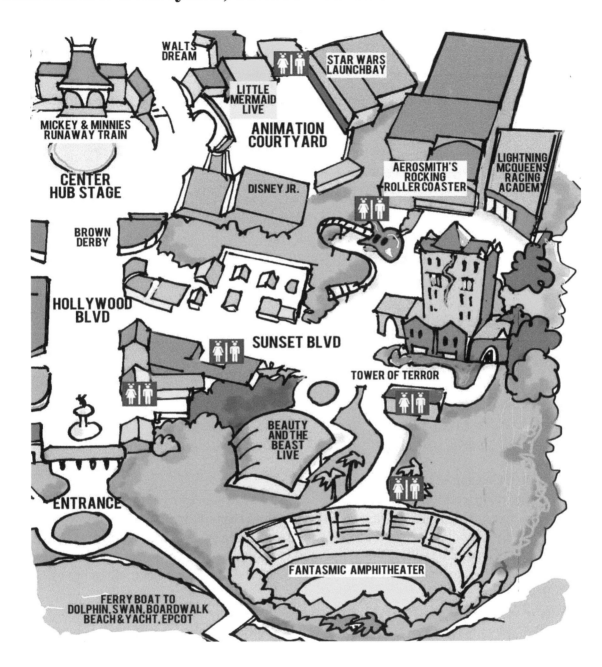

Intro to Animation Courtyard and Sunset Boulevard

A tribute to Walt Disney's enormous contribution to the world of entertainment. Here you will find some great attractions for small children, the whole family, and true thrill seekers.

Do Not Miss!

Star Wars Launch Bay

While Galaxy's Edge is a totally immersive *Star Wars* experience, Launch Bay is more of a homage to the *Star Wars* movies themselves. You won't find much *Star Wars* merchandise or movie references in Batuu, but you will here. Meet select *Star Wars* characters here. Think of Galaxy's Edge as a chance to live out your *Star Wars* adventures. While at Launch Bay, celebrate the movies themselves. **Tip!** You have not lived unless you hug a Wookie.

Other Attractions
Voyage of the *Little Mermaid*
Live musical theater tells a condensed version of Ariel's story through song, live performers and puppetry.
Disney Junior Dance Party!
Geared toward little ones who love the Disney Channel, this show features lots of Disney Junior characters. Pure joy for preschoolers with a little extra steam to burn. Great photo opportunities for their parents!

Animation Courtyard Restrooms
You will find restrooms tucked away back to the side of the *Star Wars* Launch Bay.

Sunset Boulevard
Some of this park's best attractions lie along this street—it feels like you are venturing into the glamour of old Hollywood.

Do Not Miss!
***Beauty and the Beast* Live on Stage**
A Broadway-style musical tells the story of Belle and the Beast, performed in a covered open-air amphitheater.
Rock 'n' Roller Coaster Starring *Aerosmith*®
Fans of the classic Space Mountain roller coaster will be blown away by this rocked out, all-in-the-dark trip across a mythical Los Angeles to attend an Aerosmith concert. Magnetic levitation launch technology catapults you from 0 to 60 in a breathtaking two seconds... and I do mean breathtaking. This coaster has a few inversions and is definitely not for the faint of heart, but those who dare will be rewarded with an incredible ride! Height requirement: 48 inches (122 cm).
The *Twilight Zone* Tower of Terror
This beautifully creepy old hotel is the perfect blend of theme, thrills, and chills. It is home to one of Disney's scariest attractions. You'll take a service elevator that not only goes up and down, it moves forward through one of the upper floors of the hotel before dropping guests through a series of completely unpredictable plunges. The drop sequences are different every time you ride, but you can count on at least one full thirteen-story drop to the bottom of the shaft. Again, not for the faint of heart. Height requirement: 40 inches (102 cm).

Other Sunset Blvd Attractions
Lightning McQueen's Racing Academy
A larger wrap around screen video experience. Immerse yourself in a 15-minute *Cars*-themed adventure. Great for younger fans of the *Cars* movies.

Dining Along Sunset Boulevard

Sweet Spells

Quick-service and snacks. This is more of a bakery than a restaurant, but they do have good sandwiches along with the baked goods you might expect...and some really, really, good cinnamon rolls. Mobile Order.

Toluca Legs Turkey Co.

Quick-service and snacks. This is the best spot in Hollywood Studios® to get that famous Walt Disney World® turkey leg. It's so big, and sooo good! Mobile Order.

Anaheim Produce

Quick-service and snacks. If you're craving something healthy to snack on, this is the spot for you. Fruits, veggies and other healthy refreshments. Mobile Order.

Rosie's All-American Café

Quick-service. Not too far from the Rock 'n' Roller Coaster® and the Tower of Terror. Burgers and fries are the main attraction here. Mobile Order.

Catalina Eddie's

Quick-service. Pizza and salads.

Fairfax Fare

Quick-service. Gourmet hot dogs, smoked spare ribs and chicken.

Sunset Boulevard Restroom

Halfway down the street on the right across from the Anaheim Produce there are restrooms near Sunset Club Couture. Further down the boulevard you will see an odd looking dark stone building adjacent to the entrance to Tower of Terror and the entrance path to the Fantasmic amphitheater. Down towards the Rock 'n' Roller Coaster®, you will find restrooms near that attraction's exit. On the other end of this plaza, near Lightning McQueen's Racing Academy, there is even another restroom.

Disney's Hollywood Studios® Special Touches

Most Disney Parks offer at least one "kiss goodnight," but some nights at Hollywood Studios®, you may be lucky enough to catch two, maybe three nocturnal spectacles!

Do Not Miss!

Star Wars: A Galactic Spectacular Fireworks

On special nights, Disney takes pyrotechnics to a whole new level with this musical tribute to the *Star Wars* movies. It's not just fireworks overhead, but synchronized projections, lasers and columns of flame – one of our favorite firework shows on the property!

A Celebration of Animation

Running on the surfaces of the Chinese Theater you can see an impressive projection show taking viewers back through the musical history of Disney's amazing animation.

50th Anniversary Tower of Terror Projection Show

Depending on the pandemic situation, these night time shows might come and go, but Disney has promised an all new 50th anniversary-inspired projection show for Tower of Terror to celebrate the resorts historic achievement. It should be amazing!

Fantasmic!

This is not a firework show and you can't see what is happening from outside the massive amphitheater. Even after many years, this show still packs in capacity crowds, so you do want to queue up when you see the lines developing. Fantasmic is a live-action celebration of Disney animation. Yes, it is starting to show its age, but if you want to see some impressive showmanship mixed with mist projections and big fire effects, this is still worth checking out. Especially if you have never seen it before.

Fantasmic Food Offerings

The giant arena that surrounds the Fantasmic stage has its own concession stands. Be warned, these stands get overwhelmed quickly before the show. Bring your patience. It might be smart to stock up on snacks before entering the amphitheater.

There are no restrooms in the Fantasmic amphitheater area so plan accordingly.

What's Next for Disney's Hollywood Studios®?

The completion of *Star Wars* Galaxy's Edge and *Toy Story* Land ends a massive expansion and transformation of the Studios. This also marks a decisive shift of the Studios away from being movie and television production grounds, to more of an adventure park. There are plenty of rumors about more things to come.

The next big thing to happen at Hollywood Studios® is the attachment of the new *Star Wars* Galactic Cruiser hotel experience. A completely interactive, immersive two-night adventure which functions as a luxury cruise ship. Guests can leave their themed cabins (featuring windows out into space) to participate in an assortment of interactive activities.

As long as the *Star Wars* galaxy continues to grow with incredibly popular new series and movies, the potential for expanding this part of the Studios is limitless.

Disney's Animal Kingdom®

Overview of Disney's Animal Kingdom®

Disney's Animal Kingdom® is becoming my favorite of all the Disney Parks. What used to be a "maybe" on many people's vacation plans has become a full-fledged, don't-miss park. Disney has added some out-of-this-world, new attractions (literally, thanks to the opening of Pandora:

The World of *Avatar*) and is offering a wide array of nighttime entertainment for the first time since its opening! Disney's Animal Kingdom® is now easily a full-day park, and quite possibly a two-day park.

Getting to Disney's Animal Kingdom®

All transportation to this park from all the Disney Resort hotels is by bus.

Our Tips for Visiting Disney's Animal Kingdom®

Disney's Animal Kingdom® is like no other theme park you have visited. The Imagineers wanted visitors to have the true experience of discovery while exploring this massive park. You won't find many big signs here pointing you toward attractions, and many of the trails leading to animal exhibits are virtually unmarked. This park rewards those who are bold enough to explore those unassuming walkways. Finding this park's many surprises can be half the fun.

With Pandora's current runaway success, if you can't get Genie+ for this section's standout attraction; Flight of Passage, try to get to the park when it opens and queue up right away. The Na'Vi River Journey is beautiful, but short. It serves up the nighttime Pandora experience for those who might not be able to stay in the park after dark. If you can, you'll want to explore Pandora during the day and then come back at night to see it all magically illuminated with its stunning bioluminescent plant life. If you are staying at a Disney Resort hotel, take advantage of Early Access to experience Pandora first thing in the morning.See the rest of the park during the daylight hours, but make sure you see Pandora both in daylight and after dark.

The Oasis and Discovery Island

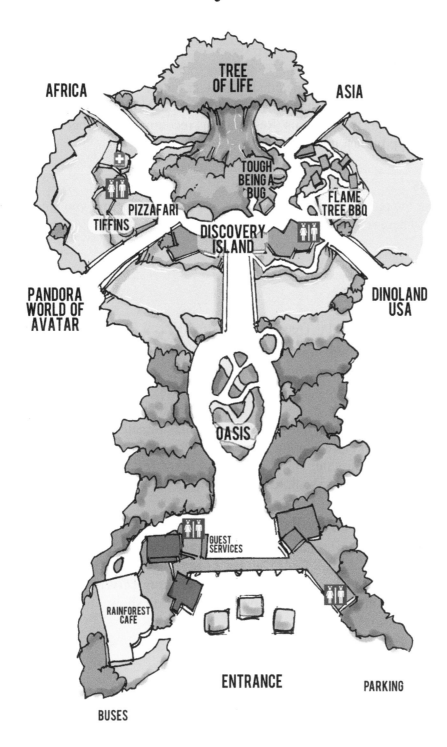

Intro to The Oasis and Discovery Island

Just inside the main entrance to Disney's Animal Kingdom®, the Oasis is a small collection of shops, amenities, and animal exhibits.

Oasis' Animal Exhibits
Here you can see the giant anteater, wild boar, muntjac, and other smaller creatures.

Oasis Dining
The Rainforest Café
Table-service. Dine amid audio-animatronic creatures under jungle foliage. The café is located at the main entrance and stays open later than the rest of the park, making it a nice spot to enjoy a meal after a long day observing real animals. Reservations recommended. Check the Walk Up Wait List in the Disney app for last minute seating.

Oasis Restrooms
This entrance plaza for the park has restrooms located just to the left before you enter the park turnstiles and security. There is also a set of restrooms just inside the admission area to the left near guest services.

Discovery Island
This island holds the park's spectacular Tree of Life landmark, as well as some fun attractions and cleverly concealed animal exhibits.

Do Not Miss!
It's Tough Being a Bug!
Located in the roots of the Tree of Life, this fun and funny 3D-animated Pixar presentation that shrinks the audience down to an insect's point of view. Fun for all, but those who don't appreciate surprises might not enjoy this show. This queue takes you right to the base of the amazing Tree of Life. See the amazing sculpted animals up close.

Discovery Island Animal Exhibits
Watch Galápagos tortoises, African-crested porcupines, kangaroos, lemurs, and cotton-top tamarins at the base of the Tree of Life. **Tip!** There is a nature path near the entrance to It's Tough Being a Bug! That will take you much closer to the amazing-carved, and sculpted trunk of the Tree of Life without queuing up for the It's Tough Being a Bug show.

Discovery Island Dining
Tiffins
Located next to the bridge into Pandora, Tiffins specializes in African-inspired dishes and offers one of the finer dining experiences in the Animal Kingdom. Serving lunch and dinner. Reservations recommended. Last minute possibilities within the Wait List in the app might get you into this upscale spot.
Nomad's Lounge
Outdoor seating on the riverside deck of Tiffins. Enjoy the restaurant's full menu or lighter fare from the lounge menu. A rare quiet hideaway from the bustle of the rest of the park.
Creature Comforts-Starbucks

Snacks. You can get your favorite caffeinated beverage here. There is also a large selection of baked goods! Mobile Order.

Flame Tree Barbecue
One of our favorite quick-service spots in the Animal Kingdom. Big portions of authentic, smoked, barbecue-rubbed ribs and chicken. Yum! Mobile Order.

Pizzafari
Quick-service. Obviously pizza is the featured item here, but they also serve sandwiches and salads. The dining area is adorned with beautiful colors and designs. Mobile Order.

Discovery Island Restrooms
Just past Pizzafari on the path to the left of the Tree of Life you will find restrooms along with the park's guest services office, Baby Care Center, and First Aid Station. If you take the walkway to the right of the Tree of Life, towards Dinoland USA, you will find a second set of restrooms across the way from Flame Tree BBQ.

Pandora—The World of *Avatar*

Intro to Pandora-The World of *Avatar*

When Disney announced their partnership with filmmaker James Cameron to make his cinematic creation *Avatar* into a section of a theme park, people weren't sure how to react. At the time, *Avatar* was already almost a decade old. It may be one of the most successful movies of all time, but could a war-torn, environmental, science-fiction story translate into a charming land within a Disney Park?

Well, after years of construction, the bridges to Pandora are open and the answer to that question is an enthusiastic, YES! Disney wisely made the park's Pandora set decades after the movie's war between the humans and the native Na'Vi inhabitants. Disney's post-war Pandora is calm, peaceful, and almost hypnotic. Every inch of the area is covered in lush, exotic plant life. It is nearly impossible to tell what is real and what is a creation of Disney's Imagineers. It is all strangely soothing, like you've wandered into a secret garden where everything is new and inviting.

You MUST experience Pandora during the day AND after dark!

Do Not Miss!
Flight of Passage
This may well be the best attraction in all of Walt Disney World® right now, and its queue is both massive and necessary. You'll climb high into the mountains until you reach a research base where humans are studying the planet's famous Ecrons – flying dragon creatures also known as Banshees. As the story goes, you must be transported into the body of an Avatar just as your Ecron is about to take flight. I will not play the role of a spoiler here – this is one of those attractions where you should just experience it fresh without knowing too much about it. I will say that the ride is like the best dream of flying you have ever had. It's very exciting, but somehow so smooth that it isn't nauseating the way other rides can sometimes be. Well worth the wait in line, even if that line is more than two hours long. It's definitely worth trying to get a Genie+ Lightning Lane access if you can, but even if you can't, you still need to experience this incredible adventure! Height requirement: 44 inches (112 cm).
Na' Vi River Journey
This is definitely a world-class attraction. It is a relatively short ride which makes us question if it is worth the long line to see it. This is the best place to see the mythical animals of Pandora. Many of them come to the riverbank as you drift along with the current. The ride ends with one of the most amazing audio-animatronic figures ever created. This gives you a nice preview of what the entire Pandora area is like after sundown. I wish this attraction was just a little bit longer.

Pandora Dining
Satu'li Canteen
This large sci-fi themed building is meant to be the old RDA mess hall, with unique counter-service options that are native to the alien planet. Choose your protein (meat) or go vegetarian; a variety of side dishes make for a delicious and healthy meal combination. This is quickly becoming my personal favorite counter-service in Animal Kingdom. Serving breakfast seasonally; lunch and dinner year-round. Mobile Order.
Pongu Pongu
This refreshment stand features alien-looking concoctions and sells both kid-friendly and adult beverages (have your ID handy). Collectable drink containers are available, but not required. Check for Mobile Ordering.

Pandora Restrooms

You can find restrooms on either side of this alien land. One set of restrooms are near the exit to the Flight of Passage attraction. The second set of restrooms can be found across from the Na'vi tribal drums and up the path from Na'vi River Journey.

Africa

CONSERVATION STATION

PANGANI
TRAIL

TRAIN TO
RAFIKI'S

KILIMANJARO
SAFARIS

HARAMBE
STAGE

HARAMBE
MARKET

FESTIVAL
OF THE
LION KING

TUSKER
HOUSE

TAMU
TAMU

ASIA

PANDORA

DISCOVERY ISLAND
TREE OF LIFE

Intro to Africa

Wandering across the bridge, you'll feel like you are being transported into the African village, Harambe. You'll find the park's premier animal attractions here, as well as some fantastic African culture and flavors.

Do Not Miss!

Kilimanjaro Safaris

Safari vehicles take visitors into an expansive environment teeming with real wildlife. Once the vehicle enters the African plains of the adventure, there's rarely anything standing between you and the animals. I have been told this single attraction is almost as big as the entire Magic Kingdom®. **Tip!** There is a special behind-the-scenes walking safari. Check availability and pricing with your hotel concierge or with the reservation agent when you book your trip. **Tip!** Try to be first on the vehicle. Views from the driver's side tend to be a bit better than views from the passenger side. **Tip!** A breezy morning, or even a passing rain shower, can often make the animals on the safari more active!

Festival of the *Lion King*

In 2014, this show moved to a brand-new theater in the Africa section of the park. It's a broadway-style musical with incredible singers, dancers, acrobats, and even aerialists, performing songs from one of Disney's most popular films. This has been rated the number one live show in all of Walt Disney World® for many years!

Africa's Animal Exhibits
Do Not Miss!

Pangani Forest Exploration Trail

A trail featuring underwater hippo viewing, an amazing encounter with a troupe of gorillas, and an astonishing collection of African fish and birds.

Africa Dining

Harambe Marketplace

This brand new section of the village mimics a real, central African marketplace, with a blend of authentic Africa and Disney magic. Mobile Order.

Tusker House Restaurant

Table-service. Buffet-style African and American cuisine and home to Donald Duck's Safari Breakfast. Reservations recommended. Check the Walk Up Wait List in the Genie app for rare openings.

Kusafiri Coffee Shop and Bakery

Snacks, fresh coffee, and baked goods right on the edge of Harambe. Mobile Order.

Harambe Fruit Market

Snacks. A healthy selection of fruit and refreshments. Mobile Order.

Tamu Tamu Refreshments

Quick-service and snacks. Good selection of sandwiches and salads. Mobile Order.

Africa Restrooms

Located across from the Harambe stage, you will find a set of restrooms. There is another set of restrooms in a stand alone building just down the path from the *Lion King* arena.

Festival of the Lion King — Animal Kingdom

Conservation Station

An old steam engine train takes guests into some of the behind-the-scenes areas of the Animal Kingdom®, including a petting zoo and a peek into the veterinary facilities that care for the park's animals. The rumor is this section of the park may soon be closing, making way for something even more captivating. **NOTE:** Since this area of the park allows guests into close contact with animals, there are restrictions on food and drink items.

Drawing Lessons

Repeated throughout the day, a real Disney artist will teach you the techniques they use to create some of your favorite Disney animal characters.

Habitat Habitat!
See cotton-top tamarins and environmental messages along the trail from the train station to the Conservation Station.
Conservation Station
Peek into the veterinary facilities that keep all of the Animal Kingdom® creatures healthy and happy. There are interactive presentations here throughout the day. One of the highlights of visiting this area is the affection section.
Affection Section
Get hands-on with exotic and domestic animals from all over the world. Kids love this area!

Conservation Station Restrooms
Inside the lobby area for Rafiki's Planet Watch there is a set of restrooms.

Asia

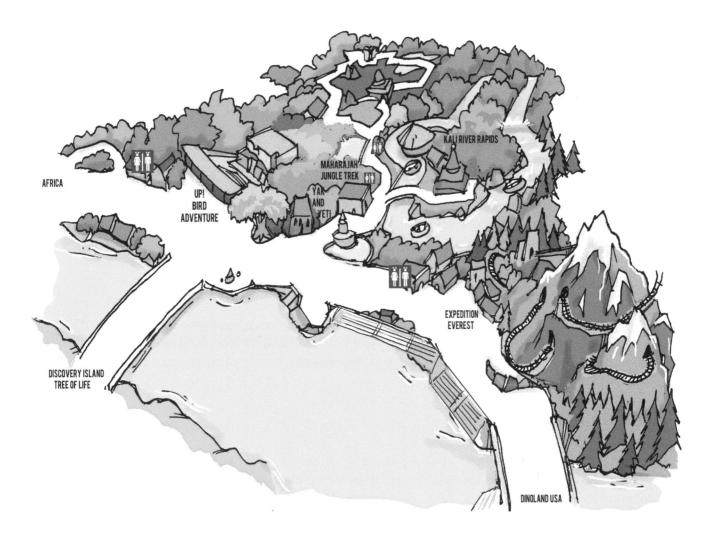

Intro to Asia

Passing into this side of the park really feels like you have walked into a Southeast Asian jungle village. This vast area hosts two of the park's biggest thrill attractions, as well as some excellent animal encounters.

Do Not Miss!

Expedition Everest

Everest is an incredible roller coaster experience which has the tallest peak of Disney's thrill ride mountains. Join an expedition to rescue a lost team of explorers who may have encountered the wrath of the legendary Yeti. A mountain train takes you high into the Himalayas. Then, on a heart-stopping race, escape the rampaging snow monster back down the mountain. Height requirement: 44 inches (113 cm).

Kali River Rapids

Some water rides warn you about getting a little wet. This one promises you will get soaked...and you will. A whitewater raft takes you down a big plunge with a huge boat-swamping splash, followed by more water effects downstream to complete the dousing. Height requirement: 38 inches (97 cm).

Tip! Use nearby lockers or waterproof plastic bags to keep your water-sensitive belongings dry.

Tip! On a chilly day, you might want to avoid this ride...but on a hot day you might want to ride it twice!

Asia's Animal Exhibits

Do Not Miss!

Maharajah Jungle Trek

Komodo dragons, fruit bats, and tigers, oh, my! Discover wildlife as you wander through ancient palace ruins. This year, the Jungle Trek welcomed newborn tiger cubs. This is a must-see, don't miss this secluded corner of the park!

Other Asia Attractions

Bird Show

This has gone through more than a few name changes since it opened so I am not giving it a proper name here. Bird shows are held regularly in this small auditorium up the road from Everest. Relax in a cool, shaded area as you watch live exotic birds perform natural behaviors with entertaining trainer/presenters!

Asia Dining

Yak and Yeti Restaurant

Table-service. This is my favorite sit-down restaurant in this park. It has good, mostly authentic Asian choices; exotic without taking you too far off the culinary map. Reservations recommended. Check the Disney app for last minute openings with Walk Up Waiting List.

Yak and Yeti Café Take Out Window

Quick-service. Want to sample some of the dishes Yak and Yeti offers but in takeout form? Queue up to this window and order up!

Asia Restrooms

Just up the path from the Bird Show amphitheater, across from Mr. Kamal's snack stand, you will find restrooms. Just across from the entrance to Kali River Rapids, you will find another set of restrooms. There's another set of restrooms across from what used to be the Rivers of Light Amphitheater near Anandapur Ice Cream truck. The *Finding Nemo* Musical Theater doesn't officially reside in Asia but it is close and there is a set or restrooms back by the theater's exits.

DinoLand U.S.A.

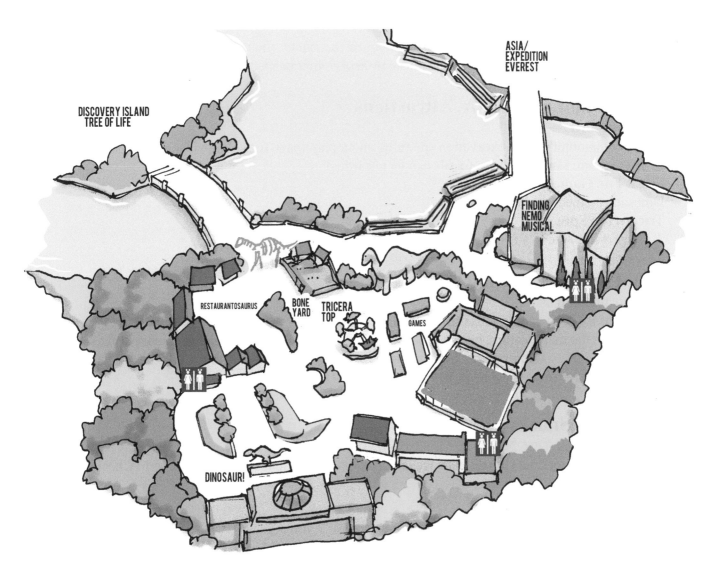

Intro to DinoLand U.S.A.

Everything in a Disney Park has a story. A whimsical carnival celebrates our long-lost friends—
the dinosaurs—in this unusual mix of midway fair and paleontology research. The premise here
is that after a research institute discovers a way to travel back in time to see real dinosaurs, the
enterprising owners of a nearby gas station create a roadside dinosaur-themed carnival to
capitalize on the situation.

Do Not Miss!
DINOSAUR!

Enjoy some prehistoric off-roading as you travel back in time to save a friendly dinosaur species
from certain extinction. Watch out for the much-less friendly ones you will meet along the way.

This bumpy ride through the dark jungles of the past is great fun, but may be scary for your smallest dino-lovers. Height requirement: 40 inches (102 cm).

Finding Nemo - **The Musical**

This very popular, broadway-style show is fun for everyone, with its blend of incredible puppetry and live performers, you will be humming the catchy songs for the rest of your day. The songwriting team that brought you the music of *Frozen* first penned the tunes for this attraction!

Other DinoLand U.S.A. Attractions

The Boneyard

A wooly mammoth fossil excavation site turns into a play-maze for young visitors, complete with a gigantic sandbox where fossils can be unearthed.

Fossil Fun Games

Dinosaur-themed carnival games.

TriceraTop Spin

A Dumbo-like ride in a friendly dinosaur shell.

DinoLand U.S.A. Dining

Restaurantosaurus

Quick-service. You get the sense that paleontologists really do hang out in this big cafeteria. Burgers are the main feature, but there's also chicken and salads. Make sure to check out the almost hidden Restaurantasaurus Lounge just adjacent to the restaurant. Added in 2021 to expand seating and offer some great adult beverages. Mobile Order.

DinoLand Snacks

Din-Bite Snacks

Ice cream, sundaes, and churros. The ice cream cookie sandwich is the stand out here! Check for Mobile Ordering.

DinoLand U.S.A. Restrooms

There are restrooms located on the dead-end side of Chester and Hester's Dinosaur Treasures gift shop. There is another set of restrooms located on the backside of Restaurantosaurus. There is a restroom located near the exit of the *Finding Nemo* Musical theater too.

What's Next for Disney's Animal Kingdom®?

Disney is trying to expand entertainment offerings here so that they can extend the guest experience later into the evening. The challenge for this park is they cannot do loud fireworks at night out of respect for the animals.

The addition of Pandora opens up an unearthly nighttime experience with its incredible bioluminescence illumination. There is more than just Pandora to experience at night – there is an evening version of Kilimanjaro Safaris featuring more nocturnal creatures which happens during late afternoon into evening. It's fun to visit the savannah during its prolonged sunset, created nightly by some impressive theatrical lighting, The Tree of Life comes alive with music and magical projected animations. Everest is certainly even more thrilling after the sun goes down.

In 2021, the Animal Kingdom will roll out Kite Tails in the water amphitheater that used to host the short-lived Rivers of Light show in Asia. Kite Tails will be a daytime offering featuring a multitude of flying colorful kits of all shapes and sizes, representing many of Disney's favorite animal characters.

Disney Parks are always in a state of flux, but we predict some pretty significant additions to Pandora once the sequels are released in theaters, rethinking of the Conservation Station area and maybe even a significant facelift to DinoLand U.S.A. Stay tuned!

Disney Springs®

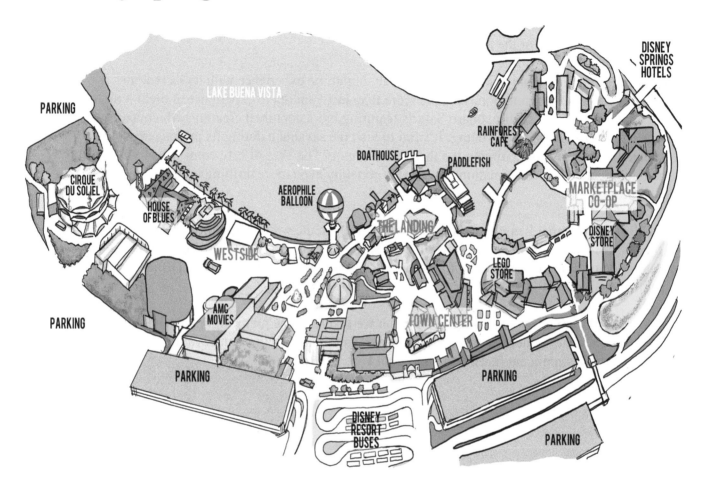

Overview of Disney Springs®

In 1975 it started out as the Lake Buena Vista Shopping Village, then the Disney Shopping Village, then the Walt Disney World Village, then The Walt Disney World Village Marketplace, and most recently; Downtown Disney. This identity crisis seemed to be caused by a lack of cohesive theming and a compelling reason to draw guests away from the parks. Finally in 2015, Disney Imagineers tied the whole complex together. Disney Springs® was born! The Spring's story is that this area was the site of a beautiful old fresh water spring around which a charming little Florida-style community grew. What used to be an afterthought, is now a full-blown vacation must-do destination.

Perhaps the best part of Disney Springs® is that entry and parking is completely free (at the time of this printing).

Our suggestions for Disney Springs®

The Springs are not set up like the parks. Disney Springs® has multiple entry points depending on whether or not you have driven to the Springs or took one of Disney's Resort Hotel buses. While Disney's buses do drop you off close to the center of the property, depending where you park might have you entering in completely different parts of the Springs. But unlike the parks, the flow of your visit is not important here. The fun of the Springs is exploring. It is the discovery of a new shop, a new aroma, a new taste. I think Disney Springs® is the perfect place to spend a travel day. Maybe your flight into Orlando doesn't arrive until mid day. Why waste a whole day's park admission on a partial day when you have this amazing place to visit with no admission cost at all?

Most people treat the Springs as the best place to relax after all the parks close at night because many of the restaurants and bars here stay open later. There are so many cool things to do here, you might want to schedule a whole day to enjoy all the amazing options.

Navigating the Springs

Disney Springs® is divided into districts. Unlike the parks, there is not necessarily a giant thing anchoring the center of the property to help you decipher where you are at any given time. A building might block your view of the massive Aerophile balloon ride. You might not be facing the giant volcano at Rainforest Cafe. You might be on the opposite side of the Springs and not spot the giant white circus tent shaped building that houses Cirque de Soulei. I highly recommend you have your smart phone remember where you parked. Or maybe take a reminder photo of the parking ramp level you left your vehicle in. Maybe make a mental note that the giant Coca Cola store is near where the resort buses load up at the end of your visit. I am going to try to include one or two easy to identify landmarks in each district so that you can find yourself on the map and maybe assist in finding the specific things you want to locate,

Lets start exploring…

Town Center

Town Center is one of the main shopping hubs of the Springs. Anchored by large Uniqlo and Under Armour stores, between which you'll find dozens and dozens of unique trendy clothing and gift shops. It's one of two access points to the Disney Resort bus transportation station

Here are the Town Center store listings at the time of printing…

Town Center Shopping

Uniqlo-Casual- Apparel and accessories
Under Armor-Sportswear
Anthropologie-Apparel and accessories
Ever After - Jewelry
Rustic Cuff - Apparel and accessories
Melissa Shoes- Footwear
Alex and Ani® - Jewelry
Francesca's® -Apparel and accessories
Zara - Apparel and accessories
L'Occitane en Provence - Health and Beauty
Lululemon® - Apparel and accessories
Pandora® - Jewelry
Edward Beiner - Eyeware

Na Hoku-Hawaii's Finest Jewelers
Levi's - Apparel and accessories
Volcom - Apparel and accessories
Orlando Harley-Davidson® - Motorcycle style
Ron Jon's Surf Shop® - Beachwear
Lovepop - 3D Greeting cards
Superdry - Apparel and accessories
Stance - Apparel and accessories
Shore - Apparel and accessories
Sephora - Jewelry
LaCoste - Apparel
Luxury of Time -Watches and accessories
Coach - Apparel and accessories
Mac Cosmetics- Health and beauty
Origins - Heath and beauty
Tommy Bahama - Casual wear
Johnston & Murphy - Apparel and accessories
Fit2Run - Running attire
American Threads - Apparel and accessories
UGG - Apparel and Accessories
Columbia Sportswear - Apparel and accessories
Sugarboo - Apparel and accessories
Everything But Water - Swimwear
Vera Bradley - Apparel and accessories
Sperry - Apparel and accessories
Lilly Pulitzer - Apparel and accessories
Free People - Apparel and accessories
Johnny Was - Apparel and accessories
Kate Spade - Apparel and accessories

Town Center Dining

D-Luxe Burger- Quick-service
T-Rex - Table-service
Sprinkles - Cupcakes
Frontera Cocina - Table-service
Blaze Pizza - Quick-service
The Polite Pig - Quick-service
Amorette's Patisserie - Bakery
BB Wolf's Sausage Company - Quick-service
Coca Cola Store and Lounge - Quick-service

Town Center Restrooms

There are restrooms located near both major entrances coming into the Springs from the main resort bus drop off. You will also find restrooms near the Polite Pig restaurant. There is another restroom on the southwest corner of the Uniqlo Store. Restrooms can also be found near the Blaze Pizza restaurant. Additional restrooms are available near the Coca Cola Store and Lounge.

The Marketplace Co-op
This section of the Springs is sandwiched between the giant volcano at Hard Rock Cafe and the Lego Store. Between them, you will find many other shops and dining including the world's largest Disney Store.

Marketplace Entertainment
Marketplace Carousel - A small children's ride
Marketplace Train - a kiddie train
Marketplace Stage - A good place to find on-going, live entertainment

Marketplace Shopping
Art Corner - Gallery and DYI projects
World of Disney - Apparel, toys, and accessories
Wonderground Gallery - Art gallery
The Lego Store - Toys
Tren-D - Apparel and accessories
Once Upon A Toy - Toys
Star Wars Trading Post - Apparel and collectables
Disney's Wonderful World of Memories - Personalize apparel
Bibbidi-Bobbidi Boutique - Health and Beauty
T-Rex Store - Apparel and toys
Goofy's Candy Company - Candy

Marketplace Dining
Rainforest Cafe -Table-service
Wolfgang Puck Express - Quick-service
Starbucks - Quick-service
Ghiradelli Soda Fountain - Quick-service

Marketplace Restrooms
There are restrooms on the south west end of the World of Disney store. More restrooms can be found near Tren-D. There are restrooms adjacent to Wolfgang Puck. And restrooms near the Marketplace bus loop on the furthest eastern corner of the property.

Disney Springs

The Landing

I do not know if this was intentional or not, but many of the Spring's best dining spots are collected on this island. To the north there is the expanse of Lake Buena Vista, while restaurants on the south side overlook the beautiful springs themselves for which the area is named. If you want good eats, the Landing is your best bet.

The Landing's Entertainment
The Boathouse Amphi-cars
There was a very brief moment in automotive history where some car companies actually made a very limited amount of cars that could double as a boat. These are real vintage cars that have

been restored. They've been brought back into service for tours of Village Lake and provide great views of the Springs from the water. This is a very unique, paid experience.

The Landing's Shopping
Happy Hound - Pet accessories
There Ganachery - Quick-service
Shop for Ireland - Gifts and housewares
Sanuk - Apparel and accessories

The Landing's Dining
The Boathouse - Table-service
Terralina Crafted Italian - Table-service
Paddlefish - Table-service
Erin McKenna's Bakery - Baked goods
Vivili Il Gelato - Quick-service
Jock Lindsey's Hanger Bar - Table-service
Morimoto Asia - Table-service
Morimoto Asia Street Food- Quick-service
Chef Art Smith's Homecomin - Table-service
STK Orlando - Table-service
Pizza Ponte - Quick-service
Paradiso 37 - Table-service

The Landing Restrooms
There are restrooms adjacent to Morimoto Asia. Additionally, there are restrooms located across the walk between Paradiso and the Edison.

Westside
The Westside of the Springs sheds some of the 'old Florida' in exchange for more modern entertainment offerings.

Westside Entertainment- Do Not Miss!
Cirque Du Soliel® Drawn to Life
Located in the giant, white, circus tent-shaped auditorium at the farthest west point of the Springs, this is a bonafide *Actual Factual Magic* Must-Do! Get your tickets in advance of your trip. This permanent Cirque Du Soliel® venue offers a one-of-a-kind show created through a partnership with Disney called Drawn To Life. This new show was all set to premiere just before the pandemic hit so performers have been honing their crafts for more than a year to give you a jaw-dropping performance now. Drawn to Life combines Disney's famous artistry with Cirque's incredible acrobatics. If this show is a fraction as good as its predecessor La Nouba, it will be worth a special visit to Disney Springs® to witness in person. Tickets available through DisneySprings.com

Other Westside Entertainment

Aerophile Balloon Ride

Perhaps the most recognized feature of the entire Springs, this giant observation balloon can take a sizable crowd of people very high into the sky for breathtaking views of the surrounding area. This experience is very weather dependent and may not be available if threatening weather or high winds are in the area. This is a paid experience and might not be something people with a fear of heights should attempt.

House of Blues Concert Stage

This small concert venue hosts some very big names in music. Keep an eye on their website of DisneySprings.com to see who might be playing during your next visit.

Splitsville Bowling

Splitsville is listed here as both entertainment and dining because this modern bowling venue offers some surprisingly good eats before, during and after trying to get that perfect strike. This is a paid experience.

AMC Movies at Disney Springs®

This upscale movie multiplex offers a wonderful dine-in movie experience. Order your meal and have it brought to your spot in the theater just as your feature starts. Very cool. Paid experience. Tickets available through the AMC website or at the box office.

Westside Shopping

House of Blues Store - Accessories and collectables

M&M World - Candy and collectables

Pele Soccer - Apparel and accessories

Super Hero Headquarters - Comic themed apparel

Star Wars Galactic Outpost - Apparel and collectables

Sosa Family Cigar Co. - Cigars and accessories

Westside Dining

Starbucks - Quick-services

Sunshine Churros - Quick-service

Everglazed Donuts - Quick-service

Jaleo By Jose' Andres - Table-service

House of Blues - Table-service

Splitsville - Bowling and dining

City Works Eatery and Pour House - Table-service

AMC Dinner and a Movie - Dining served to your theater seats

Westside Restrooms

Restrooms are available between Starbucks and the westside food trucks.

Disney Dining Plans and Table in Wonderland

If you think all you will find to eat at Walt Disney World® are chicken strips and burgers, you're in for a real treat. Literally. You can certainly find traditional amusement park food usually done so much better than any other place would prepare such things, but you will also discover a whole world of culinary delights. Everything from familiar comfort foods, exotic fare from all corners of the globe, and some of the country's finest dining venues. I'm not kidding. I am talking about world-renowned chefs and world culinary award-winning restaurants!

If you are among the many people who come to Walt Disney World® as much for the food as for the attractions, this chapter is for you! Our food author, Kat, has compiled listings of our favorite Disney restaurants. But first let's go over one of the unique ways to experience the wide-ranging food options of Walt Disney World®: Disney's Dining Plans.

The Disney Dining Plans

The Disney Dining Plans are options you can add to your vacation if you stay at a Walt Disney World® Resort hotel. These plans can give your vacation an all-inclusive feel. The plans are a point system that can be used any way you choose, but they are intended to provide you two or three meals, snacks and drinks for every member of your party for every day of your stay. Here are the dining plan choices…

Note: At the time of this writing the Disney Dining Plans have not yet resumed after being halted during more restrictive pandemic times. However, we do expect this service to return soon.

Quick-Service Dining

This plan allows everyone in your party to have two counter-service meals and one snack every day of your stay. It includes a refillable mug (one for every member of your family or group) to be used at the hotel. The cost for this plan is $60 per person, per night, $25 per night for children 3 to 9 years old.

Regular Dining

This plan allows everyone in your party to have one table-service meal, one counter-service meal, and a snack every day of your stay. This plan includes a refillable mug (one for every member of your family or group). The plan costs about $80 per adult, per night, $30 per night for children three to nine years old.

Deluxe Dining

This plan allows everyone in your party enough points to have three meals a day, with any combination of table or counter-service. It includes a refillable mug for each member of your family or group to be used at the hotel. Adding this plan costs about $125 per adult, per night, $50 per night for children three to nine years old.

Dining Plan prices may vary but they were accurate at time of press.

Things to note about the Disney Dining Plans

- This is very important. PURCHASING THE DINING PLAN DOES NOT GUARANTEE YOU ACCESS TO ANY RESTAURANT! You still must make advanced dining reservations if you want to experience the very best of Walt Disney World's restaurants. Make your reservations for special dining experiences as early as 180 days before the start of your vacation (60 days during pandemic restrictions) by calling 1-407-WDW-DINE or by booking through the MyDisneyExperience website or Disney Genie.

- Some plans will now allow you to add alcoholic drinks too. Check the details of each plan and add this feature if you choose to partake in adult beverages with your meals.

- Think of the Dining Plans more as a convenience than a money saver. When you do the math, the dining plans cost close to what it costs to eat at the same restaurants without one of the plans. Sure, If you ordered the most expensive items on every menu every time, you would save some money using the plans. But this might not be the best way to enjoy meals on your vacation. The real bargains come when Disney occasionally offers the Dining Plans for free as a perk for visiting off-season times of the year. These free dining periods are typically offered in early autumn and in mid-to-late-winter. Keep your eyes open for these great offers.

- A "meal" typically includes an entree, a side, dessert, and a drink (separate from the refillable mug).

- A "snack" is typically a treat, piece of fruit, or drink costing up to roughly $7.

- Gratuities are not included with the table-service meals.

- The refillable mug is a nice perk at your hotel, but you should note that the refill stations are typically located in the hotel dining areas, which may not be close to your room. Also note that the mugs are metered when refilling by an embedded computerized chip to prevent people without these mugs from abusing the refill privileges.

- The refillable mugs do not apply to locations outside of your hotel area. Do not bother bringing these mugs with you to the theme parks or water parks.

Tables in Wonderland Membership

For those who live nearby or who really plan to make their Disney vacation all about the dining, you might want to consider purchasing a membership with Tables in Wonderland (TiW). This discount program is only available to Florida residents, Disney Vacation Club members and Disney Annual Pass holders. In other words, very frequent Disney diners. The membership card covers the cardholder and up to nine guests on the same check. The TiW card gets you 20% off dining and drinks. The membership gives you free valet parking at the Disney hotels and parking at the theme parks, with the intent of dining. The TiW card can be used in conjunction with the Disney Dining Plan for items not covered by the plan, like alcohol.

Walt Disney World® has created some of the best dining experiences anywhere, but not all the best restaurants are easy to find—in fact, some seem downright hidden. Our culinary expert, Kat Garbis, put together a list of her top choices from all over the property, to help you make great decisions with your advanced dining reservations and steer you in the right direction when you just need something to grab and go.

Take it away, Kat...

The Best of Disney Dining

By,

Kat Garbis

In any vacation, food is such a key element to a great experience. At Disney, there are so many amazing options available to you regardless of budget and time. The best part? The ability to have so many different cuisines, dietary needs, or experiences at your fingertips.

Like most people, I love food. In this version, I leaned in on my experiences and expanded on the food section in this book. As I thought about what to change, what to keep, I said to myself "there are so many different reasons why someone would dine at Disney." Depending on where you're from, your background, your budget — everyone's experience will be different. So I took time to curate what could be valued — whether you're from a small town in America, New York City, or perhaps you're not even from the USA and are looking for some guidance all around.

I spent a lot of time crafting not only my personal favorites on the list — but even the small, foodie bites that could be appreciated as you stroll through the parks. There are so many amazing food options at Disney. From fresh corn on the cob with African spices in Animal Kingdom, potstickers while watching acrobats, warm empanadas while listening to a mariachi band.... The food experiences are endless and you get the opportunity of sampling cuisines and cultures from around the world — all the way to seven-course fine dining at the Grand Floridian while likely to see a couple get engaged.

In many ways, I did a tear-down, rebuild of the food section from our last edition. This time around, the book is formatted by park or destination, popular tourist spots, personal favorites, and must-do recommendations.

I then further segmented by table-dining and casual quick-service spots for a few reasons: First, sit-down dining and grab-and-go are different experiences. One offers service, requires additional time, and likely (but not always) has more high-end food thus costing more. However, just because
you aren't sitting down to dine doesn't mean you can't find something awesome to enjoy either. That's where I come in — helping you balance budget, time, dietary needs, and favorites. If we're talking about it, it's a favorite of ours. If we labeled it as "do not miss" it means we strongly recommend you check it out.

Note: The only area of the book we did not segment like this was Epcot because World Showcase was best to be laid out by country vs. dining type.

While, yes it is true, there's a lot of info you can find on social media. In fact, I encourage you to still look on social media and check things out. Yet with social media, not everything is as personalized, easily found. Joe and I? We're your Disney experts that have taken the time to curate these lists. No matter where you dine, you know what to expect. Think of me as your foodie fairy godmother guiding you on a tasty journey.

I firmly believe that a Disney vacation is about making memories.

So many memories can be made over a meal. We want to help you with those moments. Whether that memory is of your newborn infant meeting Mickey for the first time at a dinner table, your child meeting their favorite Disney Princess, or seeing their favorite *Star Wars* character represented on a cupcake. Perhaps you found a great wine spot and enjoyed the company of those around you, creating the fondest of memories.

Food makes people happy and can create some of the best moments. Disney not only is known for its amazing food offerings, but experiences. Put it all together? You have some good times ahead.

And…bad food or not so great experiences, well, that can also cause some memories too. Not quite the ones we're after. Note: If we skip a restaurant, we felt there were other like-options that we would better recommend. We also may agree to disagree with the status quo, and that's OK too. Or there are select items mentioned that we felt deserved a shout-out. I try to keep an open mind here at *Actual Factual Magic* — just like the rest of our team.

We've done our best to stay current with the menu items, but please know they can change at any time. Several of the items we have recommended have been long-standing menu items so it's unlikely they would get removed entirely, but it could happen as menus get updated, altered, or changed. Even if there are changes, we trust our recommendations and would still encourage you to try places out even if menu items are not quite the same during your vacation.

That being said, I have PLENTY of amazing options to choose from regardless of budget, diet, food restrictions, stay duration, and I can't wait to guide you through them.

What to know:

With the 2020 pandemic continuing onward into 2021 (ugh, I know, I don't love it either but it's reality), Disney has had the highest regard for cleanliness and safety. That also means you have to do your part as a Disney guest. Please note, the pandemic is continuously in evolution as we figure out normalcy in our daily lives and enjoying our vacations at Disney.

Before we jump right into the foodie favorites, a few things to keep in mind as you visit Disney Parks and Disney Springs for the foreseeable future:

- A temperature check may be required upon entry to a Disney Resort, Disney Park, Disney Springs, or restaurant. If your party's temperature is above 100 degrees Fahrenheit, you will not be admitted to the restaurant (or park) as a precaution to keep staff and other guests safe.

- Depending on the phase or current guidance, masks may be required by guests and staff unless you are actively dining or eating. If we're in a phase where a mask is required, it's required for any persons admitted over the age of two. While it's important to enjoy your dining experience, we're still in the midst of a pandemic era. You're on vacation and want to enjoy each experience, but keep in mind etiquette and safety: If we're at a heightened risk time, keep your mask on when you're not dining, or to keep it handy to put back on if a staff member approaches your table to take orders, provide beverages, food, or to clean. If all is good and guidance says otherwise, you're welcomed not to. Or, if you're thinking "who knows, better be safe just in case," the mask guidance above is respectable regardless of phase.

- Give yourself at least an hour before your reservations if you're not already in the park, resort, or Disney Springs. It used to be a recommended "arrive 20 minutes early" but with safety measures in place, limited staff, adjustments, social distancing, capacity limits, it can be hard to predict if you will need 15 min or a full hour to make it to your reservation. To make sure you don't lose your reservation, give yourself an hour to get to your restaurant. Worst case, you get there early, take a little walk, or shop around close by. Trust me, you don't want the stress or disappointment of missing your time slot, so get there early. It's challenging to reschedule nowadays, and there's no guarantee they'll be able to seat you due to the current climate. I am only human, the Cast Members are human too, and I *have* been turned away by not making my reservation on time. Disney never wants to do that, and they work to provide options, but it was ultimately up to me to get there on time. Will you starve? No. But you may miss out on a reservation or unique experience. If you are running behind, it's best to call ahead, to see if they can try to hold it but there are still no guarantees — especially with high-demand restaurants.
- Keep in mind if you're an international traveler, the drinking age in the USA is 21+...sorry....
- Disney is hyper-conscious of cleanliness and food allergies and dietary restrictions. If you have a food allergy, communicate to your server and make a note of it in your reservation.
- For those with plant-based diets, Disney has put a lot of focus on several dietary needs, but is expanding vegetarian and vegan guests.

Pro tip: Dine within a park or the location you'll be spending the day at. If you wish to, let's say, leave a park and go to Disney Springs, you may even want to give yourself a little more than an hour to get to transportation and then to your next destination as you'll need to go through entry safety regulations again.

Note: Some experiences may not be available during your visit due to the ever-changing health climate. Please be sure to double-check the Disney Parks app to verify if a restaurant or dining option is available during your visit.

Ok! Since we have all that out of the way, let's chat about dining: Lucky for you, Disney has plenty of incredible options.

Dining at Disney Springs®

Disney Springs® (formerly known as Downtown Disney) is an outdoor shopping, dining, and entertainment center.

Disney Springs® is a goldmine for food. You have options from food trucks to exquisite fine dining experiences. Disney Springs® is flexible in the sense you can come for one grand meal, stack up on some treats, or create your own seven-course meal walking around and sampling multiple quick-service options. If you're like me, you want the best of both worlds: I usually like to start at food trucks, work my way around the fancy restaurants that usually have a no-frills to-go menu, and then work my way to one of the glorious dessert options.

If you find yourself here, you're likely a foodie, want to go shopping, want a break from the parks, or looking for different scenery in the Disney area. Depending on what you're in the mood for, there's everything from small snacks, culinary cooking experiences, casual, or fine dining.

In this section, we've listed out places we'd recommend or are popular for various reasons. We'll start with favorites and have them divided by table-service and takeaway options.
What's fantastic about Disney Springs®, many of the restaurants have both table-service as well as grab-and-go options.

What does this mean for you? Well, if you want to try food from well-known chefs, like Rick Bayless or Wolfgang Puck, you can easily sample from their no-frills menus (which in my opinion, still have frills, but won't burn a hole in the wallet), or you can have an upscale date at their table-service options. Having the ability to do luxe dining or takeaway from world-class chefs is one of the many reasons why I love to guide people to Disney Springs®. Let's start with the table-service and work our way to other dining options.
Note: Most places in Disney Springs® participate in the Disney Dining Plan. So this could be a good way to leverage the plan while enjoying some dining experiences. However at the time of publish, the Disney Dining Plan has been paused.

Table-Service & Bars Favorites at Disney Springs®:

As mentioned, many of the restaurants here offer both sit-down and takeaway. But, not all — and that's ok!

My goal is to inform you of your options, share some of our favorites, and help determine what could be a good experience for you. Just know if it's in this book, it has a reason to be here and you can't really go wrong. You have basically a restaurant-mall of world-class chefs.

So let's start with some of our favorites in no particular order....

The Boathouse
I like this place for several reasons here at Disney Springs:

First, the ambiance is casual and fun. You get a seaside feel with the decor of anchors and fish along the walls. Being located along the water helps you feel like you're dining along the seashore as you smell the fresh water. To building on the name "boathouse," they have actual rides you can take on boats that are like a car, driven right on the water. Like your own personal little water-taxi joyride. There's a fee for them ($125 for 3-4 people), but it's worth it. It's fun if you are super early for your reservation, or want to go after a meal. Just don't get seasick. You also don't need to be dining there to go on one of these, if you're just passing through and want to partake in the water ride, you can.

There's a bar indoors while you wait, but, if you decide to go to the back of the restaurant and outside past the patio, they have an outdoor bar on the docks. You can certainly eat there too, but, I found myself enjoying a nice drink on the water. Gives you a break from the activity inside. I usually recommend hitting the bar in the back outside for a post-dinner drink. You don't want to overstay your welcome and hold up a table, so this is a nice option if you're enjoying your time here and not quite ready to go.

If you like seafood, this place is your jam. It's a more casual option than Paddlefish (another great seafood option, we'll get to it later) and delivers a great experience for the whole family. The portions are quite large — offering you a very satisfying meal with possible leftovers, or making meals easily shareable to sample more of the menu. Favorites of mine are some fresh oysters, the lobster bisque, coconut shrimp, peel and eat shrimp, steamed clams with garlic wine, grilled mahi-mahi tacos, crab cake, lobster roll, truffle fries, shrimp andouille mac and cheese, stuffed lobster tail. I've been here a few times and have been fortunate to try much of the menu and haven't been disappointed. From their steaks to their award-winning burger, you'll find something to enjoy.

If you want steak, my recommendation is to skip over to STK Orlando if you can. Know that the steak at Boathouse is a great option, but, they're not catching many steaks in the sea, if you're catching my drift. Just know if you're the only one in your party that wants steak and everyone else is all about seafood, you'll still be quite happy here. If you're feeling fish, or I can convince you to get fish, this is the spot. For the kids, they have the usual staples of burgers, macaroni and cheese, etc. What I will say, most kiddos like this place but tend to change up the usual kiddy diet of chicken nuggets and get the popcorn shrimp.

Be sure to save room for their key lime pie in a mason jar. For their cocktails, I enjoyed their Lake Squall which which was a tropical elixir of rum and passion fruit.

Morimoto Asia: *Actual Factual Magic* Do Not Miss! *Kat's Favorite!*
Nestled in the lovely Disney Springs®, Morimoto welcomes you to dine in one of the finest restaurants in Disney. When you walk in, it's easy to be enchanted by the light fixtures with yards of crystal streaming from the ceiling. If you walk up the lantern-lit staircase, you'll see the stairs continues on and transforms into the bar and seating — for real. Whoever was the architect is a genius and had quite the imagination. Alongside the bar on the second floor are mason jars filled with lights that are strung along with the ceiling as you enjoy a cocktail. They have your usual suspect cocktails, as any bar would, but you should aim to have something from their list. I had a

seasonal drink that was very refreshing with cucumber in it. If I were to compare, it was like a mojito with fresh mint and sneaky sake. I digress, the sake snuck up on me after ….Okay oversharing time is over. Anyways! My colleague had an old-fashioned with smoke. It was a pretty cool experience as they brought out a smoker and smoked the whiskey in front of us. I like to think I walked up that staircase and ended up in cocktail heaven.

We enjoyed the upstairs, got a tour, and saw some private dining rooms as well. In case we ever came back with more of our work colleagues or perhaps we just wanted a private dining space, the second floor has a few spaces for a more intimate setting.

We sat on the first floor and got a view of the ducks hanging dry for peking duck. Naturally, we ordered some. The duck was roasted beautifully. It was very moist (something that is challenging when cooking duck, it can be very easy to dry out) and had the gorgeous burnt orange coloring. It came with two sauces: a plum-hoisin-based and an apricot sauces. I loved both but especially enjoyed the apricot sauce. I found the sweet, apricot jam really complemented the poultry well.

Peking Duck — Morimoto Asia — Disney Springs

We sampled quite a bit here: We started off with the saffron-sticky wings. They did not disappoint. They had a light, crispy fry to them and the perfect amount of heat in the sauce. We also opted for some edamame because, vegetables? They were bright green, perfectly steamed and salted, and were a good balance to the sticky wings.

From there, we had the peking duck and the shrimp lo mein for our entrees. I thoroughly enjoyed the shrimp lo mein for a few reasons: One the noodles were perfectly cooked (they weren't soggy or too hard). Oftentimes, lo mein noodles can be swimming in sauce and then the dish can quickly become unappetizing. They really have a great balance of flavors to offer — clean, sweet, or some heat you have options. I also loved the larger pieces of green onion added to the stir fry. It not only was a welcoming pop of color to the plate but you get to enjoy the vegetable itself vs. it being a sliver or two added as a garnish.

We left here painfully full — the best kind of pain to be in. Tho expensive, we felt we got our money's worth for the meal based on portions, quality, ambiance, and service. The staff was incredibly friendly and also helpful when it came to recommendations.

T-Rex

Okay before you start judging me and sayin "Kat why are you recommending this" remember I said "we have recommendations for everyone." This one gets an *Actual Factual Magic* mention because it pleases the kids and gives them a good experience. Like, if you have sat there with your tiny human and bargaining with them saying "please eat something," this is a good spot to get them to eat something without much pleading. The food here is fine and predictable: sit-down experience with burgers, pizza, chicken tenders, etc.

I like to recommend this place as a lunch option for when you're traveling with small kids. They enjoy the dinosaurs and all the chicken nuggets their little hearts can handle, and then perhaps mom and dad have a date night or a place of their own choosing. Honestly, this place is nearly impossible to skip on a Disney trip because if your child likes dinosaurs, guess what, you're dining here. The good news? They do have a bar for the adults while kiddos can dig up dinosaur fossils. Just be sure to bring some hand sanitizer since the fossil area can be a bit of a petri dish.

Note: If you go to Animal Kingdom, they also have a dinosaur-themed restaurant. They are not the same. So you may need to plan for two dino-themed meals during your trip with kids.

Paddlefish

If you're looking for a seafood restaurant that is a bit more upscale and more sophisticated atmosphere, Paddlefish could be your seafood option for the night. The restaurant is staged like a ship with bright wall lights, blue paint, white leather chairs and wooden tables. I'd say in some ways, it rivals with Boathouse. The main difference to me is that Boathouse is more casual and family-oriented than Paddlefish.

Paddlefish is open for both lunch and dinner. Think of them as upscale seafood with southern flairs. Some of our favorites are the warm crab cake, breaded calamari, and if you're feeling curious, give the lobster corndog a try. It really is a lobster dipped in corndog batter and fried.

I'm a huge fan of their chilled & raw seafood bar. Honestly, I have done this place more times for an appetizer or two, like a happy hour. Coming here for a happy hour to taste a few apps and get some bubbly is always a good plan and makes for a nice date night or grown-up gathering. Anything on their raw menu is great. I love their ahi poke and crab ceviche.

If you stay for dinner, you won't be disappointed. Their king crab legs and whole lobster are impressive and will grab anyone's attention if they see it passing by. If you're feeling something else, additional favorites are their shrimp pasta, salmon with the miso vinaigrette, and the mahi-mahi. Aside from the pasta, the salmon and mahi-mahi are light yet filling options. Great choices for health conscious guests.

A bright seaside option for those who want a fancy fish night.

STK Orlando

Disney Springs® has so many fine dining options. However, if you are looking for the steakhouse feel, to be wined and dined, this. is. the. place.

The atmosphere is modern, with bubble light fixtures hanging from the ceiling. Most tables are rounded in some way so everyone at the table can see everyone. It's a dimmed and sophisticated setting. I have one of these locations by me in Chicago. This is a "dress up nice and look amazing" option. I recommend sprucing up if you're coming from the parks. If you live in a big city, the menu here is virtually similar. If you're unfamiliar and perhaps don't have local access to one of these, they're a real treat and I recommend this to any steak lover out there.

If I come here, I usually can be found with the seafood platter at my table. I like how their menu is parsed from small, medium, and large for steaks. Their pricing is comparable to most steak houses. If you have enough hungry people willing to share, get the tomahawk steak. It's 34 oz and can easily feed 3-4 people with sides and appetizers. It's so impressive and beautiful when it comes out charred and au jus. Or, if you want to go your own way, any steak you choose will be lovely and skillfully prepared. For entrees outside of steak, the miso sea bass and the lobster linguini are other personal favorites. Oddly enough, tho it's vegetarian, I really enjoy the mushroom truffle tagliatelle. It's perfect as an entree, or, grab it as a shareable as you cut through some steak and share some carbohydrates with your friends.

Along with the amazing menu and food, this place is all about service. The staff is well-trained and experienced in fine dining. To me, that's part of what the STK portfolio strives to offer and makes this place great for special occasions or business.

Tho expensive, if you want to try this place but not break the bank, be sure to stop in during their happy hour for half-off cocktails and some menu items that are between $5-$8 on average.

Raglan Road

If you haven't been to a pub in the UK, this place looks like they transplanted a pub from Ireland over to Disney Springs®. This place is just a good time all around, the food is wonderful and you can catch live music and Irish dancing while you eat. Epcot® doesn't have "Ireland" in the World Showcase, but Disney Springs® sure does — right here at Raglan Road. Basically, it's loud here so if you're looking for a good time and to party, Raglan Road is where it is at.

If you like beer, you have come to the right place. While they do have mixed drinks here, I'd say their beer menu will satisfy many. And of course, let's talk food. I would say their fish and chips are competitive with what you'd find at Rose & Crown at Epcot's World Showcase. But their menu overall - I think wins. From their wings to their warm shepherd's pie, they knock it out of the park.

One of my favorite places to get a burger on Disney property is at Raglan Road. In my opinion, they serve burgers how they should be served: a big juicy beef patty with a bunch of fixings piled a mile high. If it's a challenge to eat it, they're doing it right. Do not skip dessert here either. Their lemon curd tart, or 'fluffy lemon clouds' is just wonderful. They don't have a large dessert menu here, it's the lemon tart, a brownie, and their bread and butter pudding — all winners in my book. This is a place where time flies because you're having fun.

I came here once in a sour mood, I did not leave in a sour mood. It's just a great place with wonderful staff. Honestly, the staff here is a ton of fun and has cared well for my party each time I have visited. An absolute favorite.

I recommend to end your night here. Have a meal, get dessert, throwback a few beers, watch the live entertainment, and close down Disney Springs and catch an Uber or bus home. Just, don't catch your flight the next morning or run a marathon - it's going to be a bad time. Trust me.

Jaleo by Jose Andrés:

This is a favorite for several reasons: First, I like Jose Andrés as a person. I haven't had the pleasure of meeting him, but, you have a world-class chef with two-Michelin stars, he's an author, self-made chef, charitable by staying involved in humanitarian efforts, and, oh yeah, great food.

There aren't a lot of Spanish dining options in the Disney area, in fact, this may be the only true Spanish cuisine option. This is a tapas-style restaurant so plates are small; designed for a tasting, small bite, or to share.

For those familiar with Spanish cuisine, you're in for a real treat as you'll spot some common tapas favorites, with the Jose Andrés twists. Like the fried potatoes, gazpacho, tomato bread, paella, cheeses and meats. I also might be an expert at crushing the piquillo peppers stuffed with goat cheese. Just saying, if there's an Olympic sport for eating those, bright red peppers with warm cheese, I'm your gal.

If you've been to Spain, especially Barcelona, you'll be able to identify a lot of familiar plates and flavors. For those of you who haven't, or looking for some guidance on what to try, I'd recommend to start with something fresh, like the apple & fennel salad with Manchego cheese for a clean starter.

The fried potatoes with spicy tomato sauce are great. I'm hesitant to call them "french fries" (because they aren't) but think crispy potatoes with a tomato sauce usually spiced with a smoked paprika that makes your nose curious.

This was my favorite menu item Spain, and my favorite here, but the garlic shrimp tapas are a must-do. Think a little piece of crostini with grilled shrimp that has a touch of the charcoal and garlic. It sounds simple, but it's a winner.

I'm a fan of cheese, meat, and wine so be sure to splurge a little on some of the meats and cheeses offerings.

If you can, be sure to get the paella. It's basically rice, seasoned with broth, garlic, herbs, saffron, and usually topped with shellfish. It's a great meal to share.

PS: They have croquettes here, but it's on the kids menu. Be like me and order a bunch for the adults.

Like most restaurants in Disney Springs®, they have a to-go option as well, Pepe's by José Andrés, a sandwich shop. I personally recommend the sit-down dining experience but if you are pressed for time, check out Pepe's.

Terralina Crafted Italian
There's a couple of Italian spots in Disney Springs®, but this one is the one I recommend. I think I gravitate to this one because it checks all the boxes: Great food, great staff, great ambiance, food value, quality – when you add it all up it sets you up for a good time.

I'd say Disney as a whole has really good Italian options, however, this one wins for Disney Springs recommendations. I think this place is great for those who want "familiar Italian fare but nice" and has a straightforward menu. This place has a lot of Tuscany vibes to it.

I love their antipasti here. Some of the favorites from our team are the antipasti tower: It's impressive and contains lots of yum. And by yum, that is inclusive of various salamis, cheese, olives, peppers and breads. I think it's perfect for a little happy hour with some wine, or makes a satisfying starter for those of you coming in borderline hangry.

Their calamari fritti, mussels, shrimp scampi, eggplant fries, and bruschetta are all favorites in addition to the antipasti tower. As you can see, the *Actual Factual Magic* team enjoys happy hour here.

Moving right along, their wood fire pizza is also quite nice. I like getting this as a starter to share as well. Their spicy capicola (think spicy pepperoni) is a lovely option if you want to venture off from the margherita.

They do the classics here quite well. I'd recommend either the eggplant or chicken parmesans hands-down. While we're on the topic of chicken parmesan: If you come here for lunch, get the chicken parmesan sandwich, however, be prepared to have a food baby and the need to nap shortly thereafter. Back to dinner: I'm also a sucker for their seafood fettuccini. Be sure to check out their wine specials to pair with your meal.

Wine Bar George: *Actual Factual Magic* Do Not Miss!

See, this place is a tricky — in a good way. I love to come here for happy hour. But whenever I come for happy hour, guess what happens? It's not just a lite bite and a little wine. It turns into a lot of wine and a six-course tasting menu meal on accident. It's one of those "oops, oh well, here's my credit card. Sorry credit card."

They have "bites and boards" from 2:00-3:00 PM Sundays and Saturdays - like a mini weekend, happy hour menu. Or you can just kind of make your own any night of the week, to be honest.

For the foodie in your party, this place is a great spot. I honestly love everything on here. When I went, we felt we ordered "basically the whole menu" which is easy to do, as much of it is easy to share.
The menu is Greek and Italian with modern French vibes. Honestly, just get everything:

Hummus, olives, burrata, saganaki (cheese that is lit on fire - I kid you not), shishito peppers, a giant platter of charcuterie boards to start. Then, get the skirt steak and the sea bass to share (because why not) and wash it down with wine. Does it sound expensive? Yep. But will you have fun? You sure will. Obviously, I recommend this for more of an "adults night out, here you're the oldest babysit your siblings at the hotel and watch Disney movies" kind of night (or hire a Disney babysitter). But legit, this is a great spot to just lose track of time, enjoy the company, ambiance, good food, and drink. I usually trust my server and the team here with the wine recommendations. They have a master sommelier on staff, so you should absolutely trust them for the wine recommendations when you visit.

Enjoy!

Wolfgang Puck

If you want to try a Wolfgang Puck restaurant, this is a really good opportunity to do so. While the Wolfgang Puck brand is everywhere these days (canned food, frozen, airports), you may feel like "maybe something else" and that's ok. But I like to try to find something for everyone because I also understand, not everyone has access to try the wonderful, world-renown Wolfgang Puck "wherever." So if you have not tried Wolfgang Puck and want to try his food, I think this is an excellent opportunity to do so.

It's a classic, favorite place to dine. You can't go wrong here. From their avocado toast to their chicken and waffles with blueberry compote for brunch, all the way to the pizzas on their dinner menu — you'll be happy here.

I favor this place a lot for a "take care of me" lunch option. It's a nice escape from all the fried stuff (I mean they have a few on their menu but it's not what they're aiming for).

Favorites for me are the truffle potato chips, crab cakes, calamari, tuna tatare, and grilled bruschetta. Basically, all their apps are a home run.

For soup and salad, I gear people towards the chicken and chili soup, Chinese chicken salad, and the burrata and heirloom tomato salad.

For their pizzas, which are quite nice, I am a fan of the BBQ pulled pork, mortadella, prosciutto, and sausage options.

For entrees, I've enjoyed their burger, their double-cut pork chop, and the ribeye. Other favorites that I think really like to guide people to are the grouper, half chicken, salmon, and the tagliatelle. All of these in my opinion speak to the Wolfgang Puck experience and flavor profile which would be upscale, familiar foods, with clean flavors.

Chef Art Smith's Homecomin': *Actual Factual Magic* Do Not Miss!

I have a soft spot for this place, mainly because I am a sucker for southern-style food. They're open for brunch or dinner. Come for either as both offer what they specialize in: Fried chicken.

Let's start with brunch — I'd recommend grabbing one of their delightful cocktails from their list. Their *Southern Mary*, twist on the Bloody Mary, complete with bacon, fried green tomato, and olives. Or if you are feeling more refined, a *Florida Crush* or *Princess Mimosa* will do the trick.

For food: I recommend getting a few items and create your own family-style share plate. The short rib hash, hush puppy benedict, hallelujah biscuit, and fried green tomatoes are all wonderful options. To me, the winner of brunch here would be the fried chicken and donuts because you're on vacation and you should get their fried chicken and donuts because you can. If I were to order one thing on the menu, it would be that.

Moving right along: For dinner, their *Thigh High Biscuits* are just little bundles of chicken magic. First, the chicken thigh is the best part of the chicken to fry, tucked in a biscuit with a honey-blended hot sauce. I also enjoyed their golden and flulffy hushpuppies (I think this may be one of the few if not only place on Disney property I've encountered them). You could get grilled chicken here — but why? Unless you have a dietary restriction, I would say go here to just annihilate your diet. Get the fried chicken and donuts for dinner, or some of their traditional fried chicken with mashed and biscuits.

While there are many places to get dessert at Disney (and especially Disney Springs®), be sure to get a slice of their hummingbird cake. Or, you can do their chocolate pecan pie…. or both…

Just go here and destroy your diet, walk it off at a park. I've done it each time. No regrets. YOLO as the kids say. You're welcome.

The Edison

If you're looking for peace and relaxation, don't come here. If you're looking for live music and to be entertained, come here! They have live music every night of the week. I'd say this place is more of a "bar" first, and restaurant later. While they have good food here, I'd say this is more of a favorite for me to enjoy music, their amazing cocktails, and get some small bites.

That's not to say they cant satisfy any late-night cravings — because they sure can. They have your staples here: fries, calamari, chips, salsa, chicken tenders. Some menu highlights are their burgers: Both the Edison and the Bacon Mushroom Swiss are incredibly satisfying and well portioned. The Edison and Raglan Road have some of the best burgers in Disney. I'd say this is a bit of a live-music meets gastropub if you can imagine it — or experience it. From the specialty cocktails to acrobats in the air, to their layered chocolate cake, it's a good time. A perfect way to close out a night. They do have a kids menu here too if you wanted something that is for more "mom and dad first, little Sammy later."

Frontera Cocina

Chicago native, Rick Bayless, has a satellite restaurant in Disney Springs, Frontera Cocina, a playoff of his Chicago stores, Frontera Grill and Xoco. This establishment has been around since 2016 and offers casual, yet modern Mexican cuisine. I'm a huge fan of Rick Bayless. He is from my hometown, charitable, an author, has a food line with some of the best salsas (I use his tomatillo salsa whenever I make breakfast tacos)— and his food is awesome.

I enjoy this place for a few reasons: The food is not only fresh and flavorful, but their cocktails and mixologists know what they're doing. If you find yourself in Disney Springs Monday - Wednesday, they have drink specials for $5. Can't beat it. Sometimes mama needs a drink - especially a drinker $5 because you're on vacation, want to treat yourself, and also spent all your money on buying princess attire at the boutique.

Some menu favorites: If you're from the midwest like me, you may naturally gravitate to the bacon guacamole and chips. Maybe it's not even a midwestern thing, but more of an American reason to get this is because bacon, and bacon. If you're an international traveler, you may enjoy this twist, maybe not. We just garnish things with bacon out in the states. I can't explain it. We even dip our bacon in chocolate. But yes, you can find bacon in your guacamole here.

I like this place for a lunch option: Their salads and tacos are all home runs. Oddly enough, again you're in Florida, but their soup with roasted corn and poblano is really good. I am not even the biggest fan of poblano peppers and I really enjoy this comforting soup. For it being Florida, Disney Springs® offers some comforting soups and Frontera Cocina is one of them.

I'm a sucker for the enchiladas here. I think it's the chipotle chicken seasoning he has that really makes it challenging for me to order other things when I come here. I also love the carne asada.

It's one of the more expensive items on the menu, but I find it creative and worth it. I love how it is paired with plantains and the cotija cheese. And yes, you should get the addition of grilled shrimp.

All around a win here for a casual dinner or lunch option by a world-class chef.

Quick-Service Favorites at Disney Springs®:

Along with fine dining at Disney Springs and amazing sit-down options, you have some pretty solid quick-service options too. If you decide to snack your way through Disney Springs® by day, and close out with table-service by night, that's a solid foodie plan. Or, if you're thinking, "Hey Kat, my foodie godmother, I just really want to eat all the things." You got it. You can accomplish that with a blend of dining options and snacking your way through here. If you do that, sharing with your mates and family is the key to success in covering a lot of foodie ground.

Let's start with a few options, and work our way through our list.

Disney Food Trucks:

A newer addition to Disney Springs®, and a growing crowd pleaser, are the Disney Food Trucks. Unless you are in a major city, like New York or Toronto, this could be the first or one of the few times you experience a food truck. Walk up, order your meal, and then the food is prepared and served to you from the vehicle. It's a restaurant on wheels that is perfect for food on-the-go. Or, grab your snack and have a sit over by one of the relaxing fountains.

In this day and age, these tend to be satisfying for a few reasons: Takes care of the hunger quickly, not as expensive, good portions, and these are a safer option to enjoy food for those of you looking to minimize possible illness exposure while dining out. For those not quite yet comfortable with indoor dining, are high risk, or simply want to enjoy the outdoors, you don't have to go inside anywhere. Honestly, whoever thought to bring in food trucks here, deserves a medal. It was a good plan and a really nice, easy way for businesses to keep moving forward at a lower cost to the owners.

Currently, Disney has three that can usually be found at Exposition Park.

They are:

- 4 Rivers Cantina Barbacoa Food Truck
- Mac & Cheese
- Hot Diggity Dogs

I'm going to start with my favorite food truck:

4 Rivers Cantina Barbacoa: *Actual Factual Magic* Food Truck Favorite!

First off — have you ever seen a person unhappy with tacos? That's a trick question. It's never happened. It's impossible. Tacos make people happy. This delightful truck has possibly one of my favorite quick-service menus at Disney Springs®. They'll have your traditional favorites like tacos, burrito bowls, and quesadillas for the kids. But, why did they make our list being a food truck?

Taco Cone.

Yes. You read that right. If your brain imagined an ice cream cone but a tortilla, filled with taco goodness, of seasoned meat, sour cream, cheese, and greens, you imagined it correctly. Satisfying, tasty, and social media worthy.
Second, where they won my heart over, they have birria tacos on their menu. Birria is a type of taco that has been seared and dipped into a red, spicy, beef broth sauce. They're not available just anywhere, but they do have them here.

Mac & Cheese
Um....need I say more? It's mac and cheese, the ultimate comfort food. But mac and cheese with some additional comfort food fixings like barbecue brisket, seafood lobster-shrimp, or chili? Yeah. They have all those. It's like comfort food fusion.

I prefer to stop here on my way out, package it to-go, and reheat it at my vacation rental for later. I literally will leave with a bath bomb from Basin, enjoy a bubble bath, get in my comfy clothes, turn on a Disney movie, and enjoy a nice reheated bowl of mac and cheese. Isn't that the perfect way to cap a day? The answer is yes. My personal favorite is the bbq brisket.

Hot Diggity Dogs
Another food truck favorite is Hot Diggity Dogs. Similar to the Mac & Cheese food truck, they have fun toppings here too like the chili or street corn (like for the *Santa Fe Dog*). Being a Chicagoan, I'm partial to them because they offer a Chicago-style dog, which in my opinion, is the correct way to make a hot dog (mustard, relish, sport peppers, tomato). Ok, fine, I may be biased. Oh, and be sure you have a relative or a friend nearby to share their house-made chips.

Inexpensive, delish, and you have the option to get a big hot dog here too (~12 inches). For you social media lovers, their menu options are impressive to show your friends at home.

Amorette's Patisserie: *Actual Factual Magic* Do Not Miss!
This place has possibly some of the best dessert in all of Disney. Paris in Epcot rivals with this one — I'll get to that recommendation later. When you have Parisian desserts, Disney-themed treats, and a splash of elegance, this place takes the cake - literally.

It's a quick-serve patisserie cafe located in the heart of downtown Disney Springs®. Amorette's is a bright, friendly, classic-Parisian-style dessert shop with the Disney magic twist. They boast their latest creations in the windows where you can see bakers decorating speciality cakes for the day.
I usually waddle my way over there after a hearty dinner and find room for a Disney-themed cake.

These desserts are exquisite and for the price? Are an exceptional option. As someone who has been to France and taken cooking classes in Paris, this place doesn't mess around. Their mini-cakes are a very popular option to share as well as their Mickey and Minnie cakes.

We had tried the espresso-coffee custard dessert which was rich, creamy, woke me up from the caffeine, and even had edible gold on top.

Aside from their must-try desserts, if you're in the Disney Springs® area and are open for a lunch
spot that isn't in the park, they offer cafe-style sandwiches and crêpes. My favorite sandwich is their carved turkey on focaccia.

I regularly shop with my eyes: I get something for immediate consumption, and then something

to bring back to my vacation rental for later. This is also a great place to get a celebratory cake for a loved one...or just because. It truly is a lovely bakery with dessert and cafe options.
Note: In the past, they have offered cake decorating classes so you can go and learn how to make some of these delicious treats. These classes vary and are offered seasonally. For any die-hard foodies who love to not only eat but cook, these classes would be a Disney foodie's dream. They're usually conducted early in the morning. Due to the pandemic, they have been either on pause or incredibly limited. If available, when you go to Disney Dining's website to book reservations, you can book a "reservation" here for the class. It's unclear when these will return, but check with your concierge if this becomes available during your stay.

Morimoto Asia Street Food

In a hurry but want to try Morimoto? Or perhaps couldn't get a reservation and still want a taste? Or maybe you have a hankering for Asian street food. They have a stand right outside their main restaurant door for quick food to go. Some of my favorites are the spring rolls and ribs. Their ribs are so satisfying too: tender and slathered in sauce. You will need napkins ;) It's a nice way to sample while walking around. Their street-food menu is not the same as their fine dining menu, however, you can't go wrong at Morimoto.

Gideon's Bakehouse: *Actual Factual Magic* Do Not Miss!

Another (and newer) dessert option is Gideon's Bakehouse. I best describe the vibe at Gideon's is like "the home decorator for both Edgar Allen Poe and The Haunted Mansion showed up and added steamed-punk flair inside the bakehouse."

Their menu is heavy on chocolate and portions. They are known for super-sized cookies and cake slices. Some of their known menu items are their peanut butter chocolate swirl, chocolate chip cookies, and triple chocolate chip cookies.

Think stacked Oreos and a mound of dough on top. Seriously, mound of dough is not hyperbole here. You have an oreo, which is already a cookie, with another cookie built on it. It's like cookie inception.

For chocolate and peanut lovers, their cakes can be found with Oreos, Reese's, or Andy's. Their menu offerings are quite different than Amorette's but when it comes to decadence, they are right there. A must-try!

Everglazed Donuts

Say it with me: Fruit Loop Donuts. If you're visiting from the West Coast, you may be familiar with Voodoo Donuts. I'd say these are on par with similar offerings where they find a donut, glaze it, and top them with cereal breakfast favorites. Not all their donuts have cereal toppings, but I'm a sucker for Cinnamon Toast Crunch and they sure have that. To no one's surprise, it's fabulous. I call it "breakfast fusion." You have both donuts and cereal, already breakfast items, and they're mashed together into a little something mightier. Some other favorites from our team are the *Nutella Bella, Strawberry Jelly Deluxe*, and *Mounds Coconut Dream*. If you're not feeling a donut, they do have breakfast sandwiches as well. And if you're like me where you're on vacation and would like a drink, they also offer spiked coffee.

Hint: Get the *Glazed & Confused*. I actually love stopping by here for breakfast before going to the parks or water parks.

The Daily Poutine

Poutine isn't impossible to find at Disney but there are only just a few spots that offer it: Epcot Canada (which requires a park admission) and The Daily Poutine, which doesn't require a park ticket. Similar to the other foodie spots at Disney Springs®, they have a classic offering, but also other twists. So if you want to have classic poutine you can, or if you want it showered with cheese and bacon, pork, beans, and cheese — they have several options available.

The Basket at Wine Bar George

For those who enjoy the sit-down experience at Wine Bar George, but want something for on-the-go or simply the experience of building your own picnic basket, that's why this makes the list. With the ability for more of a clean-eating option and to change up your Disney experience, you literally can build your own picnic basket which is, honestly just adorable. It has a $60 minimum for the picnic basket, but with wine, it's easy to hit that minimum. Find a place to picnic at Disney Springs, or perhaps at your resort. Seriously, who doesn't love charcuterie?

Aside from building a basket, you can also have a little charcuterie grab-and-go. For those who also have an eye for healthier options, they have hummus, chicken skewers, and a cheese box.

Food isn't the only thing to grab and go here. Try the frozé. For dole-whip lovers, try the *Frozcato* which is made up of the *Pineapple Dole Whip*, moscato, and vodka. Memories are made from this drink. Or if you have a few…several memories can be made.

I like to take this basket, and picnic by the beach over at the Polynesian. For those of you in need of a romantic idea, you're welcome.

B.B. Wolf's Sausage

If you love meat, this is your place to stop by. This may not be everyone's cup of tea, as they have not only hot dogs, but some gamey meats, like lamb sausage, on the menu as well. However, they do their best to accommodate even non-meat lovers and even have a plant-based sausage option.

For those of you that haven't gone to Casey's Corner at Magic Kingdom®, or want a similar experience, I'd say this is their cousin at Disney Springs®. Similar to Casey's they do have foot-long hotdog options which make them not only filling but also make great food photos for your social media.

Some Actual Factual favorite menu items are the bratwurst sausage with sauerkraut (reminds me of Germany in Epcot's World Showcase, the *Texas Chili-Cheese Dog*, and the *Hawaiian Island Dog* complete with grilled pineapple. I know there are arguments out there if pineapple goes on pizza — I believe it goes on pizza…and hot dogs. I mean, pulled pork is usually marinated in pineapple. I get this may be a stretch, but it works. Pork + pineapple = yum. The math is simple.

To get a sampling of their menu, I recommend the *Three Little Pigs* which are mini versions of their specialty dogs: *Pastrami, Hawaiian, and Texas Chili*.

Cookes of Dublin

This one is a fun one to me because it has a lot of favorites: Burgers of all kinds, fries, chicken tenders, and of course fish and chips. This tends to satisfy both parents and kids in my opinion and also won't burn a hole in your food budget. It has traditional Irish fare and their fish & chips are a similar option to those found at Epcot's World Showcase: United Kingdom pavilion. My go-to recommendations here are fish and chips and the *BBQ Dream Burger*: which is basically a hefty beef patty, topped with smokey barbecue sauce blended with Jameson, onion ring, Dubliner cheese, and crisp arugula.

Wolfgang Puck Express

Like several of the options listed in Disney Springs®, if you want to dine at a Wolfgang Puck restaurant, but perhaps don't have time, or it is not part of your current dining plans, this is a casual quick-service option that has better options than "I just need food" but want something better than just a plain ol' sandwich.

I'm a huge fan of their soups, which may sound weird to recommend considering Florida heat, but, for a nice soup and salad, they have some tasty options. I really love their sandwiches here too. I love the rotisserie turkey with pepperoncini aioli. Oddly enough, my favorite here is a vegetarian option: The whole wheat hummus wrap. It's just incredibly refreshing to eat: cucumbers, hummus, arugula, feta, olives. I feel like if you're exhausted from the traditional fried options, this shop is a welcomed break.

Be sure to split one of their pizzas as an appetizer. The roasted mushroom with goat cheese is on point and my personal favorite.

Ghirardelli

Ok — before you say "Hey, these are basically everywhere, not unique, why are they on the favorites list?" Honestly, I had to put them on the favorite list for that reason. I get these are in almost every major city, but ya know what? They are always busy. Why? Because they are delicious and a predictable favorite. You just can't go wrong with Ghirardelli ice cream.

Go get ice cream here and some chocolates to bring back home. They're originally from San Francisco and found their way to have a booming spot at Disney Springs®. *The Ocean Beach* (salted caramel sundae) and their *Land's End* (warm brownie sundae with thick fudge) are my favorite menu items. If you want — you can always get a sundae in a welcoming waffle bowl. Also, their sundaes are massive. Sharing is highly recommended.

Magic Kingdom® Dining

So let's level set: The Magic Kingdom® is a theme park and the majority of options are fast food. Now, that's not to be said that you can't find good eats here. I tend to lean on the Magic Kingdom® more for snacks and social media-worthy foodie pics. We do have a few standout dining options here, and some snacks that will wow you. If you're looking to maximize your time at the park and leverage your Disney Dining Plan, you can easily eat your way through here on quick-service dining, or have a lovely sit-down dinner with princesses. The good news, you have options. Since the changes in the last year with the need to focus on health, most people are not too keen to leave the park to dine, only to come back to it later and go through entrance line again. If you fall in this mindset, not to worry, let us guide you.

Best Table-Service at Magic Kingdom Park:

While Magic Kingdom® itself doesn't have a ton of sit-down spots, we've listed our top three. If you choose to not leave the park, these would be our recommendations based on food, service, experience, and overall value. We often like to recommend visiting a nearby resort for sit-down dining as they're a quick monorail or boat ride away. The amount of time to re-enter a park can be unpredictable, but if you don't stray too far at a nearby resort, you'll be a-okay.

It really depends on what you want: Get a break from the park, or perhaps just ensure you can get a good meal and not have to leave. Regardless, we got you covered. Let's chat if you stay:

Liberty Tree Tavern:

This non-character, family-style restaurant is tucked in Liberty Square at The Magic Kingdom®. I feel like this is a real crowd-pleaser on many different levels: First, like any Disney Park, if you've got a food allergy or dietary restriction, they take such good care of you here. They do everywhere, but for this place, we had a vegetarian in our party and they didn't leave hungry. They had some kind of vegetarian pot-pie that was fabulous - and filling (I got to try some since they struggled to finish it — we were pleasantly surprised by the portion size).

I couldn't help but notice that at the surrounding tables, kids were enjoying their meals here too. Sometimes it can be a struggle to even get the kiddos to eat, but apparently not at Liberty Tree Tavern.

As far as food quality goes, this one is always on point. From the fluffy mashed potatoes to the juicy roasted chicken, the food is always coming out at a steady pace and fresh. You can always order more if you need to like most of the all-you-care-to-enjoy menus. I appreciate coming here before the parade for a filling dinner _after_ Big Thunder Mountain Railroad. Don't go before. It'll be a bad time.

It's going to have your "Sunday dinner," supper-style option. In some ways, it's like Thanksgiving every day here. Who wouldn't want Thanksgiving dinner? Instead of turkey, just think chicken for the poultry option. You then have stuffing, mashed potatoes, and salad. I loved the fact that I could eat something "like mom makes" for family dinners in a Disney Park. Sure you have the hustle and bustle of a Disney theme park, but you can't help but feel cozy with the woodwork in the hallway and the comfort food at your table.

Steak Entree — Cinderella's Royal Table - Magic Kingdom

Cinderella's Royal Table: *Actual Factual Magic* Do Not Miss!
If there is someone in your family in absolute need of meeting the Disney Princesses, they've come to the right place. Cinderella's Royal Table is the Chef Mickey's of the Magic Kingdom® (great food and face characters).

You walk into the castle and are in an enchanted dining area with high ceilings and windows — a dining hall fit for royalty. If you have children wanting to meet a princess and share some special moments, this is the place to do it. This is also a great option if you're celebrating something special — a birthday, honeymoon, engagement — this is a place where they believe in magic (and good food).

Their menu style is a bit different as they try to do more of a "fancy tasting experience" vs. the usual grand buffet. Some folks may argue that they'd prefer to hit up a buffet for the value, but then again, this place has *all* the princesses. So, keep in mind you're paying for access to them here vs. standing outside in the heat with 60+ minute wait times for *each* princess. Depending on where we are with the ongoing health crisis, if character dining is not occurring, they still work to make it special by Cinderella greeting guests safely from a short distance.

The food has upgraded in execution and quality since it first opened. You can find entrees including duck, beef tenderloin, and chicken all paired with some kind of vegetable and sauce that compliments the main entree. For those with a sweet tooth, their desserts are really one of a kind here. The *Clock Strikes Twelve* is their play on a chocolate mousse with praline (um yum, right?), and hazelnut gelato. My favorite, and likely more for grown up pallets, would be their pot de crème which is currently a coffee custard with passionfruit.

This is another one to book with as many days in advance with a calendar reminder.

Jungle Navigation, Skipper Canteen: *Actual Factual Magic* Do Not Miss!
A growing favorite for those looking to dine at Magic Kingdom® is the Skipper Canteen located in Adventure Land. A casual dining spot that has a lot of different fusion flavors with modern twists, based off the *Jungle Cruise* ride and movie.

Popular items are chicken with sweet chili sauce, Thai noodles, and curry vegetable stew. I also enjoy the pork with jasmine rice. Their entrees are well portioned and well-executed. If you're undecided when you come here, I gravitate towards the steak or the fish. The fish is pretty impressive so if you're also torn between those two, get their fish.

I love that their menu is of variety and you'll love taking photos of each colorful entree that comes out.

Depending on your server, you'll get some dad jokes with your meal. Since the recent theatrical release of the *Jungle Cruise*, I anticipate longer wait times, so be mindful of that. But certainly a do not miss!

Be sure to try the corn pancake appetizer for dinner!

This place is also becoming well-known for their cocktails and full drink list. While they have alcohol drinks that are all quite refreshing, I actually really enjoyed their non-alcoholic menu a lot, specifically their *Punch Line Punch* - fruit juice and mango puree.

For alcoholic drinks I would say my pick would be their sangria.

Best Quick-Service Dining Options at Magic Kingdom®:
The Magic Kingdom® is littered with quick-service options — and several good ones. I've done some trips where I simply just get quick-service meals and made my own little tasting menu of quick bites.

Whether you want to dine-in and be pampered, or not waste your time with table-service because you have to see it all, or, you're just a foodie and MUST TRY ALL THE THINGS. Whatever your reasonings, let's make sure you have the best of everything and can create your own perfect experience. Most people I talk to, tend to want a balance of quick-service and table-service.

We tend to lean on the nearby resort hotels for a sit-down option, but, sometimes you just don't want to leave the park, and we get that too!

For foodies who love to post on social media, you can find some impressive and tasty items through quick-service dining at Magic Kingdom®.

Main Street Confectionary: *Actual Factual Magic* Do Not Miss!

As soon as you walk into the Main Square at the Magic Kingdom®, an inviting smell of chocolate catches your nose and stops most people in their tracks.

Here you'll find chocolate-covered strawberries, pretzels, and cupcakes, but they're most known for two items: Their character-themed Rice Krispy treats and their taffy apples.

They have an open kitchen so you can often find yourself in awe while watching these delectable treats being made by Cast Members. They have mini Rice Krispy treats, or you can get the ones we get: The giant Mickey-shaped Rice Krispies are as big as your head. Many are dipped in chocolate or plain.

Most of us tend to only have taffy Apples in the fall and winter seasons but this shop has them year round. There are so many fun designs on the taffy apples. Many of which resembled the wizard's wardrobe in *Fantasia* or Minnie's dress. They also have giant apples with no theme but just to appreciate there is a giant apple covered in caramel, chocolate, and M&Ms because that's what's possible here. **Pro Tip:** Grab items to-go on your way out of the park and go back to your hotel room with them. If they stay in your bag, the chocolate will melt and you'll have some sad-looking sweets. I may be sharing from experience. Or, why wait? Just eat them in the park.

From traditional gift shop items like mugs or Disney-themed kitchen accessories, you can find those here along with some park-made sweet treats. My favorite collectible I once purchased here were *Alice In Wonderland* tea cups. The good news? Someone with some pixie dust told me they're expanding this area.

Casey's Corner

Craving a hotdog at the Magic Kingdom®? Casey's Corner is for sure the right place to go. Now, you may say to yourself "Why on earth would I pay ~$13 for a hotdog?" Two answers: Because Disney makes it possible and therefore you can. All you have to do is believe in yourself and you too, can eat a foot-long hotdog. They do have standard-size hotdogs as well, but honestly, when you're here and you see people with it, you can't help but think "Go big or go home. My home doesn't have hotdogs like this." And yes, I took a picture with the hotdog against my arm just to show that Disney isn't messing around.

Footlong Specialty Hot Dog — Casey's — Magic Kingdom

Not only do they have footlong hotdogs as a possibility, but they even have some dressed-up hot dogs, like mac and cheese or chili cheese, to name a few. If you're feeling more carnival food, they also have corn dogs.

I'm from Chicago. It's basically in my genetic coding to have a Chicago-style dog (mustard, relish, onion, hot peppers, tomatoes, celery salt). Tho last I checked "Chicago-style" isn't on their menu, you can certainly come close to building your own as I did. If you want some fast food that will fill you up, this is the place.

Plaza Ice Cream Parlor

I like to think of this place, where, if Mary Poppins had an ice cream shop in America, this would be it. The plaza has a sit-down dining restaurant here available for those who want to relax and have a bite to eat. However, I recommend usually getting some ice cream to-go from their quick-service ice cream bar to have while wandering the park (or in times of the pandemic, in designated areas). This is more your traditional, old-fashioned ice cream parlor that will have you time travel back to a nostalgic early 1900s era.

If you're wandering and seeing people with delicious-looking ice cream on or not far from Main Street, they got it from here. **Hint:** Be sure to get a waffle cone or waffle bowl.

Tortuga Tavern

You come here for giant turkey leg noms and you look like a prehistoric caveman (or in my case, cave lady) eating one. Seriously, you'll look like a total cave person badass walking around the park with a giant turkey leg in hand. They look intimidating to eat — and they are — but they sure are tasty. Be sure to share with at least one friend. I'd say they're good for 3-4 people to be honest. Or not, maybe you just want that big ol' leg all to yourself after burning off all those calories walking through the park.

A few things to note if you haven't had one: They are smoked turkey. So if you're thinking it's going to taste like Thanksgiving turkey — NOPE! It, in my humble opinion, tastes more like ham. So if you do not like ham, smoked turkey legs may not be for you. Personally, and this may sound weird, I like dipping mine in BBQ sauce. Sometimes they have them at the stand, or a nearby location has some sauce handy. Or, maybe you're also like me and have fast-food sauces hoarded from various restaurants readily available in your purse for this exact moment in your life.

I love the smoke on them and the light caramelization on the skin. It's a real treat. I enjoy to eat them, but I have never finished one on my own. My partner and I could barely finish one together. I'd recommend getting it as a snack to share with the family as you stroll through the park, or as an appetizer to share as you get some sides at one of the local fast-food stops and make a mini-meal out of it. You can find them at the water parks, Epcot®, and Magic Kingdom®. I think you should get one to try! Tho, you probably should not eat them before riding the teacups....

If you want to sample a sweet, try the rum cake.

Cheshire Cafe

This place really has one item that foodies seek: *The Cheshire Cat Tail*. This place fulfills a few goals: Guests need a bite, they also want to get a *Cheshire Cat Tail* because there's some serious *Alice In Wonderland* food worship happening here, and it is very social media worthy. In short, they're flakey pastry dough with chocolate, drizzled with some pink and purple sugar glaze. You only need one since they appear never-ending, so be sure to have friends or family willing to share.

On mornings I happen to be in the Magic Kingdom®, I like to grab one of these to count as breakfast.

Gaston's Tavern

I suppose if your kid ever wondered what a tavern was like, and you wanted to be transported to the one in *Beauty and the Beast*, hats off to the architecture team here that brought this place to life. In the back part of Fantasyland, you'll find a Gaston water fountain, and to no surprise, behind it is Gaston's Tavern.

This is another "quick bite and foodie spot" option. You go here really for the cinnamon rolls. So if you're craving a cinnamon roll, this is the place. You are easily tempted here by the giant plate of warm, cinnamon and sugary dough. For those ultra *Beauty and the Beast* fans, they also serve the "grey stuff that's delicious" mentioned in the movie. Which is a yellow cupcake with a grey buttercream frosting.

Note: This place does not serve alcohol. But, if you want, try *LeFou's Brew*. It's not beer, but it's a frothy marshmallow apple cider blend that has become a fan favorite. I almost think of it as a liquified taffy apple. Personally, it's a little too sweet for me, but, several folks I know truly enjoy it.

Aloha Aisle

You come here for one thing: Dole Whip. I suppose you can get some at Storybook Treats as well, but this is like...the original. You come here. This is the authentic experience and why this one gets the shout-out for *Pineapple Dole Whip*.

Upon entering Adventureland, just adjacent to The Enchanted Tiki Room, you will find Aloha Isle. They serve a pineapple-vanilla soft serve that helps you beat the heat and enjoy something refreshing, while not overly sweet. This has grown in popularity, so much so, that Polynesian Resort and every major Disney location now offers it.
I got one and my travel buddy was like "I don't want anything" and consumed pretty much the entire thing we had to get another.

Sleepy Hollow

This is a foodie favorite if you love waffles and or funnel cake.

If you've been doing your Disney homework and saw a waffle sandwich with fresh strawberries on the internet, this is the place to get it. Sleepy Hollow is another foodie favorite and they are well-loved for their carb creations.

Funnel cakes with strawberries and whipped cream, or their ever-popular warm waffle sandwich with Nutella and fresh strawberries make for a happy snack in Fantasyland. The smell of freshly fried funnel cake dough will enchant your nose and you'll find yourself suddenly craving something from this stand and you weren't even hungry.

Best of Magic Kingdom® Area Resort Dining

If no one has told you, "it's okay to take a break from the theme parks." I'll be that friend telling you, "take a break from the parks, go enjoy some signature dining at the Magic Kingdom® Resorts. The Magic Kingdom® is within easy access (via monorail, ferry, or bus to several of Disney's signature resort hotels that contain some of Disney's best dining experiences. Do yourself a favor and enjoy one or more of these restaurants during your vacation.

The Polynesian Resort & Spa:

Whenever I think about the Polynesian Resort & Spa, I always think of all the amazing vegetation upon arrival. Whether you are fresh off the monorail or arriving by vehicle up front, there are tropical plants everywhere. It's so relaxing to walk in and see the waterfalls. You get to the main house which has two floors of shopping, dining, and at the center are blue and yellow lanterns hanging from the ceiling with palm plants all around. Basically, the goal was to make you feel like you're in Hawaii and French Polynesia. I always relax every time upon arrival. It smells floral, fresh, and you mentally transport to the tropics. For those looking to go to Bora Bora without the passport, you're in luck. Themed with Hawaiian and island cuisines, you'll find flavors and fusions throughout all the dining options here. Hint: Must love pineapple.

O'hana: Actual Factual Magic Do Not Miss!

This used to be a best-kept secret. Many Disney guests are probably wondering, "What is so special about O'Hana?" Lots.

It's the one meal I am constantly dreaming about whenever I am about to visit Disney. This is one of those places where you must set a calendar reminder to book in advance from your intended visit. It's that good.

There are two experiences with O'Hana at Disney's Polynesian Resort. Both are very different.

First, there's breakfast: Breakfast is with your favorite Disney characters decked out in their best Hawaiian gear. Mickey shows up with a Hawaiian t-shirt. O'hana breakfast is a fun, family-style Hawaiian meal to get your day started before hitting the parks. A little kiddy at times with the entertainment (usually a musician singing and playing a ukulele). For food, I loved getting breakfast here. The menu is family-style and has your everyday staples: eggs, bacon, biscuits, fresh fruit, and then some Hawaiian flavors like pineapple sauce and island-style loaves of sticky-sweet bread. The waffles resemble Stitch from *Lilo and Stich*. With a full belly, I like to hop on the Monorail in a few short stops, start my day at the Magic Kingdom®.

My most favorite part tho is dinner: Dinner at O'hana is truly like a different restaurant by night than by day. This is a nice way for adults to unwind or have a great meal with the entire family and take a break from the character dining.

First, let's talk about the drinks: In case you have a long wait or perhaps you want to just be a complete glutton like myself, you start with their drink menu. They do have many of the common drinks you can find at the water parks or other areas, but their two standouts in my humble opinion are the *Pimm's Punch* and the *Lapu Lapu*.

Neither drink is for children, but you know what, it's time to focus on you. Start off with a *Pimm's Punch* and drink the island, or go straight for what I enjoy: The *Lapu Lapu*. It's a rum-based tropical drink served in a pineapple with a little umbrella. You can get your pineapple refilled and just keep enjoying the vacation in pure liquid form. I usually just hit up the bar at the Polynesian my first night in Disney (regardless if I'm staying there or not) because I always feel like I'm on vacation with a *Lapu Lapu* in hand from the Tambu Lounge (the bar attached to O'hana).

Now that we've got our drinks settled, let's talk about dinner at O'Hana. You come here to get meat. Lots of it (sorry vegans and vegetarians, tho Disney and the restaurant can be accommodating, and they would be here no doubt, this restaurant experience is geared for carnivorous friends and family members).

O'hana is Disney's churrascaria. What's that? Basically, lots of meat cooked on a long skewer we're talking about 3' skewers of freshly cooked meat. Restaurant attendants come around to your table, offer you the meat they have, and give you as much as you like. They offer varieties of chicken, shrimp, pork, and beef. They also have fabulous sides: pineapple bread, mixed greens, noodle salad, veggies to name a few.

Note: This exact experience may be slightly adjusted during the ongoing health crisis. What I can say, is you can expect delicious meat that came from a skewer cooked over fire.

This restaurant surprises me because I have been to several churrascaria-style restaurants and every time, O'hana wins. The meat is always *very* fresh. Each meat is also perfectly cooked at the right temperature: Chicken is juicy, pork is tender, and the beef is served at multiple temperatures but I love the medium-rare — it's always a family favorite. I don't know what they do with the shrimp, but they are some of the best cooked and flavored shrimp I've ever consumed. They've got some juice, sweet, and a little bit of heat. I'm pretty sure I ate a whole school of shrimp last time I was there. Sorry shrimp.

Whether you're going here as an adult group, date night, or perhaps this is a night with the kiddos. I think of this as "the adult foodie sanctuary" or "mom and dad want to use their bonus money for a good dinner here." Between excellent service and quality food served fresh from the grill, if you don't leave here with a food baby, you did O'hana wrong.

Kona Cafe

Kona Cafe serves up all three meals at the Polynesian Resort. It's a non-character dining option with Polynesian-themed favorites.

Foodie favorites here are the *Tonga Toast* (banana-stuffed French toast in cinnamon, sugar, and strawberry sauce) or the *Macadamia Nut Pancakes*. You can't get breakfast options like this anywhere else in Walt Disney World® so this is the spot to load up.

Many of the dinner favorites include *Coffee-Rubbed Steak*, ahi tuna, or the pork chop. They also have a "daily catch" which is something that is non-Disney traditional. Most Disney dining options do not offer specials so the fact this one has an option that changes daily makes it inviting as they often do an upscale fish that elevates the overall dining experience.

Trader Sam's

If you're exiting the Main House towards the back of the building, and you veer to the left of the Volcano Pool, you'll find yourself en route to Trader Sam's Tiki Lounge. It's a hip little dive known for its cocktails. They also have really unique drink ware - beyond the typical tiki cup. Some of them, you get to keep as a souvenir. I like to come back and get a second drink so I can make a set to bring home.

If you are lucky enough to merit a spot and have the patience to wait out the line, you'll find

Pineapple Dole Whip — Magic Kingdom, various parks

yourself enjoying some of the best tiki drinks in Disney. They do have a few light bites here. The food menu had adjusted a few times, but the personal favorite are the pork tacos.

My personal favorite drinks here are the *Uh-Oa* (like uh-oh) (with a really neat souvenir cup) and the *Spiced Island*. This place is more known for the drinks than the food. It has had some stellar food favorites in the past, I loved their chicken wings and fried green beans. I would recommend getting a snack while you drink here because let me tell you — those delicious fruity drinks sneak up on you.

Pineapple Lanai: *Actual Factual Magic* Do Not Miss!

This little stand is basically where you can get the *Pineapple Dole Whip* glory at the resort and not with all the park traffic. You may still get a line here, but it's far more bearable and you have another option to get the famous *Pineapple Dole Whip* as soft serve, a rum floater, or as a pineapple float.

The Grand Floridian

Gracing Florida with its Victorian influence and southern charm, you have the exquisite resort that is one stop away from the Magic Kingdom®. The Grand Floridian is comfort, service, and luxury. If *Alice and Wonderland* or *Mary Poppins* could have their own hotel, it would be this one. This place is packed with character dining options, high tea, and world-class dining experiences.

This is a property where if you're staying it, you have access to some of the best hotel dining in Disney. And if you're not staying at The Grand Floridian, be sure to make time to check out at least one restaurant or lounge here.

Grand Floridian Cafe

We chose to dine here for breakfast and lunch during a few of our visits and were happy with both. This is fun for the whole family or even couples. Many families could see this as a letdown if you didn't score a character breakfast next door (since there aren't characters here), but the food here is a few notches up. Many folks seem to find this as a breath of fresh air since it is quiet and doesn't have the characters or activities over loud speaker system.

Breakfast: Tho a sophisticated restaurant, they do a great job tucking in the Disney details. Nothing beats starting your morning meal than ordering a cappuccino with the Mickey Mouse symbol. Before hitting the parks, we got ourselves a meal to start the day right: Crab cake benedict and their french toast. Both were excellent so we went split each. The benedict was splendid - lovely crab cakes topped with a nice thick hollandaise and served with a seasonal salad of mixed greens and tomatoes. Their french toast was to perfection and had a vanilla bean butter dolloped on top. This is certainly one of those "eat your heart out" breakfasts that are a few levels up from the buffets. Not that the buffet food is bad, there are some pretty darn good spots, but this is one of those spots where you sacrifice the character dining and get elevated food. Their pancakes also were fluffy and divine. Needless to say, our tummies were quite satisfied.

Salmon Entree — Grand Floridian Cafe — Grand Floridian Resort & Spa

Dinner: We felt dinner was more geared for adults than kids. Of course, Disney caters to families but if you're looking for a more quiet evening for a nice dinner at the resort, this is a good spot for it. It was a quiet evening in, but we were just a few steps away from prime firework viewing at the docks. The seared salmon with green beans, steak, and mashed potatoes were menu favorites. For good food near the Magic Kingdom® that doesn't require park entry or characters, this is a spot that accomplishes both.

Afternoon Tea: They also have a very elegant tea time. I have only done this once. It was truly lovely and the desserts were exquisite. It's one of those "it's nice if we have time to do this." Otherwise, there are other things you can do or spend your foodie dollars on. I recommend doing this with adults - or children who would appreciate something like this. This is a perfect activity to do at the hotel on a rainy day, feel like a princess, or if you want to just relax and have some chill time and sweets. I also recommend doing this if you have a longer Disney stay (around 5-7+ days). They offer chocolate-covered strawberries, swan-shaped profiteroles (so pretty to look at), and macaroons to name a few with tea sandwiches.

Narcoossee's

This fine-dining option available for dinner only at the Grand Floridian resort is a recommended option for seafood. If you want upscale Florida, this is it.

Menu standouts are shrimp and grits, calamari, crab cakes, and lobster bisque. Any of their seafood entrees are winners. Guests love the surf & turf options that allow for upgrades and multiple options on the steaks (like you could do sirloin or upgrade to a fillet) or choice between salmon, shrimp, lobster tail, and more.

They're also one of the few places that have succotash for any fans out there, or folks looking to try this southern delicacy.

The kid menu options are also flexible and well-priced for a fine dining option.

Victoria & Albert's

Victoria & Alberts is the ultimate fancy, upscale, dress-nice, reputable restaurant in Magic Kingdom® and Walt Disney World®. This is one of the few restaurants that actually require a dress code of slacks, dinner jackets, or cocktail dresses. Most people come here to propose, celebrate something very special, or just really want a fine dining experience.

This is also one of the dining experiences that is a tasting menu with courses. You can find items on here such as caviar, Alaskan King Crab, Kobe Beef, and quail to name a few.

You can expect usually an eight-course menu (inclusive of dessert).

This may break the bank depending on the size of your account, however, it is one of those "meals you won't forget" for a dining experience and usually accompanied with a memorable celebration.

If you've been to New Orleans, while they're not quite the same, this place reminds me of Commander's Palace.

The Enchanted Rose

Disney has been upping their cocktail game by adding lounges to resorts, like Trader Sam's at the Polynesian, and additional ones over by the Swan and Dolphin. The Enchanted Rose, is a bit more upscale than Trader Sam's, but the concept of a lounge addition is similar.

This lounge has more of your traditional finds: Old Fashions, Manhattans, etc. But I do encourage you to try their featured drinks. I'm a sucker for St. Germain, so naturally the *Floral Bitter Beauty* is my go-to. The *Island Rose* is also a gratifying drink. I thought it was a unique combination to mix pineapple and lime with rose. It gave a nice drop of elegance to already refreshing flavors.

If you do end up snacking here, I really like everything here. I am a fan of the mini brisket sliders topped with blue cheese. We already know my love for mac and cheese as I've stated it earlier in this book, but when you add crab and breadcrumbs? Sold. Throwing back a drink and taking mac and cheese to my room with sweatpants. Are you noticing a trend with me? Mac and cheese leads to sweatpants. I try to be inspirational.

And I was also pleasantly surprised by their flatbread.

Where this place really grabs your attention? The ambience. A location that is well lit with windows and you get drawn in by the giant chandelier in the center of the main room.

I feel like the kids get to have Cinderella's Table in the Magic Kingdom®, and this is the exclusive, refined version for grown-ups.

1900 Parkfare: *Actual Factual Magic* Do Not Miss!

For either meal option, we love this restaurant! Breakfast or dinner, when you tally up ambiance, food quality, characters, and service, you may be spending top dollar on a meal, but it checks all the boxes.

I can't say enough good things about food quality. I love coming here after walking off miles in the parks for dinner and enjoying their main entrees. All the different sides and options ensure there is something for everyone. For breakfast you'll find an assortment of baked goods, omelettes, bacon, sausages, yogurts, bagels, the list goes on. For dinner, salads, soups, roasted chicken, beef, and fish.

I have seen so many children get lost in the moment of meeting their favorite characters here. Mainly because many of the face characters are so real — from their looks, costumes, voice, all the way to how they interact with you. For children, it really brings these characters to life — and they do a great job staying in character and professional. I remember looking over and saw a sweet three-year-old girl dressed as Cinderella wanting to give Prince Charming a kiss on the cheek. Prince Charming politely declined the kiss of course, but held her hands and told her she was a lovely princess and that kiss is for *her* prince charming, that he was Cinderella's prince.

The restaurant reminds you of a fancy merry-go-round as there are horses everywhere, like in *Mary Poppins*. Once you're in, you can start with your meal or wait for the closest character to come by to say hello. Depending on breakfast or dinner, characters could be Alice in Wonderland, Marry Poppins, or Cinderella and Prince charming.

Just like O'hana, this is one you want to set the calendar alert in advance to ensure you get to dine here.

The Contemporary Resort

The first stop on the monorail when departing the Magic Kingdom® is the Contemporary Resort. It's comprised of the main building and the Bay Lake Towers. A modern slanted structure with lots of windows, the monorail floats through the resort. It's starting to get some major renovations as when it was first built, what was once contemporary, is now considered nearly vintage: Think purple, yellow, red, and orange patterned carpeting in the original decor. Anyways, it's a short ride (or walk) from the Magic Kingdom® and it's nice to get a break from the park as we have some highly recommended dining selections here. This place offers a balance of great food for family and kids, as well as some adult fancy dining with a view.

Chef Mickey's

At Chef Mickey's — Everyone is a kid. Both for breakfast or dinner, Chef Mickey's is an all-you-can-care-to-enjoy style of American-new dishes (formerly a buffet). This place is so kid-friendly — from menu items, to characters, to entertainment.

This place is a long-time Disney favorite. I am well into my adulthood but this was a place I would frequent in my childhood. The atmosphere is bright and fun, in the center of the Contemporary Resort. Watch the monorail cars pass through the open air as you wait for your table or wait for a character to arrive.

This place has a really solid family-style with many favorites: Carved meat, pasta, soups, salads, and a dessert bar that is sure to leave you wanting a little bit of everything. You really come here though for the characters. This is my "fast pass" to see all the characters in the Mickey crew. So you're paying top dollar for access to Mickey, Minnie, Goofy, Donald, etc. There's also a lot of sing-a-longs and games over the PA system depending on the evening. Regardless, it's a good time and a great way to get your kids with characters in one spot, over a meal, vs in the long park lines. I want to be real with you, it's very kid-forward ambience with songs and entertainment, but I'll suffer through the kid songs for a great meal.

If you are here with kids: there's a lot of Disney magic with the characters to be had here. I feel like tho there are many tables for the characters to visit, I always found myself smiling ear-to-ear with the quality of time the characters would spend with us during dinner — something you may not get at the parks. Whether it's Goofy making faces that instantly put smiles on faces, or Mickey coming around to give hugs, this place can't be beaten.

They're also very detail-oriented and bring special care when it comes to birthdays here. I strongly recommend that if you're in Disney World celebrating a kid's birthday, this is the place to do it. Over the sound system, and napkins twirling in the air, the whole crew will wish your child a happy birthday and everyone will know it.

What I loved most? This place gave a sense of community. If it was someone's birthday or there was some kind of interaction here, strangers would come up wishing folks a happy birthday, or congratulations if they recently got married.

Overall, a must-do for kids— especially with children or for a birthday celebration.

California Grill: *Actual Factual Magic* Do Not Miss!

This is another dinner-only, upscale dining option in the Magic Kingdom® Resort area. Found atop the Contemporary Resort with lovely views of Bay Lake, you can enjoy lots of fresh, clean, and prime favorites here:

From sushi, artisanal wood-fire pizza, truffle-goat cheese ravioli, and braised short rib wontons to name a few favorite appetizers.

They have so many stand-out entrees here including the grouper, jumbo scallops, short rib, and steaks.

Honestly, you can't really go wrong here. It's been around for several years and continues to deliver any time I have visited.

For wine lovers, they have a lot of California Sonoma and Napa favorites. While it is the "California Grill" it wouldn't be complete without the California wine pairings. So be sure to sample their vineyard favorites.

The Wilderness Lodge Resort

The drive into the Wilderness Lodge Resort is a long road lined with tall trees, making you feel like you're traveling through uncharted woodlands. This hotel is a salute to the wild west. You walk in and you have Native American totem poles, you have log cabin vibes, and you're surrounded by nature. I love going through the lobby and to the back where you see the walking paths and small creeks. What I love most? You will find wild turkeys roaming around. It's so neat! You'll be on your way to the pool, or grab a coffee and the next thing you know you're crossing paths with a wild turkey. I love the details like that. While you are in the USA, this hotel doesn't have as many dining options but tell you what, they are fun dining options with good food.

Whispering Canyon Cafe - *Actual Factual Magic* Do Not Miss!

Whispering Canyon Cafe is a family favorite of ours for many reasons:

First, the food, though pretty familiar, you always know what you're getting and it's always hot and fresh. This place is always fun and the hosts are always in character. They're fun and love to playfully troll diners in a Disney way: For example, my brother showed up wearing his favorite basketball jersey, Michael Jordan. So they kept referring to him as Michael Jordan throughout the entire meal. So if you wear sports attire, don't be surprised if you're addressed by the person on the back of your jersey throughout your entire meal. Or, they asked my friend, "What does she like to do in her free time?" and they said, "She's an artist and loves to draw." Our waitress brought me crayons and a coloring book from the kid's table. Some family-friendly, professional trolling here.

They also love when guests ask for ketchup. If you ask for ketchup be prepared for lots of shouting and a large donation of ketchup brought to your table. In fact, I dare you to ask for ketchup.

In this wild west-themed restaurant, they have an all you care to share option for family-style dining, or you can order a la carte.
They're open for breakfast lunch and dinner and are right in the main lobby of the Wilderness Lodge.

I have yet to have my family order from the a la carte in the 30+ years we have been coming here. The family-style always seems to have something for everyone and can please pretty much everyone in the crowd. They have many of the breakfast staples: Eggs, bacon, waffles, sausage, and my personal favorites: their biscuits and gravy. I came here after doing the *Star Wars* Half Marathon. Let me tell you, after burning all those calories, those biscuits and gravy were pure Disney magic.

If you find yourself here for lunch or dinner, be sure to try their ribs — they are doused in BBQ sauce. It's messy and so good. I tend to lean on this place more for breakfast, but know you'll have a very filling dinner here as well.

Geyser Point: Wilderness Lodge

I love to guide people to this casual, outdoor grill. It's a bit off the beaten path, not in the main building, and it's just a very calming atmosphere. It may make you feel like you're visiting a family or friend's cabin in the midwest with a peaceful lakefront with the timber trees.

The food here is solid — Whether you get a fresh salad with salmon or one of their grilled burgers, chicken wings, the food here won't disappoint you. I like to guide people here tho, for the drinks. It's a little oasis to come grab a cocktail, have great service, kick back, and relax. Depending on the time and which park has its night show, you may be able to sneak some firework views here without huge crowds. I'll admit, as the trees get taller sometimes the firework views are a bit obstructed, but you can still see a little bit of the glitter in the sky.

Disney's Animal Kingdom® Dining

The nice thing about Animal Kingdom, while they do have the staple quick-service options — ice cream, chicken nuggets, burgers, they have a lot of food you won't find in other parks because it is very inclusive of different cultures in the regions and their flavor profiles. So yes, if you have some picky eaters in your party, you'll still find things for everyone here, but, take advantage of snacking through this park. I would say Animal Kingdom® and Epcot® give you visas to eat around the world and try food and various flavor profiles, you may not normally get to try depending on where you're from, upbringing, or where you have traveled to.

Animal Kingdom® contrasts to Epcot® in a few ways: Yes, Epcot® has several countries in World Showcase to sample lots of amazing food and cuisines, but Epcot® has very little African flavors, no Indian flavors. Epcot® does have some Asian countries (Japan and China), you get to try additional flavor profiles like Nepalese and Indian in Animal Kingdom®.

I feel like these two parks balance provide balance to the growing flavors Disney is offering. So for those of you with worldly-curious pallets, you can enjoy different profiles with each park in different ways.

Another little surprise with Disney's Animal Kingdom® — I feel like it is the unsung hero of some pretty awesome drinks in Disney. Over recent years, Disney as a whole has upped their alcoholic beverage game, but we're proud to highlight some nice spots to grab a drink in the parks that go beyond your usual bottle beers or well drinks.

Best of Disney's Animal Kingdom® Quick-Service:

Dawa Bar

Let me tell you something, it is easy to spend a lot of money in this little hut-bar. And I'll tell you exactly why. Gentle reader, come learn how to spend a lot of money at this little corner bar:

First, their drinks are some of the best I've had at any Disney Park. I had a two hour wait between my Fast-Pass for Pandora and had to find a way to pass the time, because there was a long wait everywhere, I was tired of waiting in line.

My all-time favorite recommendation here is their *Jungle Juice* — and no, scratch the thought of whatever you drank from college basement. This is, legit and delicious. I don't know what is in the jungle juice, but beware of the schnapps and vodka…they ambush you.

The Lost on Safari drink is also really a nice option on a hot day, and for those who are like "I want a Long Island" they have twist on that here too.

Dawa Bar also has some craft beers as well as some decent wines. It's a win all around and a great way to wait out rain, or a two hour wait for Pandora. That being said….

Conveniently, there is the popcorn stand across from this bar. So to make sure you don't get drunk off your Disney-loving-behind, be sure to get some snacks from across the way if you're going to camp here like I did and wait for a Pandora ride, while watching the Cast Members do some acrobatics. Or, the Harambe Fruit Market is a short walk too. So be sure you don't put yourself in a situation where you could get escorted out of the park due to having too much of a good time waiting out the Pandora lines if you camp out at this little treasure.

Harambe Fruit Market: *Actual Factual Magic* Do Not Miss!

So this place is perhaps not like the typical recommendation because it's mostly fresh fruit, but ya know what? There's something really nice to just grab a freshly roasted ear of corn, dipped in butter, spices, and have a gentle stroll, or a break. It's just a nice pause from chicken tenders. It's always fresh, and they make it kind of fun. It's like a mini farmer's market to grab some corn and enjoy. For a break from the fried fun, enjoy this little bite here. No other parks have this so eat your healthy-foodie heart out. Plus, the way they prepare the ear of corn with the husk pulled back makes for a nice photo.

Tamu Tamu Refreshments

Each park has some variation of this stand, but this is your *Pineapple Dole Whip* stand. So if you want the legendary *Pineapple Dole Whip* cup, cone, float, or with an alcoholic runner, this is your stand to get it and that's why it makes the list.

Pongu Pongu

This little stand in some ways seems like its small menu is random, and it kind of is when you think about it, but it's got that nice mix of yummy bites that make a foodie happy and also has some fun twists to drink. Found in Pandora, you can either grab a sausage biscuit (yum) or french toast sticks for breakfast.

They also have a sweet lumpia (Filipino spring roll) filled with cream cheese and pineapple. You can get it at any meal period and you should. Flakey dough filled with gooey cream cheese? Ok!

Finally, this place wins the little social media foodie fun because they have some pretty imaginative beverages here that really play into the sci-fi Pandora scenery. Kudos to whoever came up with this concept because it's pretty creative. Let me share:

Their mixed drinks all have boba balls, so if you have a hankering for boba tea, this is a good way to satisfy that craving. They have the *Rum Blossom* (rum, apple, pear) and *Mo'ara Margarita* (tequila and lime) and both have boba balls. I didn't particularly prefer one over the other, other than tequila is not usually a long-term friend. But if you need a break from actual alcohol or the kiddos want one too because they are tasty and look cool, they have an alcohol-free one: the night blossom which is basically like the rum blossom, minus the rum. They do have a lot of sugar, FYI. This is very much drinking your dessert. However, if dad wants a hearty beer and none of this frozen-slushy-like object with boba, no worries. They have some ales readily available too and a pretzel with beer—cheese dip.

Restaurantosaurus

If you notice a trend, I like to recommend places with hot dogs, but like *good* hot dogs. And Disney does a great job with that. This place has your typical American fare: hot dogs, burgers, and chicken nuggets. In addition to the usual suspects, they also have a really nice Cobb salad (I came to Disney on a diet once. It didn't last long, but I nonetheless, I enjoyed my Cobb salad here), and they also have fried shrimp.

For those of you who haven't had a footlong hotdog yet either, this is another stop on your Disney foodie itinerary to enjoy one. You can find this in Dinoland USA. This section of the park is really for the kiddos, so if you find yourself dining here because you can't pry your dino-loving-kiddo away from fossils, know that you can still enjoy this quick-service establishment.

The Smiling Crocodile

This little stand is by Discovery Island and the main ingredient is pulled pork. You can get pulled pork tamales, tacos, or — get this — a pulled pork sandwich but the buns are jelly donut cut in half with some slaw. Yes, you read that correctly. You either love it or you hate it tends to be the consensus, but most adventurous bellies will pay the $6.99 to see if they do. While I have had fried chicken sandwiches with glazed donut buns, this is a new one for me. I am not sure I would order it again, but there are folks out there, who *love* this dish. I like the concept and I like that you can't really get this anywhere else. I mean, it's pulled pork and a donut. I personally would recommend ordering it without the slaw or on the side.

But for all the foodies who want to try the unique food options that Disney offers, be sure to try this. It is very filling, I don't even want to know the calories, so maybe share with one of the kids or your significant other.

Mr. Kamal

Between the walkway that bridges Africa and Asia together in the back of the park, is Mr. Kamal. This is a little snack station that has been previously known for samosas. Recently, they have on their menu seasoned french fries, hummus, and falafel.

Currently, they have seasoned fries (I don't know the exact flavoring, but I feel like it's a mixture of salt, pepper, and then perhaps paprika or a red pepper spice). I could be wrong, but they're seasoned and that's all they tell us. They're then topped with tzatziki (cucumber yogurt sauce) and sriracha. Being Greek, I have never seen sriracha paired with tzatziki, so the pairing is a little odd to me, but I'll admit the heat from the fries and sriracha complements the cool cucumber sauce. We'll call this fusion. I'm more of a hummus and veggie kind of lady when it comes to their menu, but if you're open to trying something different, this could be something you may like.

It's grown to become a little snack-foodie favorite amongst park-goers.

Flame Tree Barbecue

So you want BBQ? Good. This place is legit and right at the center of the park — Discovery Island.

I have a soft spot for BBQ and when you want something that is quick, delicious, and comforting, this is a favored spot to eat. One of the things I like most about Flame Tree Barbecue is you can get combos. I can honestly never really decide between just one food item, so the fact this place offers combo plates allows you to sample a bit more of the menu.

This place is a solid option for ribs. They have St. Louis ribs or you can get a half chicken….or do what I do and get the combo so you can enjoy both. If the Smiling Crocodile is too adventurous with a pulled pork and jelly donut, you can certainly enjoy a sweet and smokey pulled pork here with a traditional bun.

They also have mac and cheese topped with pulled pork here as an entree. My foodie tip is to order it as a side to share. It's super filling, you won't have sweat pants nor a couch nearby, so you may as well enjoy it but in a smaller portion that can easily be achieved by sharing it.

For those who are vegetarian, fear not. They have a plant-based options here for you too.

Yak & Yeti Local Food Cafes

I usually urge people to enjoy the sit-down restaurant Yak & Yeti but perhaps you don't have the time or you've done too many table-service options for the day. Lucky you, they have a quick-service option too.

I like that they have all three meal periods here: If you want a breakfast bowl with eggs and potatoes, an English muffin, or fruit salad, this place has some decent quick-service foods.

For later in the day, you can enjoy sweet and sour shrimp tempura, a Korean fried chicken sandwich, A Kobe cheeseburger, tikka masala, or a honey chicken stir fry. **Tip!** The fried rice portion is quite large and inexpensive. I recommend getting it for it being filling, tasty, and frugal.

For quick-service, it's a fan favorite for this park. My personal choices from the list are the Korean fried chicken sandwich and the shrimp tempura. Don't forget to enjoy the mango pie.

Disney's Animal Kingdom® Table-Service Favorites:

Animal Kingdom doesn't have too many sit-down options, similar to the other parks. Plenty of great grab-and-go, or "stroll and dine" as I like to call it. But if you go for table-service here, be sure to check out our favorite establishments.

Tusker House: *Actual Factual Magic* Do Not Miss!

A little background story: My brothers and I overslept during one of our Disney visits (hey, every once in a while you need a break from the 7 am running to the parks, early chaos, and need to sleep). So we basically slept through breakfast. We were arriving at the park at about 10:30 AM. Not that there weren't going to be food options, Disney always makes sure there is food available, but, on that particular day we had a croissant and a coffee to hold us over until we were awake enough to consume real food. We had done drink-around-the-world at Epcot the night before. We've all been there. And if you haven't, you'll see.

Anyways! The point of the story is, a casual family-style option that is perfect to cure any World Showcase hangover. Though the menus are not entirely the same, there is some slight menu and flavor overlap with Boma (I'll get to this restaurant later), and I consider them close cousins.

My absolute favorite in this park is Tusker House for lunch or dinner.

To start, I enjoyed the chutney and hummus dips. The dips are sweet and hints of spices carry through. The hummus is creamy and refreshing on any hot day. The tabouli was also revitalizing and complimented the dips. They have a wide variety here. I opted and most enjoyed the spit-roasted chicken as well as the roasted pork.

Be sure to finish with some bread pudding. If you're here for a casual meal with the kiddos, they do have kid selections too. I might have snuck a chicken nugget or two on my grown-up plate for myself.

A casual family-style spot with great food to fill up on before wandering through the parks or catching a parade.

Yak & Yeti Restaurant:

This place makes me happy. My belly treats this place like it's a buffet, and my wallet wishes it were a buffet because I always spend too much money here — but it's worth it. Note: It's not a buffet, I just want it all. This is a place for anyone who just loves Asian flavors. I strongly recommend going with a group or if you're attending as a couple, basically, just share everything and make your own mini-buffet at the table. There are so many solid menu items that it's super easy to make your own dim sum.

All the small plates are a treat: the potstickers, egg rolls, firecracker shrimp, and the fried green beans. I love that the options have a light fry and get dunked in a sauce that balances the flavors.

Apparently, the Korean fried chicken and the ahi-tuna nachos are "meant for two" but this 5'3" woman can probably decimate each of them alone — especially the Korean fried chicken. I almost always get each of the small plates and then 1-2 shareable dishes when I come here, depending on how many people are dining with me.

Some entree favorites of mine are the *Miso Salmon*, *Bhaktapur Duck* (one of the few places in Disney to get duck), *Coconut Shrimp, Honey Chicken*, and *Korean Beef* from the wok.

If you somehow have room for dessert — check out the fried wontons with pineapple and ice cream. From a value standpoint, while it's not inexpensive, you can do well here. If you find yourself enjoying this place, it's easy to go from a moderate spend to "whoops, but I'm full."

Tiffins & Nomad Lounge: *Actual Factual Magic Do Not Miss!*

Tiffin's is a favorite for casual table-service dining with some good eats. For those looking for something a little more refined in the park, look no further than Tiffins.

Some menu favorites are their bread dish appetizer — their ginger and pear chutney is just a friendly welcome to the tastebuds.

This place has some incredible main courses that have a lot of Indian and African flavor profiles. You can enjoy their butter chicken for something comforting and warm: I was in Disney during the winter months. It was a little brisk and this warm bowl of comfort put a smile on my tummy.

Their surf and turf of African spiced tenderloin and scallops do not disappoint and are a nice twist to the traditional seared-style. Or, you may enjoy their tamarind-braised short rib.

They're most known for, or guests are regularly impressed by, their whole-fried fish. The fish is not only fun to look at, but a real treat and wonderful to enjoy. Social media lovers, this is a fish to brag about. Get your smartphones ready for pictures.

This place does justice to any vegetarians in your party: From appetizer-friendly options to the African-spiced tofu with tomato chutney.

If you're looking for a drink, and perhaps are short on time, or can't commit to a full meal, wander over to the Nomad Lounge and leverage Tiffins' menu. I find that Disney has been very intentional with adding lounges to the entire resort and I'm okay with that.

Disney's Animal Kingdom® Resort Dining

This resort is such a wonder. When they first announced they were going to open the lodge and their intention for it to have its own savannah, I couldn't wait for it to open. You literally can stay here, look out your window, and see giraffes. Growing up in the midwest, we don't have giraffes. We just have squirrels and raccoons. I mean, it's surreal. It's magic. It's so peaceful to just sit back and see these darling creatures walk around, snack, or care for each other. If you stay here, you can wake up to this during your entire stay. I find people that stay here, always come back to spend at least one night here on future trips — just to experience this again and again.

Whenever I come here to dine, I always come early to just stare at the animals. It's pleasant and part of the experience. If you have a 30 min wait for a table, suddenly it doesn't matter while you just watch the giraffes. I highly recommend staying at this resort or at the very least, making a trip here. The food is outstanding and they have adorable animals. What more could you ask for?

Boma: *Flavors of Africa - Actual Factual Magic* Do Not Miss!

This is a personal favorite of mine. I've never been to Africa and hope to go someday. Until that day comes, I always make a stop to go to the Animal Kingdom Lodge for dinner. In case you don't make it to the Animal Kingdom Park for any reason, this is a great way to enjoy the surrounding area and food.

We try to go just before the sun goes down to still see the giraffes walk around the grounds — truly a magnificent sight to see. Or, you can go for a nice long walk to walk off the full belly.

Once you get a chance to wander through the lodge grounds, you can enjoy flavors of African cuisine at Boma. It's a family-style/buffet restaurant enabling you to fill-up before your off to see the fireworks.

The menu here rotates. Before 2020, it was a buffet, but it is now family-style, and may flip between each, so keep that in mind. I got to sample the seafood gumbo and the chicken-corn chowder. Both were excellent and flavorful. The chicken-corn chowder was exceptionally comforting. The broth was nice and thick, stuck to my stomach in the best way possible. I intended to only have one serving of it, however, once my partner dug his way into my bowl, three bowls later we had to tell ourselves "now, now, there is so much more to eat here." But that just gives an idea of how good it was. We had to leverage self restraint and I'm still not sure we did a good job of that.

I sampled the couscous salad along with a few other sides such as the mashed potatoes and even the spiced sweet potatoes (I loved these — a must try if they are available).

From the meats, we enjoyed the roasted salmon and the pork. They had a beef option as well that my partner had seconds of. All meat options were cooked to perfection and flavorful. We prefer our beef more on the rare/medium-rare side but if you are looking for more of a well-done option, they can get you a cut like what you are looking for when it's your turn in line. The carving station is where it's at and you should absolutely try the various sauces to complement your juicy cut.

We finished up at the pastry station. They have several mini cakes and chocolates. We loved the guava cake but I was fond of the mini chocolate cakes with white chocolate drizzle. They reminded me of zebras. I'm hesitant to call them zebra cakes, but if you see something like that, go for it. You'll know what I mean.

Overall, a great spot to try out African flavors if you don't make it to the park. Or perhaps, you loved what you had in Animal Kingdom you wanted similar flavors at one of the resorts.

Disney's Hollywood Studios® Dining

Hollywood Studios is like the rest of the theme parks in the sense of a greater quick-service ratio to table-service. I'd say Hollywood Studios isn't known for its food scene but that doesn't mean some great food can't be found here. In my opinion, Hollywood Studios has some good food undercover.

As you enjoy your time at the parks, you may want the best of both worlds if you're going to "not leave till they kick us out" and want to be sure you can maximize your day. My hope is with some guidance on what is in the park, you will find you don't have to leave if you don't want to and can find some bites and relax.

Or, if you want to linger in the area, the following sections will list Epcot® & Hollywood Studio Resort area dining options.

But for now, let's stick to the park and all the good eats (and drinks) they have inside.

Quick-Service Favorites at Disney's Hollywood Studios®

ABC Commissary

Hollywood Studios has a handful of quick-eat options. They all tend to vary by stand, ever-so-slightly. My all-time quick bite favorite in the park is the ABC Commissary. Their options are a little more widespread, it's a large venue, and they have anywhere from mediterranean salads to BBQ.

Our favorites were the ribs and chicken. We're not veg-heads but we felt like we needed 'a vegetable' that day so we got the mediterranean salad with hummus, feta, and olives. We were very impressed by their in-park vegetarian option. If you need a quick bite in the park, this is my usual stop.

Baseline Tap House

Behold! A bar in the middle of Hollywood Studios! We found ourselves exhausted, wanting a break from the action, and just wanted to decompress. Hey, kids need a *Capri Sun*, adults usually want booze. This is clearly something Disney is understanding of.

Baseline Tap, tho the impression it is a brewhouse, also offers more than that. I am not much of a beer person but prefer a good cocktail. My favorite on the menu was their *Wild Strawberry Lemonade*. Since that was a non-alcoholic option, we asked them to throw in some Grey Goose and suddenly, we have a refreshing adult beverage.

Service here is great — as the bartenders are always happy to chat. In fact, I can't say enough good things about the staff here. They know how to mix a drink and are just some of the friendliest bunch. Heck, I'm an introvert and enjoyed chatting away with the staff here. It's a grown-up oasis for those in the park.

Woody's Lunch Box

When you're greeted by the giant toy arch at Toy Story Land, upon entry, and with a shy left, you'll find Woody's Lunch Box.

This is another quick-service favorite and it's a play on "packed lunches." While you can get some familiar sandwiches like turkey, brisket, or grilled cheese, I feel like some of their "snack objects" are the foodie heroes of this little nook in the park.

I'm not sure if it's the pastry tarts. OK, it's for sure the pastry tarts. They're a lovely, flakey pop-tart-like-object for breakfast filled with jam.

My favorite thing to do? I just really enjoy grabbing a beer or an adult lemonade and chowing down on some *totchos*. What is a *totcho*? Let me teach you the way: They are if a tater-tot and a nacho got together and had a baby, you'd get tots, covered with chili, cheese, sour cream, and green onion. Thus, *totchos*. I suggest a fork.
Also, side note: They sell mini Babybel cheese wheels. That is important to completing any modern-day packed lunch.

If you're here for breakfast, be sure to try the breakfast bowl. It's tater tots covered with sausage gravy (like biscuits and gravy) with cheese and scallions.

One thing I appreciate about this place - Disney as a whole is very very very allergy and diet-friendly, but I feel like this place goes above and beyond in their menu offerings to accommodate people beyond the common dietary needs.

Backlot Express

I love coming here for a quick lunch. It's got mostly American fare here: Burgers, fries, but I feel like, it's a little more done-up.

I enjoy their *Backlot Burger*. It's a nice big ol' juicy burger with pulled pork, pepper jack cheese, tomato, and pickle. It's just delicious and food-coma-worthy.

Also, I love that they not only have chicken tenders, but with biscuits and gravy. It just kind of changes up the usual items of burgers and tenders. They add a twist to it which is why it makes the list.

The other two favorable options are their *California Club* and their *Cuban sandwiches*. The grilled chicken sandwich is a lighter option if you're aiming for something on the healthier side.

I don't know of any other spot in Walt Disney World® that offers a *Cuban sandwich* so if you have yet to try one, or have a hankering for one, this place offers one. They are even mindful of serving it on the flatbread vs. a regular bun. Be sure to also get a BB-8 souvenir cup here.

Ronto Roasters

One quick bite I enjoyed in Galaxy's Edge was Ronto Roasters. Judging by the name, initially, I thought it was a coffee spot. The item they serve here is a grilled and roasted sausage in a pita topped with slaw. They also have a plantain chip sampler.

It was a nice little snack spot for the "I'm a little hungry, but not starving."

Hollywood Scoops

Sure you can get ice cream at any old stand. The theme parks are known for the Mickey ice creams, fruit bars, etc. But, if you want more of a classic feel from a 1950's California-beach-themed stand, complete with striped awning, this is the place to go.

Even their type-font on their menu screams classic Hollywood nostalgia. It's right off the main strip as you veer close to the Hollywood Tower of Terror. It's like you time traveled to a 1950s ice cream shop on Hollywood Boulevard.

They advertised old-fashioned, hand-scooped ice cream. This reminds me of another recommendation in the Epcot/Hollywood Studio's Resort section (The Fountain).

Menu favorites are the *Brownie Sundae* - but let's be real, who wouldn't enjoy a brownie sundae? I have also tried their *Apple Crisp a La Mode* which is another favorite to enjoy in the autumn months.

Last but not least, for those who want to race against the heat, they also offer a delightful ice cream cookie sandwich. It's quite nice, I just encourage you to eat it quickly in the 85+ degrees Floridian humidity or the result is you end up wearing it.

Quick note: This is close to the Hollywood Tower of Terror. I recommend you get ice cream *after* bouncing around the Tower of Terror, not before. Think of that as a courtesy for you and your fellow riders.

Rosie's All-American Cafe

Ok so by now you've probably figured out that if a restaurant offers a foot-long hot dog, I'm recommending it, right? Right. This is off the main strip, Sunset Boulevard, and I swear, the details Disney has when it comes to even naming places that sound "California" is so on point. Like, I think "Oh yeah, a place named Rosie's sounds about right to be a Californian cafe."

Anyways — just as it sounds, this has your typical American staples: Chicken nuggets, burgers, and hot dogs. I would say this is similar to Casey's at the Magic Kingdom®. You can get a delicious foot-long hot dog, covered in chili cheese. Perfect for anyone who wants to feel like Sonic the Hedgehog (yes, I acknowledge Sonic is not a Disney character, but I am also a nerd like most of you reading this book and know chili cheese dogs are his favorite food).

For those aiming for something healthier, Rosie's also offers a pretty interesting salad: I think they're going for a mix of southern and northern California flavors. It has mojo pulled pork, with roasted sweet potatoes, radishes, pumpkin seeds with a spicy ranch dressing.

In all, this is a favorite quick-service option loved by many.

Oga's Cantina

In Galaxy's Edge, you can find the legendary bar that has been brought to life from the *Star Wars* films. It was pretty neat to see something you saw on the big screen in a living reality. You feel like you're on the set, or immersed in *Star Wars*. I gotta hand it to Hollywood Studios - the purpose of the park is to showcase movie magic. Well done, Imagineers. Well, done.

This is one of the newer dining options in Hollywood Studios. I think in some ways, things are still being refined. What you can appreciate here is the ambiance and the ability to be "in the bar from the Star Wars films" and the creativity around the menu to bring some of the galactic ingredients to life.

The neat thing about this bar — it's also for all ages. So you don't have to worry about the kiddos getting bounced out or missing out on the fun. So think family-friendly lounge.

Favorites containing alcohol are the *Fuzzy Tauntaun*, a peach drink with foam. Another favorite is the *Jedi Mind Trick*. It has grapefruit, rose vodka, lime juice with Ketel One, were some of the memorable flavors.

My personal favorite was the *Cliff Dweller*: It is a non-alcoholic drink of citrus, hibiscus grenadine, and ginger ale. The best part? It comes in a Porg mug which is why it is the most expensive of the drinks (especially or it being non-alcoholic), but can we say Porg mug?

All in all, you may find more upscale drinks elsewhere in Disney, but you come here to appreciate the creativity and being immersed in the bar from the films.

Best of Table-Service: Hollywood Studios

Hollywood Brown Derby: *Actual Factual Magic* Do Not Miss!

Compared to all other food options in the park, Hollywood Brown Derby, in my opinion, offers some of the top food in the park. From their bisque or lump crab cake, or any of their entrees (all the meat cuts are fabulous but we especially love the short rib), it's high-quality food. They also have a lounge for grown-up drinks. What I appreciated most, was that this restaurant had great offerings for children. Most Disney restaurants have mac and cheese, a burger, chicken nuggets (the usual) for the kids. I loved that they also had grouper and grilled chicken breast - healthier and more gourmet-like options for kids at fair prices. Undeniably, the best sit-down dining experience in the park.

We recommend all their appetizers. None of them will let you down: sea scallops and pork belly, lobster bisque, tomato & burrata salad, shrimp cocktail, charcuterie, ahi tuna carpaccio — get a few and sample away!

Hollywood Brown Derby is more upscale American cuisine, so know they do a steak properly as well as roast a chicken and sear salmon. I found all their dishes to be fresh, clean, and well-balanced.

You don't have to break the bank here if you don't want to. They're well-known for their signature burger. It's $24 which is a lot of cash to drop on a burger, but it has a mountain of meat, pastrami, a fried egg, and a delightful cognac-mustard. For lighter bites be sure to try out their Cobb salad. That's my go-to here for lunch. Or, if you're looking for a light-bite option here or just to drink, be sure to hang out in the lounge area. It's a nice place to relax and catch your breath.

For dessert, I recommend trying their grapefruit sponge cake. No one else in Disney has anything like it and I'm a sucker for fruit. For those who want more of a chocolate option, their chocolate coconut cake is divine and rich.

Hollywood & Vine

Over by Echo Lake (look for a friendly dinosaur), this is one of the family-style (former buffet) options and the only place in Hollywood Studios with character dining. So for those of you who want to be waited on, entertain the kids with characters, and enjoy a good meal, and not leave the park, this is the spot for you.

For those of you with an early start at the parks, this is a really good option in the park for breakfast. The winning breakfast item to me is the *Hazelnut-spread French Toast with Bananas Foster*. If it has been a minute since you've been to Disney, they have Disney Junior characters during their breakfast hours. This option is perfect for dining with kids at the park. If you come as a couple, you may find yourself not fully aware of some of the characters and could possibly pay a premium for an experience geared more for families with small children. Regardless, the food here is solid and I have come here as a grown adult just to get their french toast.

For all ages and audiences, I highly recommend their dinner menu here (also the same as lunch). To be clear, this location is a buffet/family-style option.

One thing that stood out to me was the menu: As someone who has been to California many times, and especially Hollywood, there was a sense of familiarity in the menu that is appreciated.

Their entree options are really where I get hit with Hollywood-dining-nostalgia:

They have a filet of beef with chive-whipped mashed, and their spice-rub with BBQ pork tenderloin with peach chutney.

What takes the cake for me are the fresh salmon with the mustard-beurre blanc or their asparagus and truffle risotto. Where you start to see the fresh-American flavors with French and Italian culinary techniques. That, to me, tastes like Hollywood.

Their desserts are great too. I enjoyed the lemon cake with fresh strawberries or the spiced berry pie with coconut cream. The cherry pie is also bound to create some cheer when it arrives. I feel like no matter what your dietary needs are, this place is very enjoyable.

Mama Melrose's Ristorante Italiano

Melrose's is an Italian restaurant with elements of California and New York food scenes fused together in both cuisine and ambiance. This restaurant is recommended for table-dining for those who are looking for some rustic comfort favorites.

You'll find a lot of the usual Italian menu items done well here: Fried calamari, Caesar salad, or their Margherita flatbread for starters.

I'd say you also have something that can please pretty much anyone in your party here as well. If someone's not feeling pasta, you can get a big ol' strip steak.

They're most known for their Italian classics. The chicken parmigiana and the shrimp capanelle (angel hair pasta), stand out as my personal favorites. Honestly, our party found we really couldn't go wrong with anything here.

It reminded me of some of the Italian restaurants I found in California. You'd have an Italian grocery/deli counter up front, and a full Italian restaurant in the back complete with Christmas lights — just like this place. I think sometimes good dine-in food can be challenging at any theme park, but I feel like of the options offered Mama Melrose deserves a top three for overall quality, value, and service. While this place doesn't particularly have a deli upfront, the resemblance of the Italian restaurants you'd find tucked away in the back is uncanny.

Oh, by the way - make room for the tiramisu.

Epcot® Dining

As my pal Joe will say, Epcot® is really like two parks in one. In foodie-land, Epcot is the capital of cuisine in Walt Disney World®. Disney Springs® is a close second.

For those who love both Disney and food, Epcot's World Showcase gives you a mini-passport to try flavors from all over the globe. In this section, we'll share with you what to expect for dining options at Epcot® and our absolute must-dos. Much of the focus for this section will be on World Showcase, the back half of Epcot®. For now, let's quickly focus on the front-half of the park, Future World.

Future World:

In my opinion, you don't go to Future World (soon to be known as World Discovery, World Celebration, and World Nature) to have a life-changing foodie experience. While we're not going to actively guide you to dine at any of the options there, know if you're hungry, or you or someone in your party just isn't an adventurous eater — that's ok, Future World could be for you. Future World has more of your cheeseburgers, chicken tenders, fries. Seeing as this is the foodie section, we're going to make you aware of the food options at the front half of the park, and then we're going to skip on over to World Showcase because that is foodie nirvana.

If you're not an adventurous eater, I strongly encourage you to sample a few of the quick bites in World Showcase (you may be surprised and you can sample the world without having to travel to it), but, if you want the more familiar items for park dining, no worries, we've got you covered:

Sunshine Seasons (Quick-Service)

Ok, the front part of Epcot®, The Land to be specific, isn't really where the food is at — but if there was one place I would guide you to dine in, it would be Sunshine Seasons.

If you come here, get the juicy rotisserie chicken or the oak-grilled salmon. This place won't break the bank, so if you're budget conscious and looking for something that's not another chicken tender, this place is a good alternative.

What makes this place awesome tho and why I like to recommend it aside from being a budget-friendly option, if you go on "Living with the Land" ride, you're taken through to a greenhouse. The vegetables at Sunshine Seasons are from the greenhouse — pretty cool, right?

So, if you decide to have some tasty rotisserie chicken and dine here, you'll get to try garden vegetables from the attached Living with the Land ride.

World Showcase:

Hi. This is my favorite park to eat in. Don't get me wrong, I love so many restaurants in Disney but I float to foodie heaven once I pass through the entrance of World Showcase. I don't know where all 5'3" of me puts the unnatural caloric intake during my time in the World Showcase, but I find a way, and you will too. Just know, you will eat here. You will drink here. You will have so much to enjoy here. Be comfortable spending a little more than usual on food here. It's so hard for me to only do one day at Epcot® because of how good so much of the food is. My little foodie soul just has an out-of-body experience every time I come here because so much of the food is on point. And that's just during a regular day at Epcot®. Just wait until we get to Food and Wine Fest or the Flower and Garden sections.

World Showcase gives you the opportunity to be exposed to countries you may not have had a chance to visit. Or, perhaps you have visited and you want to relive those fond memories as Disney gives you silhouettes of so many nations. For many, this is your chance to try lots of new foods.

Ok. I'm excited. You should be excited too. This is without a doubt my favorite place in Disney. Some people come here to "drink around the world" I challenge you to "eat around the world" instead. Plus, you don't have to worry about that one person in your party (it could be you) that just can't handle more than four drinks and you get carried off away into the sunset because you need to recover in your hotel room from starting in Mexico with tequila.

I digress, this is the place to eat. Eat everything. Share everything with your party. Sample whatever you can (safely of course). If you're thinking you should "drink around the world," eat instead — or better yet, "sample around the world" and create your own little tasting menu.

From a foodie standpoint, almost every representing country has at least one sit-down restaurant and a counter-service option. Depending on the country, some have like five options. We'll get to that later. Unlike the rest of the foodie spots in the book (broken out by park, quick-service, counter-service, casual dining, fine dining), we divided this part of the book by country first, a description about each spot, and continue with the theme from there.

This is probably going to be the biggest section of the book for a park because there is so much to enjoy. With that all said, let's get started:

Mexico

La Cava del Tequila (Lounge)
Right so there is a lounge with tequila in Epcot and if you don't watch yourself, your trip to Epcot® will end early.

Inside the pyramid in Mexico World Showcase, down the stairs, you'll find little shopping stands and of course, tequila. It's impossible to come here and not find a bachelor or bachelorette party. Most people come here as their stop to drink around the world or pass the time while they wait for their dining reservation at San Angel Inn Restaurant which is towards the back of the interior of the pyramid.

If you go here, pace yourself. The tequila sneaks up on you and the drinks here are pretty smooth. I can't tell you exactly which drink would suit you best, but I went with the *Piña Loca* - or the crazy pineapple. It was a blend of sweet, spice, and salt. Just don't drink this before you go over to Test Track. Bad plan. Go on all the rides first, let your hair down, and then enjoy the tequila mixology.

Choza Margarita (Quick-Service)
You guessed it. Margaritas can be found here. In Mexico World Showcase along the lagoon is a Margarita Stand called Choza Margarita. They have margaritas of all types - classic on the rocks and frozen. I was a huge fan of the cucumber one option.

The frozen margaritas are also delicious but I found myself unable to finish them on my own — maybe I am just weak at drinking frozen margaritas, or they were just too much, sweeter than I'm used to — but if you find yourself splitting one with a friend, it's more manageable.

What I also like about here and why I am really recommending it… they have food. I basically leave with a drink in one hand, and then a small tray of empanadas, guac, and pulled pork tacos in the other. PS: They also have elotes (Mexican-style street corn) here.

I feel like when I go to Mexico, I gravitate more towards Choza Margarita and La Cantina for food. In my opinion the street food is where it's at in Mexico World Showcase.

La Cantina de San Angel (Table-Service)
Outside of the pyramid, overlooking the lagoon and near Choza Margarita, is the Catina de San Angel, the sister restaurant, of the that has more street-style, low-cost dining option. In my opinion, where the most value is. And oh, it overlooks the lagoon so if you end your day in Mexico, guess what — fireworks and tacos!

I usually can't make up my mind which taco to get and enjoy all of them. Therefore I recommend the trio of chicken, beef, and fish tacos. If I'm the one in line buying food, you bet I'm coming back with a tray of nachos to share, guac, and empanadas for the table - because sharing is caring.

One of the underrated items I like to get, that I haven't seen in too many spots, are fried plantains. I highly encourage you get a side of these to snack on and share.

Basically if you come to this spot, it's a good budget-friendly option to share with the group.

Norway
Akershus Royal Banquet Hall (Table-Service)
"For the first time in foreeeever"…is basically all I want to bust out and sing when I come here. An "all you care to enjoy" restaurant, complete with princesses (but oddly not the *Frozen* sisters - yet they can be found nearby), this enchanted dining hall wins the hearts of kids who are so excited to meet some of the most popular princesses around.

This is the cousin of Cinderella's Royal Table (in the Magic Kingdom). They're both character restaurants with your favorite Disney Princesses floating around.

They serve breakfast, lunch, and dinner.

Their breakfast is your usual suspects of eggs, sausage, bacon, along with a potato casserole. In addition to an American-style breakfast, they offer a Norwegian charcuterie plate of meats and cheeses. The assortment has salami, cured salmon, and a variety of cheeses.

Their lunch and dinner menus are basically the same, and you may find more value in coming here for lunch to save some cash, see some princesses, and a menu that offers more variety. I personally find lunch and dinner to be more enjoyable.

I feel like any Norwegian restaurant has to offer salmon, it's a staple ingredient. I like that of the salmon dishes I've had at Walt Disney World®, theirs has a nice smokiness to it. My personal favorite are the pork tenderloin (it has an apricot sauce that is just such a compliment to that cut of meat), and the herbed chicken. The chicken is likely the safest menu item for those uncertain of what to enjoy. They pair it with a sweet potato pudding which in my opinion, is a must try item.

In short, I recommend coming here for lunch if you can. If you are unable to get into Cinderella's Royal Table in the Magic Kingdom®, give this place a try. The menu items are quite different, but know that at both you'll get a good meal and Disney Princess encounters.

Kringla Bakeri Og Kafe (Counter-Service)

So, I usually don't write raving reviews for counter-service places unless some options in areas of the parks are limited. World Showcase has so many sit-down spots so why would I draft up a quick review here?

A few reasons: If you're drinking around the world, congrats, Nordic beer is found here and it's delish. If you're in Epcot® earlier in the day, you can get yourself a *Viking Coffee* and start your day with some Bailey's in your cup — a creative way to check this off on your worldly drinking adventure.

The fan favorite here is the *School Bread*, which is a little bun filled with custard and some toasted coconut. Think almost like a coconut-cream donut. Honestly, with Epcot, you can eat here for days and it's taken me several trips to be able to write this book. So if you are at Epcot for one day, grab one of these beauts to-go, or share with your family to 'snack' around the world.

My other favorites here are the *Lefse* (cinnamon roll-like-object) and the *Eplekake* (apple cake with caramel — I always enjoy grabbing one of these if I am visiting during the autumn or winters months).

China

Nine Dragons Restaurant (Table-Service)

I usually gravitate and steer people towards Disney Spring's Morimoto Asia for really good Asian cuisine. The two places are very different, but Nine Dragons has upped its game in recent times.

I've been coming to this spot since I was a kid and it's been good to see the recent menu evolution. They've begun to add more dim sum options as of late and I think that makes the menu more well-rounded. The lunch and dinner options are nearly similar. The restaurant is located on the left side of the entrance in World Showcase.

Favorites here are the pork belly buns and the potstickers. I may be little basic, but I'm a fan of the *Honey-Sesame Chicken* and the *Kung Pao Chicken* menu items.

The *Canton Pepper Beef* is worth a shot as well. It's similar to a pepper beef you'd find in your neighborhood Chinese restaurant. For those of you not afraid of heat - try the spicy *Mala Beef*. In my case, keep a Tums nearby but worth playing with fire. This reminded me of some of the items I found in my Chinatown.

For the price point - you may find it a little on the high side. It's the upscale dining option in China World Showcase and the recent menu changes are striving to prove value. The service here is good and the waitstaff is wonderful. The food is much improved and has inclined over the years.

I think one of the things I've found here, it will satisfy a craving for Chinese food, but it's a little steep on price. Back at home, you're likely paying closer to $10-14 per Chinese dish (on average, I get it varies depending on the city you're from), whereas here it's closer to $20-$25 per dish.

Overall, I recommend coming here to give it a a try if you haven't sampled the new menu.

Lotus Blossom Cafe (Counter-Service)
The quick dining option in China is the Lotus Blossom Cafe. Just past Nine Dragons on the left side of the main entrance, you'll find the Lotus Blossom Cafe. The menu is short with three main options of *Orange Chicken, Mongolian Beef,* and *Chicken Fried Rice.*

The hidden gems in this spot in, my opinion are the ice creams: caramel-ginger and the lychee ice cream. Both are unique, flavorful, and hard to find anywhere else.

Germany
Biergarten: *Actual Factual Magic* Do Not Miss!
(Table-Service & Musical Experience)
When I was in high school, I got to go on a choir trip to Germany. I got to see so many lovely sights in Bavaria such as Oberammergau. Many of the small towns were painted white with a dark wood frame and hand-painted signs along the cobbled streets. It's always fun to re-live those moments every time I'm in Germany in World Showcase. They really set the stage on what Bavaria is like — with the Disney magic of course. You walk this similar path as you find your way to the Biergarten Restaurant that is tucked in the far back of Germany.

There's a lot of things to love about this place:

Brautwurst — Sommerfest — Epcot

First, everyone is dressed in traditional German clothing: So lederhosen all around! Also, many of the employees are college students doing a study abroad in America. It's a fun way to actually connect with people from Germany if you take a moment to speak with the waitstaff and learn about them. And if *spreken zie Deutch*, they'll practice with you.

Second, it's a party and they make it so: They have live music performers that are exceptionally talented. They perform frequently enough where each seating should allow you to catch at minimum one song. You'll hear classics like *Edelweiss* along with some polkas. And yes, if you want to dance, they have a dance floor and invite people to come up and dance. I have yet to be at a dining experience here where no one has danced.

Third, the drink menu:

I repeat: I was in high school when I went to Germany, and therefore was on high school rules when I went. That meant, no drinking even though I was technically of legal drinking age in Germany.

Fret not for those who went to Germany underaged as I once did, or perhaps you haven't been at all — but Biergarten lives up to its name and you can make up for lost time. Of course, they have your American beer staples on the menu, but please divulge in trying some German imports with a boot or a stein glass.

Now I'm not saying get hammered, this is Disney after all, but if you wanted to ever experience your own mini-Oktoberfest, this is your chance to do it.

Lastly, tho it could easily be the first reason why I love this place, the food:

It's a casual family-style/former buffet menu that hasn't changed in the 30+ years I've been going to Disney and that is totally fine by me. The food is so good, and lives up to the food I had in Germany back in high school, I crave it once I start wandering through Epcot®.

You can start with a cucumber dill salad, tomato salad, warm pretzel bread, carrot salad, and work your way through my favorites: I love their roasted chicken here as well as their pork cutlets. I also tend to go for their sausage links and sauerkraut. Perfectly juicy links with pleasantly bitter sauerkraut to compliment them — you must try these items!

Don't forget to save some room for dessert. You can get a few different varieties of sweet treats but I tend to go with the two German staples: A slice of apple strudel and two pieces of black forest cake because one slice is never enough.

If you're looking for a fun date night or a place to liven up your Epcot®, look no further. You have German polka, beer, and exceptional food. Great as a couple for a casual date in the park or with the whole group. Sorry kids, if you're underage here, you can eat and enjoy the music but you have to come back when you're older for the beer boot.

Sommerfest (Counter-Service)
No time to sit and dine? Grab a brat, sauerkraut, and beer to go right next to the entrance to the Oktoberfest restaurant. It's a convenient option if the wait is too long and you want to have a tasting of the food in Germany. When I went to Germany in 2018, you'd find stands similar to this one (minus the lederhosen) all over the cities. You could walk up, grab a brat and have a snack to go — especially around the holidays at the marts. If you have time to enjoy the fun inside, I recommend it. If not, you wouldn't be disappointed with the brats here.

Italy
I feel like Italy at Epcot® does a really good job providing guests with the ability to really sample the staple food items that Italy has to offer. I really enjoyed the atmosphere as well — from the mini Fountain of Trevi, to the patio dining. Italian cities are known for their plazas. Alfresco dining is very common in Italy. For an authentic Italian experience, try to dine outside as you would in if you were actually in an Italian plaza.

Tutto Gusto Wine Cellars and Tutto Italia Ristorante (Table-Service)
When I think of Italy, I think of pasta, pizza, and wine, and Epcot Italy provides just that.

Wine tours are huge in Italy. So many wonderful wines we sometimes take for granted, that get imported to the states, come from Italian wine regions.

Tutto Gusto Wine cellars gives you the ability to sample wines from the various regions in Italy. It's designed like you are in an actual wine cellar with brick arches and dark wooden panels. A few glasses of wine later along with Imagineer creativity, I actually thought for a second I was in Italy. Between wine, convincing surroundings and the Florida sun, you too can feel relaxed and mentally escape to Tuscany.

This is a double-duty kitchen that offers the menu at the lounge as well as in the restaurant. The food here is legit and offers "a little bit of Italy" — from meat and cheese boards to calamari, pasta, or mains. If you're looking for a dining experience or traveling with children and craving some delicious Italian food, the dining table is a great option.

My personal recommendation for this place (especially for couples) is to come for a wine flight, take a break from roaming around, enjoy a few snacks to share. That being said, they do offer three wine flights and you may find you may need a real meal if you take on a flight or two. It has been helpful they offer pasta and Italian delights to share. You can enjoy the best of both — the lounge experience and the food from the kitchen.

Of the two restaurants, this is a bit more of the upscale or finer dining experience, but both are good depending on what you're after.

This has a bigger, more refined menu.

Via Napoli Ristorante e Pizzeria (Table-Service)

OK — Pizza enthusiasts, this place is for you. If you're looking to sample authentic pizza and take a break from the mass-produced pizza at the hotels, or perhaps the pizza you've only been exposed to is American-style, this is several steps up and really does a good job being pretty true to Napoleon-style pizza as it's made-to-order and wood fire pizza.

Located in the back of Italy, near the Fontana Di Trevi replica, in a yellow building, is where you'll find this lovely little spot of Italian carbohydrates. Whenever I step foot here, it reminds me of the piazzas (plaza/squares) in Rome. Just like in Rome, you'll find cobblestone town squares with restaurants, gelaterias, outdoor dining, and a fountain in the center of it all.

They don't have a large menu here — but they stick to the basics and do them well. I usually almost always get the pizza margarita and calamari. They offer other options, like ravioli or chicken parmesan, but I say stick with the rustic pizza and fried calamari.

Grab a glass of vino, some pizza, kick back, and relax as though you were at a piazza in Rome.

Gelati (Counter-Service)

If you're walking around Italy Epcot or venturing around neighboring countries, it's impossible to not see someone enjoying gelato from the gelateria cart. These were everywhere when I went to Rome and it's a nice touch that they added right at the front of Italy World Showcase.

If you're unfamiliar with gelato, it's ice cream, but Italian-style. Italian ice cream, or gelato, is more cream, and usually doesn't have egg yolks. This is a perfect snack for some gelato in a cup or cone. My personal favorite is the *Coppa Delizia* which is strawberry, vanilla, cookies and cream, strawberry jam, and whipped cream.

However, it's almost impossible to not grab some gelato from here as you're taunted by fellow tourists walking about enjoying theirs. A favorite Italian snack for the Floridian sun, you'll probably make anyone passing by jealous with your sweet treat, and inspire them to also indulge.

If you're not in the mood for gelato - no worries. This place has some other nice options too: I love coming here for a limonata or a glass of prosecco for those looking for a quick sip or checking a box on the boozy passport.

American Adventure:
Funnel Cake - American — All the funnel cake glory! Impossible to miss this food stand based on the scent.

Block & Hans - Counter-service beer (if you're participating in drinking around the world, this is your stop).

Fife & Drum Tavern - Turkey leg stand. Every park has at least one and it's the Instagram-worthy giant turkey leg that you can enjoy while you roam around and explore.

Regal Eagle Smokehouse (Quick-Service)
So, this place is an absolute hidden gem for BBQ and sometimes overlooked in World Showcase — for the very reason I overlooked it. It's American food. I live in America, American food is found everywhere in Disney, so if you're vacation is less than five days, it's very natural to not choose the American spot to dine at, especially in Epcot®. The thing is, the food here is pretty exceptional. If you're especially an international traveler and want American food that isn't the usual chicken tenders, hot dogs, cheeseburgers, this is a really good spot to grab some BBQ. For those traveling from Texas, Kansas City, or any other location that has well-known barbecue — you may sneer your nose at this, but it's good. Or, some folks from the Southern belt tend to find they like this place because it reminds them of home. Regardless of your reasons to try or not to try — I'm a BBQ fan, and I'd say of the BBQ spots in Disney, this one takes it up a notch. They have smoked meats here. The cuts are smoked over oak for hours, meaning this place goes beyond just grilling.

Honestly, everything here is pleasing and done and feels authentic.

I am an absolute sucker for ribs and whether you're a fan of the different types of BBQ that the USA offers, I was pretty happy with these. My favorites are the ribs, the BBQ burger with the fried onion, and the smoked BBQ chicken.

Their goal is to provide a "salute" to the various types of BBQ you'd find in the USA, and as

Turkey Leg — Fife & Drum — Epcot, various parks

someone who has traveled all over the USA and hit up some of the major BBQ spots in the country, I'd say the deliver on the experience.

The portions here are big and if you wanted, you can easily share.

They do offer a salad, but I say ditch the lettuce, go for the meat sweats.

PS — If you're on a plant-based diet, try the *Jackfruit Burger.* Most of the plant-based food is some variation of Beyond Meats. Don't get me wrong, it's a great product but can feel repetitive and this is a welcomed change.

Japan

Teppan Edo (Table-Service)

The sister restaurant to Tokyo Dining is Teppan Edo. For those of you who love teppanyaki or for those of you in the US - perhaps Benihana - this is the Disney version of that. Located up the right staircase and to the back of the pavilion is Teppan Edo.

Here you have a theme of dining with good food. I like this place more than the well-known Benihana. Speaking of, if you do have Benihana fans in your party, they'd be pleasantly surprised and it's a great way to entertain everyone. Usually, someone will make a volcano out of onions with suave utensil handling here and there. It's still pretty Americanized compared to traditional teppanyaki in Japan, but it delivers. You really can't beat the kindness and service from the chefs and waitstaff. I also really enjoyed that every once in a while, someone would perhaps teach restaurant-goers some Japanese phrases, or counting. It made me feel more connected to the culture.

Some of my stand-out favorites are the calamari and wagyu beef appetizers. Tokyo Dining handles more of the sushi menu, but for those who want "the best of both," they do have a limited sushi menu here.

You really can't go wrong with any of the proteins, and they even have some combination options. I'm a fan of the steak and shrimp combination. Or for days when "I'm on vacation" and feel like blowing money, I splurge and pay extra for the scallops and a lobster tail enhancements.

This place checks a lot of boxes: I think it's fairly priced for the food you get, it's tasty, there's something for everyone here - and - everyone gets some entertainment while the meal is prepared. Can't beat that!

Tokyo Dining (Table-Service)

If you love sushi and have always been curious about restaurants in Japan Tokyo dining is for you. As someone who's been to Japan several times (I even studied abroad there), Epcot's World Showcase does an amazing job bringing Japan to life. From the gardens to the shopping, or even the snacks in the snack shop, this creates the ambiance as you climb steps that resemble the temples in Kyoto or Roppongi Hills into Tokyo Dining.

This place is for sushi lovers and does a great job. There are a few resorts and other areas that offer sushi but they seem a bit Americanized. Tokyo Dining is my sushi-craving-cure in Epcot World Showcase. You can certainly come here for lunch after watching some of the Japanese drummers at the pagoda across the way, or, do what I like to do: I love to come up here before or during fireworks. If you can, try to get a spot near the window so you can have an elevated view of the fireworks while you dine.

Oh, and if sushi or raw foods isn't your thing, no worries. They have many cooked options on the menu as well, such as udon noodle soups, tempura, or chicken and rice dishes.

And this is also a great time to practice with chopsticks if you're not an expert already.

Takumi-Tei (Table-Service)

If you are looking for a more traditional and upscale Japanese dining experience, the newest edition is Takumi Tei at the Pavilion. In Japan, omakase meals tend to be smaller portions (not always, but usually) and it lists the ingredients but it's up to the chef on how they deliver them.

This new restaurant is an upscale, Japanese experience that is now part of Disney Signature dining — so be prepared to spend money here.

I would recommend doing this once for anyone who wants to experience Japanese fine dining. Standout favorites here are *teien* (watermelon grapefruit salad), *agedashi tofu, hama no kani* (crab & heirloom tomato). The nigiri here is a work of art. Plump rice rounds with fish, edible flowers, and greens. The rice ratio is a little heavier to fish than usual, but it's truly food artwork. The mains vary in pricing from $40-$120, salmon and shrimp being the least expensive option, all the way up to the wagu beefs.

I would say if you do come here - I recommend doing the omakase tasting menu for $150 vs. the a la carte. Or, if you just want to "try it' maybe the a la carte could be the way to go. I felt there was more value in the omakase tasting menu and I loved that it also had a tea ceremony. Either way, cost-wise it could very well come out to be the same depending on what you get.

For me, this may be a "very special occasion" to come back for.
It's on the more expensive side and when I compare value, I think a lot of the value is in the atmosphere, service, and then the food. But, if you're strapped for cash, you may find yourself a little distracted by the price points.

If you come, you'll enjoy yourself; it's a very relaxing and beautiful atmosphere to dine in. The service is amazing here. I cannot find anywhere else where the service was so good. Do you need anything? It'll be taken care of promptly. Attentive staff, kind people that will make each table feel like they are important. As someone who's spent a lot of time in Japan, service is an important part of the culture. You will not be disappointed in this area.

In short, you will be wowed by the beauty of the dining areas and of the food coming to you. Sip on some tea, relax and be taken care of here.

Morocco

Spice Road Table (Table-Service)

Another option (if timed properly) you can to enjoy the lagoon fireworks by night, or simply admire the lagoon by day at this restaurant. Spice Road Table is a lovely blend of Middle Eastern

& Mediterranean cuisines. Considering the Florida heat is like the Sahara Desert, may as well dine like you're visiting the heat in Morocco for an all-around experience!

Being Greek, this spot holds a special place to me because some of the foods are similar to what I grew up with. Depending on your culinary exposure, these flavors may not be familiar to you, but that's the beauty of World Showcase — you get to try new things! What I love about Spice Road Table, is you can try the cuisine here, not break the bank, and get to try a lot of the cuisine via the samplers.

I enjoy coming here, grabbing a glass of wine, admiring the lagoon, and having a light bite.

I usually recommend the samplers here: *Spice Road Table Sampler* and the *Dessert Platter*.

The Spice Road Sampler has all my favorites on it - lamb kofta (meatball skewer), spiced chicken (with a yogurt sauce that is so refreshing on a hot Floridian day), and the tiropitakia (phyllo pastry with cheese). I sometimes also order the naan spreads if I'm extra hungry. You'll get hummus, some olives, and dips that are refreshing as you want some nourishment while you beat the heat. Then, I usually recommend getting the *Dessert Platter* which is very similar to what you'll find at Oasis Sweets and Sips. They have a walnut cake, an almond cookie with a cherry, and usually a type of baklava (flaky phyllo dough layered with nuts, sugar, and cinnamon in syrup).

And while you're outdoors, depending on where you're sitting, you may see hear music or see their belly dancer performing nearby.

Tangierine Café (Recently Rebranded to Flavors of the Medina) (Casual, Quick-Service)

Oddly enough, sometimes the street food is where it's at. If you end up not opting for table-service at Spice Road, I would say Tangierine Café is another good option for food in Morocco.

The shawarma chicken and lamb items are usually what I gravitate towards when I'm here. Mainly because both are delicious and if you're open to eating lamb, you may as well try them. Or, if you want a break from meat, the vegetarian platter is a really good option here for both those who have plant-based diets or those who just want to give it a try. After all, falafel is a staple in Moroccan cuisine and it would almost be amiss not to get it.

Honestly, no matter what you get in this little cafe it's all good food at fair prices. The portions are filling, and you get to try a few sides with your mains included. It's going to be a little more expensive than your burgers and fries, but not by much and I encourage you to give it a go. This is also one of those spots where I'll add a side or two. Try the tabouleh if you get the harissa chicken or the beef.

This is another place where I recommend sharing. This will allow you to sample much of the menu as well as potentially save money. The menu items here are flavorful (think clove, turmeric, nutmeg, cinnamon, cardamom), but not too overpowering. You'll find some familiar spices perhaps used in unique ways, or you may find you are trying new spices that are not common in your cupboard.

Be sure to stop by the Oasis Sips and Sweets after for dessert.

Oasis Sweets & Sips (Dessert Kiosk)

Something you'll find in Mediterranean and Arabic countries are sweets just as you'll find here. Whether you go to Greece, UAE, Turkey, (and of course Morocco) you'll find sweet stands that have several of these delightful treats.

My favorites are the kourabiedes (almond cookie in powdered sugar — I am legit eating one while I write this part of the book because I couldn't help reminisce a little), kataifi (shredded phyllo dough with nuts and honey), baklava (layered phyllo and nuts). I recommend getting the party assortment and pick seven, grab a cup of coffee to perk up, and enjoy. These also make great treats to bring back to your hotel room.

France

L' Artisan des Glaces (Counter-Service)

Across the way from the Maison Du Vin (wine shop), you'll see a white building with blue trimmings. That is the ice cream shop. It is quite excellent and a sweetly refreshing spot. Don't let the likely long line intimidate you — they are pros at Disney and work through that long line (usually goes out the door) rather quickly. Coffee lovers can enjoy their iced coffee with a scoop of ice cream and whipped cream.

My personal favorite and Insta-worthy treat is the macaron ice cream sandwich. I have not had this creation anywhere else. It's a lovely foodie treat and a nice play on the ice cream sandwich. The macaron shell is quite fragile so I recommend asking for a plate or bowl and eating it quickly.

Les Halles Boulangerie-Patisserie: *Actual Factual Magic* Do Not Miss! (Counter -Service)

One of the best and hidden gems in all of your foodie dreams, lies here. Located all the way in the very back of World Showcase France, you will find some of the best pastries. As someone who has been to France, this place makes my heart happy. There are so many options, they are all beautiful, and they all taste phenomenal. You will have a hard time not over purchasing here. I find myself grabbing a sweet treat for now, and another for later, and maybe a baguette sandwich for tomorrow that I'll pop in the mini fridge. I'm not kidding, this place is awesome. The fact it is a quick-service and makes our do not miss list, I promise you, it's worth it.

I almost always leave here with at least these items: The strawberry tartlet, chocolate mousse, almond croissant, a ham and cheese baguette, a cream puff, and a giant macaroon.

It's all so wonderful and it's so hard to pick just one item. Do yourself a favor, do not skip this place. It's well-priced and if there is a long line, sit through it. If you can wait for *Pandora* rides,

Strawberry Tart — Les Halles Boulangerie-Patisserie — Epcot

you can sit through some of the best treats available at Les Halles Boulangerie-Patisserie.

La Maison Du Vin (Counter-Service)
This is a little wine shop when you go further in, past the fountain in France, up the path, and to the right. I love to not only grab a bottle for the hotel room later on but also to grab some champagne and stroll around the stores and shop. This is where I usually stop when I go for a glass of wine in France. Champagne wins. All the champagnes on their offering are good. I

would suggest going for one of the dry champagnes, those tended to be my favorite.

Crêpes des Chefs de France (Counter-Service)
The little crêpe stand is on the outskirt of France (directly across from Chefs de France), where you can enjoy a variety of crêpes. From plain sugar to strawberry, or hazelnut, you can walk around and enjoy a warm, sugary, and aromatic pancake.

As someone who has been to France and loves crêpes, you will find stands like these all around Paris. Having a stand like this, representing the many you'd find on a casual stroll in Paris, is a cultural attention to detail I appreciate. Be sure to check out La Crêperie de Paris when it opens!

Monsieur Paul (Table-Service)
In my mind: Monsieur Paul is the foodie lovechild of several restaurants in Paris that I adore and miss.

This restaurant, in my opinion, does a good job not only of having fancy French food, but they apply so many of the classic culinary techniques that are visually appealing and are impressive to execute that any diner would enjoy.

Of the two higher-end dining options in France, I tend to guide people to Monsieur Paul. For an upscale and classic French-bistro experience, this place is a favorite of mine.

You can certainly order a la carte or the prix fixe menu. Either way, choose your adventure and know it will be a tasty one. Will it be a bit expensive? Yes, but from a value standpoint, I highly recommend splurging for a dining experience here.

Standout favorites from our team are the fish (the fish type usually varies) with crispy potatoes that artistically resemble fish scales along the back. It's a culinary masterpiece.

I also recommend the roasted duck if they have it. Not too many places in Disney offer duck, but if you're going to have it — in the French we trust.

A French delicacy at most Parisian bistros is escargot. I would say if you're interested in trying something new, give them a go. They are done properly here and you may be surprised you enjoy them.

I did want to comment on my appreciation for really delivering on the French sauces here. The purees are artistically done with several techniques such as dotting, smearing, to name a few.

If you've never been to France, or want to reminisce, this is a great spot for it. Bon appetit.

United Kingdom

Rose & Crown (Table-Service)

Epcot offers the best of everything. Rose & Crown was a great option for one of our trips as we had a picky eater along with us. The rest of us were itching for food in either Morocco or Japan — something more adventurous. Our one family member wasn't having it, they wanted something familiar and had zero interest in straying from known food items. If you want to eat at World Showcase and have a picky eater, Rose & Crown is for you.

"How about this, let's kick back with a beer and go to England." Sure enough, they had something for everyone. If you're looking for a stew, a burger, or even pot pie, they bring all the classics to you here at the Rose & Crown.

I opted for the fish and chips. Having been to London a few times, I've always adored a humble, flakey cod with a crispy crust alongside lightly salted fries. So I thought, "Alright, let's put Disney to the test and give theirs a whirl."
Did they sure come through here. The fish was a beautiful gold with a nice flakey crisp to it. The cod was still delicate and it was just a real treat to bite into. The fries, or chips rather, were also on point.

I consider myself well-fed and well-traveled. I'm a very lucky person. I ate some amazing fish and chips when I visited the UK. But I must admit, the fish and chips I had at Rose & Crown were on par or even better than some of the fish and chips I had at staple pubs in London. I know, admitting this is dangerous, but it's true and speaks to how good the fish and chips are here. Needless to say, the basket of fish and chips displayed in front of me didn't stand a chance. Every last bite was spoken for. And hey, even our picky eater left with a full belly too.

So whether you just happen to be hungry when you find yourself in England, you have a non-adventurous eater on your party, or perhaps you just really love fish and chips, the Rose and Crown has got you covered.

Yorkshire County Fish Shop (Quick-Service)

Unable to dine-in and kickback? No worries. The grab-and-go option gets a thumbs up. However, I don't know what it is, but the ones in the Rose & Crown are of slightly higher quality, taste better. Not sure if it's the psychology because I dined in and paid more at Rose & Crown, or the beer I had while enjoying my meal played a role, but if it's the same kitchen, I'll eat my words. Regardless, fear not, if you want to try fish and chips, you'll be happy with these no-frill options too.

Fish & Chips — Rose & Crown — Epcot

Canada

Le Cellier Steakhouse — *Actual Factual Magic* Do Not Miss! (Table-Service)

A gem in World Showcase is the Le Cellier Steakhouse. A steakhouse with French Canadian flavors that gives the experience of dining in a wine cellar. You'll find little stone arches, dark wood, and dimmed lighting to create a steakhouse + cellar experience. The wine list here is superb for all of you looking to enjoy a glass of vino. Much of Epcot® has great wine lists, but I love their Pinot Noir here and their dessert wines. I recommend if you go to drink around World Showcase, come here for a dessert wine to change it up. Depending on your knowledge of food at Disney, you either know this is one of the best spots to get a steak in Disney World. I think it gets overlooked for a few reasons: It is hidden, it's another steakhouse, and gets easily unnoticed because most people go to Canada for a beer and live music, and then move on to the next spot in their drinking game around the world.

While Disney has this listed as fine dining, the vibe here and the atmosphere are a touch more casual – but where I agree with Disney that this is fine dining is more around the quality of the meal. Usually, I say a fine dining experience has some dress code requirements, but, you're at a theme park so it's safe to show up in a t-shirt and shorts.

On to the food: Their menu here is pretty short and direct. That can be a good or bad thing depending on what you're after but just know they have something for everyone here. If you did bring a vegan to a steakhouse, they have newly added impossible dumplings to delight anyone who comes through their doors.

All their steaks are great and were cooked to each person's desired temperature (that's not easy to do). The ribeye paired with the onions and shallot whiskey butter was exquisite. While there are several solid recommendations to get a steak in Disney, I enjoyed that they have their own twist here and have touches like the shallot-whiskey butter, or au poivre sauce, truffle butter, and cheddar potato au gratin. Honestly, I half-joke that some of the best French food you find in World Showcase is not in France, but actually in French-Canada.

A must-do foodie item would be the *Maple Whiskey-glazed Brussel Sprouts*. If you like poutine, I recommend getting poutine to share here. Not too many places in Disney offer poutine, and of the places that do, I think their signature poutine brings you to Montreal.

For appetizers, I usually like the mussels and have gotten that as my meal at times. The *Actual Factual Magic* Team is divided with one of the items here, and some fighting words have been exchanged. Some of us enjoy the beer cheese soup, others do not. We're a house divided but all agree this place should not be skipped!

Go here for a steak, some poutine, and dessert. I still recommend to going over to France for desserts, but I had to try dessert here and recommend you make room for it. Our favorites are the warm pecan-brown butter tart or the cheesecake that is made with crème fraîche.

Epcot's Amazing Festivals

Food & Wine, Flower & Garden Festivals
Epcot has two major food festivals which is wild to me because World Showcase is the capital of food in Disney on any given day. But, guess what, during these festivals, MORE food options are available. Yes. More food stands, more countries, and you just snack your way through the parks.

It's almost too much to post — but some of my stand out favorites I've found in these festivals are seared scallops, butternut squash ravioli, Caribbean-style shrimp skewers, seared tuna with seaweed salad, pork dumplings, spanakopita, cheese bites, the list just goes on and is truly endless.

I usually don't make reservations the day I am at Epcot for Food & Wine Fest and just spend a few bucks here and there grazing all day.

Just know, I've never had anything bad at any of these stands. So many of them are wonderfully delicious and very inexpensive.

I encourage you to sample as much as you can during these festivals and perhaps find a day or meal period to just graze through some stands.

Drink Around the World … Or… Eat Around the World?

If none of your friends have told you about drinking around the world at Disney, I will be that friend. I've referred to it a few times already, but if you're confused, let me share: Park guests over the years have made an unofficial challenge of "drinking around the world" at World Showcase. Essentially, you're getting a drink at each country. If you see people with "drink around the world shirts" (likely unofficial Disney merchandise), that's what they mean. Now, World Showcase has 11 countries. So I'm not going to tell you to have 11 drinks in one day — but some people do it, or they share drinks throughout the day to safely manage alcohol servings. Your liver, your choices.

What I will say, I like to change it up and "eat around the world." My challenge to you is to get a snack or a bite in each country. See? More manageable, no one needs to get kicked out of the park because they got sick, no one's hair has to get held back.

So, my challenge to you is try a small food-like-object from each country. It's much easier to share, say, a puff-pastry from Norway compared to a giant beer. Plus, the kids can probably help in this challenge too.

Now if you decide to "drink around the world" be smart, responsible, share, and maybe it couldn't hurt to try my little foodie challenge to keep your stomach full.

No matter what you do — pace yourself. If you don't do any challenge, that is perfectly fine and the best way to enjoy the park. Let's be real - it's also expensive. If you need to abandon the challenge you set out to do, let it go. There are no prizes. Enjoy yourself. Don't worry about the unofficial challenges. Be well and avoid hospital visits.

Firework Shows & Dining Experiences:

Unless you want a really good view of fireworks without waiting for hours (the spots they reserve are quite amazing) or a chance to get some character photos with smaller lines, we recommend simply skipping the firework party shows from a foodie experience. Almost all the snacks can be found at quick-service dining locations or you can always catch the characters during regular slotted times. The value for these would be to see characters with shorter lines that you perhaps missed during the day, or to not fret for a fantastic firework spot. From a foodie angle, many of the snacks can be found throughout the park or weren't as unique as we had hoped.

Epcot® & Disney's Hollywood Studios® Area Resort Dining

Since these resort areas overlap, we felt it was best to combine these since many of them are en route to each other or near each other for a reservation.

Disney's BoardWalk® Area:

The Disney BoardWalk® is a comfortable area to take a leisurely stroll around on Disney property that connects to Epcot®. It can be busy, but not near the hustle and bustle of Disney Springs®, nor does it have the capacity to do such.

It's filled with dining and entertainment for all ages. I think of it as a bit of an upscale carnival feel where you can walk around, shop, get ice cream, play carnival games (like shooting hoops), and win prizes like you would at a state fair.

Of course, it's a hidden gem for some good food. Like, we're talking good food undercover. Disney's BoardWalk® connects a few hotels in the area inclusive of The BoardWalk Inn, Yacht & Beach Club Resort, and The Swan & Dolphin. We're going to walk you through some of our foodie favorites.

Cupcake — BoardWalk Bakery — Disney's Boardwalk®

Boardwalk Bakery (Counter-Service)

Disney has so many wonderful spots we suggest for sweet treats. From Disney Springs® to the World Showcase, you'll find a lovely spot with delicious snacks at the Boardwalk Bakery.

It's a charming little shop with an inviting sign that encourages any passerby to "come on in." It has so many treats it's hard to leave with just one item. Whenever I stay in the area, I end up skipping restaurant breakfasts and often do an ad hoc intercontinental breakfast of coffee and their baked goods to-go.

My personal favorites for breakfast are their almond croissant and their cheese danishes. All at are larger than normal size but at least it justifies the premium cost a bit.

Their cinnamon crumb cake and fresh fruit tartlets are also quite lovely. Where they really shine and get a lot of love, is for their cupcakes. It's impossible to leave without one. They are well-decorated, thematic, and seasonal. Say you're there in the holiday season, you'll find white cupcakes perhaps with snowflake sprinkles and tiny gingerbread cookies on top during the winter months.

I often find myself attracted to any of the cupcakes that have a Mickey-theme and covered in edible glitter. The cupcakes at the Boardwalk Bakery really are an attraction of their own. I mean, who would say no to a pink cupcake, with a strawberry, and glitter?

You'll also find other amazing treats here too: Rice Krispies, taffy apples resembling Disney characters, chocolates, mini pies. A lot of it is seasonal and can be hard to predict what will be on the menu since a lot of it is themed, but just know, it's delicious.

Flying Fish (Table-Service)

I feel like I have made so many seafood recommendations here, but it's Florida and it's Disney and both reasons mean good seafood can be found in several spots on Disney property. For those spending time on the BoardWalk® & Epcot® area looking for seafood, this is honestly a hidden gem. Think of this place as a "fish-forward steakhouse." You can certainly get steak and it has the vibe of a steakhouse. Their tomahawk cut is pretty awesome and will easily feed two or three people.

All their appetizers are a delight. I highly recommend the slow-roasted pork belly, bisque, and the snow crab croquettes. The burrata is also a refreshing appetizer too - especially for any vegetarians in your party. Nothing like a chilled ball of creamy mozzarella to liven up your senses.

This place is really known for its southern influence with seafood, which is what really makes it a little different than some of the other seafood spots we've pointed out and encouraged you to try.

The scallops are really one of the signature items that they pair with some grits and corn. Lots of places offer scallops, but not many people really know how to cook them. This is one of the few places I've really enjoyed seared scallops. We're also fans here of their oak-grilled salmon.

You really can't go wrong here. From the dazzling light fixtures to the fine food, it's a wonderful alternative to the suggestions we have in Disney Springs®.

Disney's Yacht Club Resort:

Disney's Yacht Club Resort is part of the BoardWalk® area and aims to portray a New England-style yacht club. It's a calming area that is certainly built for your guests who like boats, polos, and The Hamptons. Note: Several of the restaurants here have dress codes. Please check with the restaurant website to verify.

A lot of the restaurants here are absolutely stellar and next level from service, quality, and food. It's a pricey/upscale area, but, if you are vying for a nice experience and to be pampered, this is the area for it. Magic Kingdom® you have the Grand Floridian, at Epcot® area, you have Yacht Club Resort:

We have a few stand-out dining favorites here:

Yachtsman Steakhouse (Table-Service)

I feel like when I come in here, I'm either in a lighthouse or a big yacht. They're probably aiming for inside a yacht, considering the namesake, but regardless — you feel like you're at the seaside and will find a comforting atmosphere dawned with ship's wheels on the wall and wooden panels. This is also a spot I recommend if you find yourself in Disney for business, this is a wonderful place to take VIP clients out to.

If it's one thing that comes to mind aside from good food, it's presentation. The plates here are always beautiful — from soups to seafood entrees, the plating always has a nice touch.

The staff is friendly and at your service. It's for sure an upscale seafood/steakhouse – and one of the few that does have a dress code last I checked.

Some of the personal favorites here are the shrimp cocktail, lobster bisque, *Captain's Seafood Tower* (or *Admiral Tower* if you have enough people).

Any of the butcher cut mains are great — I tend to lean towards the fillet or ribeyes.

This is also one of the places I recommend getting the extra enhancements. I love the half main lobster or the oscar-style topping.

For all you bacon lovers out there — they also offer thick-cut bacon. Yes. Not like puny store-bought bacon. We're talking thick-cut where you question if your gallbladder can process it.

I'll admit, not adventurous enough to try the elk and was surprised to see they offer it. In fact, I am not sure any other place in Disney offers elk. For those of you who like gamey cuts, or are interested in trying it, they have it here.

For another upscale steakhouse option, that is not located in Disney Springs®, this is an absolutely stellar place. Bring your camera, the presentation is always on point here.

Ale & Compass (Table-Service)

I love the trendy vibes this place gives. Ale & Compass is your "jack of all trades" at this resort. They have breakfast, lunch, dinner, and a lounge.

I feel like this is one of your options where - it's familiar menu items with a pinch of flair. I prefer this place as a breakfast recommendation. You'd be happy with their lunch and dinner option here should you need a place to dine — but we've recommended so many other places for dinner I'd rather guide you here for breakfast.

Nonetheless, let's chat about food at Ale & Compass.

Their breakfast in my opinion is where it's at. They offer usual menu items with some "oomph" to them. Both sweet and savory options are great, but I tend to lean on the sweet side here and they do it well.

Like pancakes? Yes, they have pancakes and they're delicious. Currently, the pancakes are bacon-blueberry. You read that right. They have bacon sautéed up in the batter with some blueberries and it's delicious and you'll probably do what I did and start making them at home when you miss Disney.

And oh, did you say waffles? While they don't have Mickey-shaped waffles here (the child inside of me must have some each visit), they have waffles covered in a mascarpone cream (like what you find in a cannoli) with giant shavings of chocolate on top.

Another favorite is the *Salted Caramel Apple French Toast*. I like to make sure when I'm here in the autumn or winter months to book a reservation here and basically make sure I eat this.

Now, this is at the Yacht resort so naturally, we need some seafood options and for your savory options, I'd say skip the omelet (it's good but you can get one anywhere) and chase after the *Crab Cake Benedict* or the *Lobster Roll*.

My recommendation would be to do breakfast here and try dinner at another option. However, if you're like "Kat, I am tired of the parks, I just want to roll out of my hotel bed, and not venture far."

Ok, ok, ok, I get it. Been there.

Start with the bread rolls. They're these delightful golden puffs of carbs with butter and bacon jams. If you go for an entree, I'd say stick with the pastas. Any of the pappardelle options are worthy of a cheat day. I also recommend the *Seafood Potpie* as you likely won't find elsewhere.

Beaches & Cream Soda Shop: *Actual Factual Magic* Do Not Miss! (Table-Service)

Another *Actual Factual Magic* and overall Disney favorite is the Beaches & Cream Ice cream shop along the BoardWalk®. They do have food here too, so if you wanted a burger or a warm sandwich, their food here is also good. My personal favs are the burger and the turkey-bacon sandwich. I usually don't eat here all too often, because you can get burgers in so many spots. But, people usually come here and gravitate for the ice cream and shakes.

And if I'm going to be really honest, their dairy desserts here really are a work of art. If you like strawberry shakes, it's not your average strawberry shake, it is pink, glazed in raspberry sauce, and they top it with a Minnie-themed cupcake. It's almost too pretty to eat.

No matter what shake you choose, anticipate to just admire it for at least five minutes because of all the creativity before you even get to taste it.

Lastly, this place is known for the *Kitchen Sink*. Most people come here on a mission to eat the *Kitchen Sink* and I don't blame them.

You literally get a giant sink filled with anything imaginable from various ice cream flavors, sauces, and toppings. We're talking vanilla, chocolate, strawberry, cookies and cream, covered in cookie crumbles, cherries, brownies, whipped cream, and sprinkles. For a more manageable version, get the smaller one with the souvenir sinks and take it home with you to make your own on days you wish you were in Disney World. I like to say this place is a more upscale version of the Fountain Eats & Sweets in the Dolphin.

Walt Disney World Swan & Dolphin:

These hotels are pretty unassuming as a good foodie option but of the hotels in the surrounding area, I firmly believe the Swan & Dolphin have some of the better restaurants in the Hollywood Studios & Epcot Resorts areas that don't require a park pass or a trip to Disney Springs®. These hotel restaurants are filled with unsung hero dinner options (not to say you can't get lunch or breakfast here, but the good stuff in my opinion can be found after 5 PM).

il Mulino (Swan): *Actual Factual Magic* Do Not Miss! (Table-Service)

Located in the courtyard of the Swan Resort, this hidden treasure is an Italian steakhouse that seems to fly under the radar when it comes to food in Disney. I love this place and it's a restaurant that checks all the boxes: quality, service, value. I've come here a few times and continuously enjoy the menu, and have a high appreciation for the service.

Some favorites are the meatballs, the melon and prosciutto, or calamari appetizers. I also enjoyed their house salad - which has changed a few times. Currently, they have a mix of greens, olives, and beans. If you're feeling more the traditional route, the Caprese or Caesar salads are not only

Tiramisu — il Mulino — Swan & Dolphin

safe options, but well executed.

For pasta, all of them are wonderful. Personal favorites are pappardelle, linguine with clams, and gnocchi. But whatever you're in the mood for, all are crowd-pleasers.

As you venture down the menu, I highly also recommend steak here. It's an Italian steakhouse after all. The ribeye was perfect and had such a nice char to it. With the steak and pasta together it was just a lovely way to sample their menu. Their fish options were all a delight but if you want our friendly recommendation, we tend to steer people towards the grouper because that kind of fish is more of a Florida specialty vs. Italian. You can certainly stick to the shrimp or salmon and be perfectly happy if you're craving either. We like to recommend folks go for the grouper not only because it's a well-thought-out dish, but because you won't find that on many Italian menus (unless you're in Florida).

Fish is also done nicely here. This place is a lot easier to sample with larger parties but you can certainly cover a lot of ground if you go as a couple.

When I come here, I like to recommend sharing much of the menu so you can sample it.

Whenever I come, we always get a pizza or two for the table. Our personal favorites are the *Margherita* and the *Bosco*.

Something they have done in the most recent years was adding a family-style option vs. a la carte. I highly recommend going this route for parties of five or more — try as much as you can here.

If you love wine, this is also an excellent place to pair wine with dinner. The sommelier knows what they are doing and their staff has solid recommendations for pairings with different menu options. I recall the pinot noir and their cabs were standout options that complimented both the steak and pastas.

Fountain Eats & Sweets (Dolphin) (Table-Service)

For a casual option, I really like this place and have been coming here since I was around 9 years old. We're going to go with "that's a long time" because I'm not about to age myself.

Anyways, I like this place for a few reasons:

First: ice cream. Second: ice cream. Third: ice cr- Ok you get the hint. They are going for a fun diner vibe complete with a neon-light sign. Of the "more quick burgers and chicken tenders" options, theirs are actually quite good and have a bit more "oomph" to them vs. what you may find in the parks. What I like about the ice cream here, it not only tastes great I like the create your own option.

Another perk, this place is open pretty late compared to many Disney restaurants. If you're looking for burgers, shakes, or are in an ice cream kind of mood, I feel like this place hits the spot. It's no-frills, but sometimes that's exactly what the doctor orders.

PS: If you like Sloppy Joe's, this may be the only place on Disney property that offers them. AND if you're from abroad especially, you should for sure give the Sloppy Joe a try in the USA.

Kimonos (Dolphin) (Table-Service)

The more I think about it: Unless you're really in Japan World Showcase or hanging out at the Polynesian Resort, sushi isn't really offered in many places in Disney. I feel like Japan World Showcase does an excellent job with their sushi offering, but that requires a ticket to Epcot®. If you have a hankering for sushi during your stay and perhaps while you were in Epcot® you chose one of our other solid recommendations or you didn't have time to pop in there — Kimonos is another wonderful option in my opinion.

From an atmosphere, it's one of the more chic restaurants — wooden panels, have the Japanese robes (kimonos) hanging along the walls with lantern-like light fixtures.

If you're staying on property, this is a lovely lounge to come enjoy cocktails. Or you can do I as do and get a drink and a side of sushi while you wait for your family to finish getting ready before you head out to the parks or evening activities. I personally recommend this spot for more of a lounge/happy hour experience. If you decide to do a full sushi meal here, you won't be disappointed. The argument could be made "sushi can be found nearly everywhere or sushi isn't really all that different, I can get a California roll or maguro in New York," and you're right. So I recommend if you just want some good sushi as light fare with a drink, this is a great spot to achieve that. Perhaps you just really love sushi or you may not live in New York and don't have access to good sushi — that's partly why I recommend this spot. I'm not sure where all my readers are from, so, it's my job to provide options as you navigate through the wonderful options of Disney.

Overall, the sushi here is of a higher quality and more upscale. A touch pricey, but not out of this world in comparison to some places to dine for sushi. They do have a few cooked rolls (like the California roll and a few vegetable rolls). Overall, I recommend for a fresh catch.

Todd English's Bluezoo (Dolphin) — *Actual Factual Magic* Do Not Miss! (Table-Service)

Located in the Dolphin, another great option for a lounge and dinner would be Todd English's Bluezoo. This swanky spot complete with some of the most amazing light fixtures throughout creates an upscale-city-like atmosphere. I get lost in a wonderment, like a small child, whenever I see bubble lights that hang from the ceiling. They remind me of jellyfish just floating around and create an 'under the sea,' dream-like atmosphere. Every time I walk in here, even for a glass of wine, I feel important — not that I need to — but you just get this VIP vibe when you walk in. Even if you don't have time to dine here, or perhaps this isn't your vibe, I even recommend if you are at the Swan or Dolphin
and just in the area to casually walk by and admire the architectural design. It's one of the more modern and beautiful restaurants. But, alas, you're not here to stare at light fixtures. This part of the guidebook is for foodie recommendations.

The food here is good too. Similar to Kimonos, if you're looking to maximize your dining experience at Disney, I recommend coming here for a light bite and a drink, and go for more of the lounge experience.

Whatever drink you pick at the bar (a lot of their options are great if you decide to order from their house specialties, or you can always get your traditional Aviation). Our must-do menu recommendations are the shrimp cocktail, the sea scallops, and the pork belly baos.

If you stay for dinner, we recommend ordering from Bluezoo's *Simply Fish Menu*.

Shula's Steakhouse (Dolphin) (Table-Service)

Do you ever feel like you might break something because a place is pretty fancy and you might have a clumsy moment? I get some anxiety when getting too close, yet admire the wine wall (it's also a fridge but it's a glass wall of wine).
Disney has a lot of great steak houses. This follows a bit more of your old-school steakhouse theme, but has more of a modern atmosphere between the wine fridge and the white leather chairs and linens. Most people come to Disney for family vacations. Some people have met up with business partners or colleagues. I highly recommend this spot if you find yourself looking to have a business dinner. You certainly can bring the significant other or the kiddos here too (just

keep them away from the glass wall of wine ;)). Be also prepared to spend a little bit of a premium for the name and the atmosphere.

Our recommendations to guide you through the menu would be the NOLA style shrimp, tuna tartare, their wedge salad (the bacon jam is what did it for me), crab cakes, and the 22oz cowboy steak (please share this so you don't go into cardiac arrest).

For dessert, they do chocolate right here. From the lava cake to the seven-layer slice of heaven, or the soufflé, you're in good hands.

Caribbean Beach Resort/Coronado Springs/Old Key West Resorts/ Art & Animation/Pop/Movies:

These hotels are all pretty close to each other, and may not have the 'best of' options available. That being said, they still offer good and familiar meals for those of you staying at these resorts.

Sometimes it's just best to chill at your hotel to dine and have a meal — and that's perfectly fine. Our recommendation would be to venture off to some of the nearby resorts to dine at. We did feel that there was one hotel in the area that deserved a shout out and is "in the neighborhood" if you wanted to stay close to your resort, and that would be Port Orleans:

Port Orleans Resort:

As a huge lover of New Orleans and one day hope to have a second home down there (hey, a lady can dream, right?). There are a few unknown, amazing establishments here that are great for food and a good time. Especially if you feel like BoardWalk® may be overcrowded and you want good food, but not something overrun with too many people. I always find myself happy at Boatwright's and its wall-touching piano lounge, River Roost. Both of these can be found at the Riverside of the resort.

Boatwright's — *Actual Factual Magic* Do Not Miss! (Table-Service)

Maybe I am biased because I am using this book as a source of income to get me a house in NOLA one day, but I love this place. It takes me to New Orleans which is one of my happy places and they have so many cajun and creole favorites here, I will do my best to guide you, and not just list things, but literally, everything here is good.

For appetizers, I like the crawfish bisque and the fried green tomatoes. *The Mardi Gras Fritters* (cheese fritters) are also great with their pepper jelly.

I think you can easily enjoy any of the entrees here and often I wrestle with "Do I do the *All You Care to Enjoy*" or an entree plate.

If you want to sample as much as you can, the *All-You-Care-To-Enjoy Platter* has a little bit of everything: Ribs, Nashville Hot Chicken, Sausage, Brisket, Mashed Potatoes, Mac and Cheese,

Corn and beans. It's for sure worth the cost for the value and quality. Honestly, this is one of those places where I'm borderline ashamed for people to watch me eat. Manners escape me, and I always want seconds. I won't judge you if you do the same. It's so good.

Sometimes when I'm here, we just go nuts and get the platter + get the Prime Rib as a "side" to share because the prime rib here is so good. There have been some trips I've come here and gotten just the fried green tomatoes and the prime rib. Also, the crawfish mac and cheese is legit. Just saying, you can't get that anywhere else in Disney, but some places have similar options with lobster.

Also, do not skip dessert here. Whether you get the Mud Creme brûlée or the bread pudding, or the pecan pie (my personal favorite here), it's just all filling, well done, and satisfying.

Then, after you have your fabulous meal here, waltz on over to the River Roost Lounge for a nightcap and listen to Yeeha Bob. He will make you laugh, liven up the crowd, all while playing the piano as you sip on some cocktails. For me, I am usually nursing my food baby from dinner while listening to Yeeha Bob.

The Water Parks:

No one says they're going to go find the best food ever at a water park — it's just not a thing. There's no "swimsuit-fine dining." I want to level set with you there. There can also be the misconception of "I don't want to eat at the water park, the food is probably gross" and that's not true at all. We thought, if the *Actual Factual Magic* team can help you figure out some good options or foodie favorites if your Disney trip is inclusive of a water park — well, that's where we come in.

Disney has two water parks: Typhoon Lagoon and Blizzard Beach. For food at both, let me walk you through what's available as well as our menu favorites. Just know, there are no real table-service options at either of these. It's all stands, quick-service, counter — which makes a lot of sense because you don't want to rush to a dining reservation while you're on your third lap in the lazy river, about to be nearly drowned by the giant typhoon wave, or if you're in the long line to take the plunge at Blizzard Beach. Be sure to beat the heat with some snacks, quick bites, and drinks to enjoy your vacation, but also be sure to save the dollars and your appetite for perhaps a gourmet dining reservation elsewhere.

People often ask me "of the two water parks, which has the better food?" I tend to lean that Typhoon Lagoon has the better food, but it also could be because in my mind, if I am at a beach-like location, I'm going to want to eat more beach-islander-themed foods inclusive of pineapple, strawberries, fried shrimp, etc. So it could also be a bit of undercover psychology happening too whereas there are some "warmer comfort food items" at Blizzard Beach.

Just know, you'll be satisfied at the water parks and there's no need to fear 'water park food."

Typhoon Lagoon

This sunken-ship beach-vibe almost transports you to the islands south of the Florida Keys. You'll find some of your usual suspects here like burgers, chicken nuggets, and tacos - but with island flare like cajun spices or bits of pineapple. Atmospherically, it's quite different from its counterpart Blizzard Beach. For now, let's walk you through the options and our foodie favorites:

Typhoon Tilly's (Quick-Service)

If you're going to eat at Typhoon Lagoon, this is my favorite spot. Maybe I just enjoy fried fish too much, especially while on vacation in Florida, but for a place to eat at the water park, the food here is solid. I'd say hands-down, the beer-battered fish sandwich with chipotle slaw is a favorite of mine, as well as the fish tacos. And if you're looking for more basket-style, I also will gravitate to the *Shrimp and Fish Basket*. I try to come to Typhoon Lagoon at least one time per trip and there are my favorite things to snack on when I'm at the water park.

Snack Shack (Quick-Service)

Come here for pineapple bacon guac! You're welcome! If that's not something you're feeling, they have quesadillas and a fresh, clean shrimp salad. Our foodie favorite here is the pineapple bacon guacamole, hands-down.

Let's Go Slurpin' (Counter-Service)

My favorite pool bar in all of Disney. I don't know why. Maybe it's the atmosphere, and the folks here really know how to make a good drink. We're not going to talk about how much money I spent on *Rum Runners* here and *Banana Cabanas* but those are our recommendations to you.

Leaning Palms (Quick-Service)

This has your usual suspects of burgers, salads, chicken nuggets but with island influence and seasonings. We love the *Jerk Chicken Cobb Salad, Jerk Chicken Rice Bowl, Adobo Pork Rice Bowl,* and the *Island Crunch Chicken Sandwich*.

Happy Landings Ice Cream (Counter-Service)

Sand Pail Sundae is our recommendation here of soft serve with caramel, hot fudge, Oreo cookies, and waffle cone with Mickey sprinkles and a cherry. It's beach comfort food. **Must-Do**: Sand Pail Sundae

Blizzard Beach

The brother of Typhoon Lagoon would be the ski-resort-themed water park, Blizzard Beach.

This water park has some similarities that I've identified to you to Typhoon Lagoon, but it also has some differences in food items because even tho you're in hot Florida, the theme is ski which means winter, which means more warmer-comfort foods.

You'll find your usual suspects here of burgers and chicken tenders, but you'll also find things pizza, mac & cheese, to name a few.

Warming Hut (Counter-Service)

Of the places to dine at Blizzard Beach, this one is my favorite. I think it's because they have real food options here. Sure, you can say "more of the American fast-food favorites" but again, it's got the twists that make it a little different. I'd say this has the best food to offer at Blizzard Beach so if you're hungry, you'll enjoy this spot for a few reasons:

First, honey-butter fried chicken sandwich. It's not gourmet, but it is solid and will hold you over till you get to one of the more refined dining establishments later in the day. Second, they have loaded tater tots. First, we've established earlier in the book with Woody's Lunch Box that everyone loves tater tots. So, you have tater tots with chili, cheese, bacon, and sour cream. These are similar to the ones you'll find in *Toy Story* Land so if you just want to enjoy tots, here ya go.

Churros. Hi. Yes. This place has churros — warm, sugary cinnamon sticks of happiness.

Lastly, *Pineapple Dole Whip*. They have *Pineapple Dole Whip* here and I feel like that alone elevates any food establishment.

Donuts — Joffrey — Waterparks

Polar Pub (Counter-Service)

Similar to Let's Go Slurpin', the polar pub is its twin and you'll find my boozy favorites here too: *Banana Cabana* and *Rum Runners*. You'll find your beer here, piña coladas, and frozen lemonades too.

The grapefruit margarita is something that I enjoy here as well.

Mini-Donuts by Joffrey (Quick-Service)

I don't know how else to say this, but donuts are life. These little mini-warm donuts of happiness will bring you joy as you perhaps need to cope with your decision of doing the Summit Plummet and need to rethink your life choices over donuts. Or, perhaps you did the Summit Plummet and these are congratulatory, "I'm so proud of myself for doing it donuts." Regardless, there's a reason to have donuts and I'm in sales so I can help sell you on which reasons you need to enjoy these little bites of delight if you need convincing.

I've stopped "trying to be good" with my dieting during my stay at Disney. I used to just get the 1/2 dozen donuts but really — these are so yummy with their little sauces, you're just going to crush through them quick. I just get the 1 dozen because someone in your party will help you finish them. I may be traditional but the chocolate sauce is my favorite. Or, sometimes I just like to eat them plain.

I.C. Expeditions (Quick-Service)
— I.C. Expeditions is the first cousin of Happy Landing's Ice Cream in Typhoon Lagoon. Their menus are almost the same except for the root beer floats. Here is where you can find their version of the *Sand Pail Sundae* and the hot fudge brownie sundae.
Must do: Sand Pail Sundae

In Closing:
Know this — no matter where you are at Disney, good food can be found and enjoyed. Regardless of your budget, experiences, dietary needs, you will enjoy so much of what Disney has to offer. In this fourth iteration of the book, I wanted to provide different options because I have gone to Disney as a child, teenager, broke college student, adult, in celebration of love, birthdays, and I thought to myself — I can't just make recommendations based on all the higher-end reputable option. There can be joy in trying a brat in Germany World Showcase, a scoop of gelato in France, or perhaps gourmet dining atop the Contemporary Resort. Much of this is my years of experience, passion, and being a cook myself. While yes, much of this is my personal opinion and recommendations, you may disagree in some parts — and that's perfectly ok. I have done my best to support you and be your Jiminey Cricket, guiding your stomach (and your wallet) through Walt Disney World®.

I recognize how privileged I am and fortunate for the 30+ years with multiple trips of going to Disney. It has inspired me to travel to other parts of the world as I've eased my way into experiencing food from so many places — it's a small world, after all, right? I am so passionate about writing, food, and Disney. Being part of this book has been an absolute joy and has combined my passions. I want to thank my partner, Joe Pillsbury, for choosing me and trusting me with such an important task.

I want to thank you, the reader, for taking the time to review the food section of this book. I hope you enjoy your travels and this guide helps you in making your trip more magical (and delicious).

Please check out my other food related endeavors at www.fancyathome.com .

Thank you, and have a magical time!

Everything Else in the World

It's hard to believe that after covering four major amusement parks and over 25 resort hotels, there are still things to tell you about Walt Disney World® - but there are!

Walt Disney World® is also home to some of the planet's most amazing water parks, an entertainment complex with incredible shopping and dining, a state-of-the-art sports complex, and a wide range of recreation beyond the theme parks.

Typhoon Lagoon®
According to Disney legend, a hurricane carved out a little chunk of beach and dropped it here in Walt Disney World®. Typhoon Lagoon® features one of the world's largest wave pools—so big that people actually sign up for surfing lessons here before normal operating hours! The water slides range from tame to terrifying. Sun worshippers will enjoy the large white sand beach.

Blizzard Beach®
According to Disney, this second water park is what was left behind when a major ski resort melted in the hot Florida sun. Can you think of a better place to escape the heat of a Florida afternoon than a ski resort? Enjoy a wide range of Alpine-themed water slides and amusements, including one of the highest water slide plunges in all of Florida!

Summer Winterland and Fantasia Gardens Miniature Golf
The Disney Resort has two silly miniature golf courses perfect for those who need a little break from the craziness of the theme parks. Summer Winterland is Santa's off-season getaway. Come enjoy Christmas theming year-round. Fantasia Gardens features the absurd animal characters from Fantasia in a musically themed put-put golf experience.

ESPN Wide World of Sports®
The ESPN Wide World of Sports® complex hosts a near-endless list of sporting events, ranging from youth leagues up to the pros. Did you know this is the home field of the Atlanta Braves during their spring training season? Disney has gathered together every court, field, diamond, and pitch you can imagine. They host an impressive list of national tournaments for just about

every sport at just about every level of competition. Go to www.espnwwos.com to see what events are scheduled during the dates of your visit.

Disney's BoardWalk®

Set along the romantic shores of Crescent Lake. This area of Walt Disney World® offers a selection of clubs, restaurants, and shops with a relaxed atmosphere. It feels like old Atlantic City —the perfect place to unwind after the decidedly more hectic pace of the theme parks.

Disney's Marathons

Running may be the most popular individual sport in the world, and Disney has a series of very popular races and marathons for just about every skill level. For information on Disney's many marathons, visit www.rundisney.com.

But wait, there's even more!

Honestly, the activities available to you while you are staying at a Disney Resort are endless. If you're a sports enthusiast, check into Disney's world-class golf courses, tennis courts, or the many sand volleyball courts scattered across the resort properties, or the jogging paths that crisscross the entire property.

On most days, there are activities aimed at children usually around the main pool area of the resort. Expect party games and music. Some resorts offer scavenger hunts. And most hotels will host Disney movie screenings after dark.

Enjoy nature? Disney has nature trails near the Fort Wilderness campground where guests can bike, ride horses or take a Segway tour. The Animal Kingdom® safari area has special extended walking tours and The Animal Kingdom Lodge offers a limited after-dark version of the safari including night vision goggles. Ask at the hotel for details.

If it's fishing that floats your boat, the lakes around Walt Disney World® provide some of the best bass fishing in the country. Your hotel can arrange dock, shore or fishing excursions for you. Just want to get your whole family out on the water? Rent small watercraft – or larger boats and pontoons - to zip around the waterways.

Truly, the list of possibilities is endless. If you check with your Disney Resort hotel concierge or Certified Disney Travel Expert, you will be amazed at some of the options they can recommend! Your next Walt Disney World® vacation may turn out to be very different from any other vacation you have ever taken!

Some closing thoughts…

Why is all this so important to me? Why do I spend months out of my year researching and exploring the Walt Disney World® Resort complex when the world is filled with plenty of other amusement parks? Why do I think Walt Disney World® should be important to all of us?

The answer is one simple word: Inspiration.

There just are not many things anymore for kids – or adults – to look toward and find true inspiration in. But thanks to Walt Disney, we do have something.

Mr. Disney wasn't just trying to make another family fun park when he envisioned this Florida Project; he wanted to give the world something amazing to which to aspire.

A physical incarnation of the world as it could be if politics were set aside and money was not a factor; if dreamers were allowed to dream big dreams and engineers were set loose to turn those dreams into realities. A place that shares and celebrates the best of all the world's cultures and conquers many of the world's challenges. Where both the young and the young-at-heart can light a real spark of inspiration, and where nothing is impossible if you apply an equal amount of art, science, technology, and hard work.

When I was a kid, my heroes were NASA's Apollo astronauts. I can remember a time when the moon was the very embodiment of the impossible, but within a few short years of my childhood, I witnessed men walking on the moon.

Inspired by President Kennedy's famous challenge and thanks to the efforts of the world's best and brightest, before the close of the 1960s Neil Armstrong pressed his boot print into the dusty lunar surface. It was something the whole world stopped to marvel at and to celebrate. It brought all of us together, if just for a moment, during one of the most divided times of that century.

And then years passed where the world didn't seem to have any big examples of the impossible being tackled. Missions to the moon were ceased due to the expense, while lesser missions to earth's orbit became more routine. Pop culture replaced real culture, and kids began idolizing movies, music, and sports celebrities – which is fine, but a hit song or a slam dunk just isn't the kind of thing that makes the whole world stop and take notice.

That was the first generation of kids who grew up without the "anything is possible" attitude I'd had; they simply had no examples to inspire them, as I did. Heck, we now have some people who don't even believe the moon missions really happened. How sad must it be to grow up doubting just how powerful we can be when we all work together toward a common goal?

In the early '80s I made my first trip to Walt Disney World® as a high school student on a band trip, and I discovered that feeling of possibility again. There it was, just like the space program of the 1960s – a Herculean project that on paper would have seemed impossible.

Walt's crews transformed a swampy section of central Florida into something truly inspirational that makes the world stop and take notice daily, one family and one tourist at a time. In its own way, Walt Disney World® exists to inspire generations of people to dream big dreams; to aspire to something greater and change the world into what it could be.

It's all there, waiting for you to notice it.

Walt Disney famously liked to take a good idea and "plus it" into something even better, challenging his creative teams to do the same. They took innovations from all over the world and plussed them before incorporating them into his project.

For instance, Europe had a functioning monorail system long before the Disneyland® monorail was built. Walt's Imagineers took the concept and plussed it, giving the cars a Lear jet aesthetic – which somehow makes an over-half-century-old transportation system continue to look futuristic even today. He created a functional, practical, beautiful mass transit wonder that crisscrosses the property.

The Walt Disney World® system of monorails, ferries, buses, and now gondolas moves more people each day than the mass transit system of a major metropolitan city – but it does so with remarkable efficiency, and people are actually happy to use it. Amazing!

In another instance of plussing up, the Magic Kingdom® was one of the first construction sites to incorporate an underground – or actually ground floor, in this case – accessible infrastructure tunnel system so water pipes, sewage systems, and electrical conduits could be repaired or replaced without having to dig up the streets and sidewalks above.

Next Disney plussed the pneumatic tube systems used to move mail and bank deposits between floors in office buildings, reimagining them to handle the park's garbage removal via the tunnel system.

The Disney company has continued its forward-thinking tradition of plussing up to become one of the first large-scale operations to adopt biofuels and solar energy. Many of the property's buses and service vehicles run on fuel made from food waste collected within the park, and there are several large solar collection sites on the property – including a huge Mickey-shaped system that can be seen from orbit! Nearly all the electricity consumed on the property is now harvested from the sun.

The infrastructural aspect of Disney is certainly a modern marvel, but it takes more than innovative applied technologies to make a place truly magical.

Within the kingdom walls, Disney refers to what they do like the "Disney Difference." It's in everything they touch – all the things they do that go above and beyond what you would expect anywhere else. Sure, it's in the dramatic architecture of the castles, geospheres, terrifying towers, and oversized trees – but when you look around the property, you may notice that these big things set the stage for all kinds of less tangible Disney Differences, providing visitors and employees with a remarkable place to occupy.

When you populate these amazing places with thousands and thousands of happy, service-minded people, you create an infectious environment of positivity that is highly contagious. I've noticed that people just seem nicer at Disney – not just the reliably happy Cast Members, but guests as well.

No, it's not perfect. Kids get tired and adults get frustrated. Lines get very long and rides can break down. But for the most part, people tend to reflect on their surroundings. And at Disney, people are more relaxed, more polite, friendlier. I see people "paying forward" good deeds all the time.

Here are a few examples of this from just my most recent two trips:

- A group of strangers guarded our seats and literally thousands of dollars of camera gear for me when my niece got nervous and decided to seek me out while I was stuck in a very slow-moving concessions line at Fantasmic.

- A very tall man stood in front of me and my niece for the fireworks at the base of the castle; if he wasn't an NFL defensive end, he sure had the build for it. As the show began, he noticed my niece struggling to see around him. Without a word, he stepped behind us and pushed us into a better viewing spot in front of him. Afterward, I shook his hand and thanked him for being so thoughtful and making my niece's experience just a little more special.

- My brother and I were invited into a game of iPhone charades (the Heads Up app) with a family that kept ending up with us in attraction queues.

These are little things, but they mean a lot at the moment and they stick with you for years down the road.

Saving the best for last, let's talk about the Cast Members – the secret sauce in Disney's magical formula. They work long shifts under the blazing hot Florida sun, often in tropical humidity or drenching rains, but they are always quick with a smile and their own version of the Disney Difference. And yes, of course, I have firsthand examples of this to share with you…

- I had reservations for the Plaza Restaurant on the end of Main Street, but when I got to the greeter out front, there was a glitch in the app and the reservation no longer appeared on my phone. I explained my dilemma to the Cast Member and she assured me she would do her best to accommodate us. I was taking some dear friends to Magic Kingdom for their very first visit and I was intent on delivering a great time. We only had to wait for minutes and we were taken into the charming 1930s era soda fountain-style dining spot. My friends had a shy little girl who was already having the time of her life, but then the Mayor of Main Street and other performers entered the dining area and after taking a moment to meet the little girl, loudly proclaimed she was now the honorary Mayor of Main Street for the day. She was given a sash to wear and brought out into the street to be introduced to the crowds where her first act was to bestow bubbles from a bubble-making toy to the passers-by. And this two was celebrated and applauded by the many kind strangers on Main Street who chose to celebrate the moment with this family. What an amazing memory.

- A retired couple had a tradition of purchasing a Christmas ornament from the Christmas store in the kingdom's Liberty Square. They had been doing this since they first visited Disney as a younger couple of years ago. But on this particular trip, they told the clerk that they had experienced a terrible house fire earlier that year and sadly all their treasured Disney ornaments were lost. They asked if any of their favorite designs from the past were still available to purchase. Sadly they were not. They shrugged their shoulders and told the Cast Member, "I guess we will have to start our tradition over." And they purchased several new ornaments. The Cast Member inquired when was their first visit to the park together? "1996" they replied. They remembered because Disney had just opened the Ye Olde Christmas Shoppe. The couple asked if the clerk could carefully wrap up the bobbles they selected and ship the items to their home so they had something to look forward to after their vacation was over. And of course, the Cast Member promised to do just that after collecting a little more information. When the couple got back home they noted the package took a little longer than expected to arrive. When they opened the carefully wrapped shipping box they noticed it seemed bigger than what was necessary for the three new ornaments they bought. They unwrapped their treasures and discovered there were indeed two more objects in their package than they had purchased. When they opened up the remaining wrappers they discovered two Christmas ornaments they never noticed in the store. These two ornaments were gold with the dates 1996, 1997, 1998 and so on hand-painted artfully covering the surfaces of the small matching balls. All the years of the ornaments and visits they had lost in the fire.

- A friend and his young daughter found their stroller had gone missing while they were on the Fantasyland carousel. It was a rental stroller and they lost nothing of value, but his tired daughter was obviously upset. A nearby Cast Member noticed and radioed in for a stroller replacement. As they waited, she engaged the girl in conversation and asked her to point out her favorite Disney princess from a lineup of dolls on display at a nearby toy store. The child pointed to Anna; the Cast Member plucked the doll off the shelf and handed it to her, saying, "She's yours!" My friend was surprised and of course offered to pay, but his offer was declined. Things didn't end there, though. The Cast Member guided them through the shop's back door and whispered something to her fellow Cast Members, and in a flash, they were being introduced to the "real" Anna and Elsa! Hugs were given and an incredible, magical memory was made. When they left the princesses, a new stroller was waiting. My friend was so impressed by how the Cast Member handled their crisis, he took a picture with her and sent this story to Disney Guest Services so this act of unexpected kindness could be celebrated. He jokes that the photo of his daughter with that Cast Member has become more popular than any of the photos with the princesses.

Of course, you should never expect to get free stuff in exchange for a gripe – that's not how this works, and it would not be in the sincere spirit of these moments. You may or may not experience one of these magical moments firsthand, but I'd bet if you keep your eyes open you will witness them happening all around you.

Disney Cast Members were performing these random acts of kindness long before they became company policy. The fact that any Cast Member is encouraged to "plus" your experience any time they see fit is a big part of that Disney Difference. The fact that these moments happen as sincere acts of kindness makes them all the more special.

If you want to experience a perfect Disney moment, I think this is it. Walk to the base of Main Street, U.S.A. near the train station and face the castle down the lane in the distance. Take a deep breath. It will be flavored by the aroma of buttered popcorn and sweetness from the nearby confectionery, and at that moment, you will feel undeniable positivity.

Just standing in this place makes me happy. I can feel the troubles of the real world melt away with each deep breath. Even if you understand the psychology being applied here (there is a very good reason Main Street's comforting familiarity leads to a magical fantasy castle), the magic is tangible. This is a place where you should feel comfortable dreaming big dreams.

I hope this book helps you find your very own happy place within Walt Disney World®.

Share Your Own Walt Disney World® stories, travel tips, and favorite photos on our Facebook Group: ActualFactualMagic. Follow us on Twitter and Instagram at ActFactMagic. On Tiktok we are actualfactualmagic. Come see all our best video compilations at ActualFactualMagic.com and our YouTube channel ActualFactualMagic. We welcome you to become a part of our online community. Help us make this book even better in the future!

Credits

Joseph Pillsbury — This is our fourth edition of this book and I believe it is by far our best effort. Writing a guidebook in a pandemic is a challenge. It would have been hard enough to keep up with all the construction and additions coming for Walt Disney World's 50th Anniversary, but the global health crisis really put us to the test. I cannot thank my creative partner Kat Garbis enough for her amazing food section contribution and editorial skills. I honestly believe this book is better than any other guide book on the market thanks to our unselfish team effort. I'd like to thank my family too. My Mom, my brother and sister and their families, and of course the memory of my Dad. All have been sources of encouragement even when they do not always understand my obsession with a certain mouse and castle.

The secret sauce to this book is the same secret sauce that makes the Disney experience so magical. That of course is the contribution of Cast Members. *Actual Factual Magic* is fortunate to have contributing Cast Members in many different roles, from street sweepers, ride operators, to people in the front offices. I assure you they never pull back the curtain on any of the magic. But they offer us some of the best insights on how to plan your vacations and how to navigate the massive property once you arrive. I protect their identities here but cannot thank them enough for their roles everyday in the parks and their role making this book even better.

About Me:

Joseph Pillsbury is a Minnesota born author, illustrator and cartoonist. His fascination for Disney began with a high school band trip to the Magic Kingdom® and has only grown stronger over the years well into his adult years. He is the creator of one of the longest running web cartoons on the internet bogworld.com. He worked as a commercial illustrator with pieces appearing by many institutions and businesses including McDonalds, Jeep, AdWeek, Dragon Magazine, Libby Dam Visitor Center, Minnesota Zoo, The Science Museum of Minnesota, and many more. He wrote the award winning youth novel *The Prank* and the children's book *The House at the End of the Block*. You can see my portfolio and book listings here: www.josephpillsbury.com .

Kat Garbis —First and foremost, I want to thank my friend, partner, colleague, and co-author, Joe Pillsbury for the opportunity to collaborate on this book together. It was a little idea dreamt in a parking lot that became reality. I am ever grateful our paths crossed and we not only talked about collaborating on our love for Disney, but, we did it my friend. Thank you for your trust, dealing with me, support, and friendship. You not only love Disney, but you love to be helpful to people. It's no wonder you write a guidebook. Thank you for enabling me to combine my passions of food, writing, Disney, and friendships all into one.

To my family: Mom, Dad, Jeramiah, and George — thank you for all the good times in Disney we had growing up that shaped my love for Disney and this book. Mom and Dad, thank you for taking us to Disney World as kids and continually bringing us back over the years. I didn't know it till much later in life, how privileged I was to go to Disney as often as we did, and how each time is always an adventure and fun. I've enjoyed going back as an adult with friends, partners, work colleagues — each time is always memorable. Shout out to my Aunt Patty and Uncle Themis, and my friend and fellow Disney lover, Mike Miley, for their encouragement and support with snacks while I wrote this book. And thank you to my loving pup, Aubrie, who faithfully sat by my side as I drafted each and every page. Lastly, thank you to those who taught me to write, and challenged me to write better.

About Me:

Kat Garbis has been going to Disney for the last 30 years and became a Disney World enthusiast over the decades. It was easy for her to love a place that had "all her favorite things and brought nonstop joy." Her passion for food not only comes from being in Chicago, a foodie utopia, but is a self-taught home cook with a food blog, www.fancyathome.com. She is actively authoring a cookbook, Fancy At Home. Kat is an alumnus of DePaul University in Chicago where she studied Political Science and Creative Writing. In 2012, Kat took up a pastime of blogging on TripAdvisor. Kat dedicated her TripAdvisor account solely to her Disney travel experiences. Kat began to write reviews, tips, and tricks about Disney World, she became one of the top 6% most-read reviewers of all time in 2013 out of 100 million reviews and opinions. In addition to enjoying and eating her way through Disney, Kat loves to run and partakes in the runDisney in-person and virtual races. She has a loving yellow labrador named Aubrie and resides in Chicago.

Author, Illustrator, Photographer: Joseph Pillsbury

Food Author, Editor, Photographer: Kat Garbis

Original Cover and Title Design: Cassandra Clark

Layout Design: Luis Santiago, Joseph Pillsbury, Kat Garbis

Main Cover Photograph: Mickeys_Round_Table (Instagram)

Contributing Photographers: Kealani Burgos, Lukas Campbell, Allison Severson, Devin Kass, Kelsey Strickland, Mickeys_Round_Table

Social Media: Kat Garbis, Joseph Pillsbury, Devin Kass

Music for Video Production: Alejandro Carrera

Actual Factual Magic — The Simplified Guide to Walt Disney World is not an official publication from the Walt Disney Company®. This is an independent endeavor which strives to live up to Disney's standards of excellence. We strive to adhere to Disney's publishing guidelines. I recommend Disney's official guide to Disney World for all the in-depth details. It's a wonderful publication. I wanted to provide you with something a little different, something a bit easier to digest here. I hope you have enjoyed this simplified guide to Walt Disney World®!

CPSIA information can be obtained
at www.ICGtesting.com
Printed in the USA
LVHW021322171121
703571LV00008B/380